GYPSIES AND TRAVELLERS

Empowerment and inclusion in British society

Edited by Joanna Richardson and Andrew Ryder

First published in Great Britain in 2012 by

The Policy Press
University of Bristol
Fourth Floor
Beacon House
Queen's Road
Bristol BS8 1QU
UK
Tel +44 (0)117 331 4054
Fax +44 (0)117 331 4093
e-mail tpp-info@bristol.ac.uk
www.policypress.co.uk

North American office:
The Policy Press
c/o The University of Chicago Press
1427 East 60th Street
Chicago, IL 60637, USA
t: +1 773 702 7700
f: +1 773-702-9756
e:sales@press.uchicago.edu
www.press.uchicago.edu

British Library Cataloguing in Publication Data
A catalogue record for this book is available from the British Library.

Library of Congress Cataloging-in-Publication Data
A catalog record for this book has been requested.

ISBN 978 1 84742 894 3 paperback
ISBN 978 1 84742 895 0 hardcover

The right of Joanna Richardson and Andrew Ryder to be identified as editors
of this work has been asserted by them in accordance with the 1988 Copyright,
Designs and Patents Act.

The statements and opinions contained within this publication are solely those of
the editors and contributors and not of The University of Bristol or The Policy
Press. The University of Bristol and The Policy Press disclaim responsibility for
any injury to persons or property resulting from any material published in this
publication.

The Policy Press works to counter discrimination on grounds of gender, race,
disability, age and sexuality.

Cover design by Qube Design Associates
Front cover: image kindly supplied by www.alamy.com
Printed and bound in Great Britain by TJ International,
Padstow
The Policy Press uses environmentally responsible print
partners

Contents

Part Three: Conclusions

List of figures

Foreword by Lord Avebury

This book appears at a crucial moment. At the time of writing, the progress and modest gains made for Gypsies and Travellers, most notably in the form of increased site provision and levels of social inclusion, appear to be in jeopardy. As this book visibly demonstrates, Gypsies and Travellers remain one of the most excluded minority groups in society, yet it is feared that this situation could be aggravated through cuts in local and national funding, which are seeing the loss and erosion of valuable targeted services for Gypsies and Travellers, most notably in the shrinkage of the national network of Traveller Education Services. One of the most emotive issues has been erosion and fragmentation of the hopes built up for the delivery of a sufficient number of new sites to address the acute national shortage as had been promised through regional targets and planning strategies and the Planning Circular 01/06. Sadly, these were repealed by the Localism Act 2011.

The lessons of history on this subject appear to have been discarded. Adequate site provision, both permanent and transit, is the answer to the problem of unauthorised encampments. The Caravan Sites Act 1968, which I sponsored as an MP, required local authorities to provide sites for Gypsies and Travellers residing in or resorting to their areas. Unfortunately, the duty was repealed in 1994, and although by that time 350 or so local authority Gypsy and Traveller sites had been constructed in England and Wales, there still remained a significant shortfall in site provision. Many local authorities had ignored their statutory duty and the ministerial power of direction in section 9(2) of the Act had only been used towards the end of the legislation's life. The few directions that were issued did have some effect in galvanising backward local authorities. The shortfall remains, caused by the failure of successive governments and local authorities to ensure adequate provision. This has led to the endemic situation of unauthorised encampments and unauthorised developments, and it is essential that a policy of ensuring adequate site provision is promoted if any positive steps are to be made in tackling that problem.

Experience over nearly 50 years leads me to conclude that provision of Gypsy and Traveller sites, or the allocation of land for sites in local authority plans, is the key to reducing community tensions and enforcement costs as well as improving the life chances of a highly marginalised minority. Conversely, failure to provide sites or to allocate land for them, inevitably leads to the proliferation of unauthorised sites, with disastrous effects on the life chances of Gypsies and Travellers and disputes between them and settled communities. To achieve the goal of eliminating unauthorised encampments, financial support needs to be combined with obligations on local authorities to provide sites based on accurate and fair assessments of need with the prospect of government intervention where councils fail to act. However, the answer does not just lie in adequate provision of decent sites; a policy framework is also required that takes note of and reflects the aspirations of this minority and empowers them to help themselves. Too often in the past, policy makers have sought to assimilate and eradicate the identity and unique lifestyle of Gypsies and Travellers.

The lack of logic and humanity on this issue by the powers that be has been demonstrated to me on numerous occasions over the years. One notable example was the case of the Traveller site at Dale Farm in Essex. In England as a whole, 20% of Gypsies and Travellers do not have an authorised place to live, while in the county of Essex, of which Dale Farm is a part, the proportion is 47.4%. Despite this, Basildon Council, the authority within which the site lies, was intent on a forced eviction, even though the site prior to its occupation was a scrap yard. The Leader of the Council, Tony Ball, said that following an eviction 'the encampment might well become allotments', and when asked where the residents are to go after they are evicted, he replied 'they came from somewhere. One has to draw the line at some point. All our authorised sites are full up' (*The Economist*, 2010). Attempts to avert forced eviction by relocating those threatened with eviction to land proposed by the Homes and Communities Agency were spurned by Basildon Council and the eviction was carried out in October 2011, supported by riot police who used tasers on protestors (The *Guardian*, 19 October 2011).

Sadly, the short-sightedness and lack of compromise displayed in the case of Basildon Council are not isolated. The European Commission against Racism and Intolerance (2010), in its fourth periodic report on the United Kingdom, expressed concern about the eviction of Gypsies and Travellers. The report found that: 'An excessive emphasis on enforcement (i.e. eviction), involving often protracted and expensive litigation, instead of seeking forward-looking solutions in consultation with all members of the local community, has also been shown to damage race relations' (2010, para 153).

A continued emphasis on evictions and enforcement comes at a time when other major European countries are planning mass expulsions of Roma or demolitions of Roma settlements. Rights groups warn that these measures entail the criminalisation of an entire ethnic group, and break European Union law. Unfortunately, European states have forgotten that the criminalisation of Jews and Gypsies was the precursor to their dehumanisation and genocide by the Nazis, but this time the tide of racism may not stop at the white cliffs of Dover.

Despite these huge setbacks and challenges, I am not disheartened. This book chronicles many positive developments initiated by Gypsies and Travellers and those who are sympathetic to their cause. This gives me a sense of optimism for I know that there are great reserves of courage and resilience among Gypsies and Travellers. This determination has been displayed by many of the community campaigners who I have been privileged to work with. Let us hope that campaigners achieve their simple aspiration that Gypsies and Travellers are treated with fairness and dignity. A simple aspiration, but one that if achieved could have profound implications for the type of society we all live in.

Lord Avebury

Acknowledgements

The editors would like to thank all of the contributors for their expertise and insight; and their good humour in meeting deadlines. Special thanks are due to our colleagues at De Montfort University, Leicester, the Corvinus University, Budapest and Bristol University for their support. Thank you to our families, in particular David and Edward, Henrietta and Arthur, for your patience and encouragement.

A particular note of thanks is due to Arthur Ivatts OBE and Pat Niner OBE for their reading and comments on parts of the initial typescript, and to Dr Tim Brown at De Montfort University for his usual sound advice and comments. We would also like to acknowledge the advice and contributions made by a number of individuals and organisations: Angus McCabe of the Third Sector Research Centre helped to develop ideas on community development; Professor György Lengyel, Attila Gulyás (Corvinus University), Sara Memo (Trento University) and Marton Rövid (Central European University) contributed to discussions on the European dimension of the book. There are many other researchers, practitioners and community members, sadly too numerous to mention, who have helped and inspired us over the years to whom we also express our thanks.

We would also like to thank Emily Watt and Jo Morton at The Policy Press.

Joanna Richardson
Andrew Ryder

Notes on contributors

Thomas Acton is a campaigner for the rights of Gypsies and Travellers and was appointed an OBE in the 2009 New Year Honours List. He is also Secretary and Representative of both the Brentwood Gypsy Support Group and Gypsy Lore Society. Thomas has lectured at the University of Greenwich for over 30 years, been Professor of Romany Studies since 1997 and now holds the position of Professor Emeritus of Romani Studies.

Dan Allen is a senior social work lecturer in the Faculty of Health at Edge Hill University. He teaches on undergraduate and postgraduate social work programmes and has a research focus on the social care needs of Gypsy and Traveller communities, and the advancement of interpretive phenomenological analysis within the field of social work practice and research.

Lord Avebury was a Liberal MP between 1962 and 1970 and was Liberal parliamentary chief whip from 1963 to 1970. In 1971, he entered the House of Lords. He has a long association with Gypsies and Travellers, having navigated the 1968 Caravan Sites Act through Parliament as a Private Member's Bill. Lord Avebury is currently President of the Advisory Council for the Education of Romany and other Travellers (ACERT) and Secretary of the All Party Parliamentary Group for Gypsies, Roma and Travellers.

Sarah Cemlyn is a former social worker and senior lecturer in the School for Policy Studies at Bristol University where she is now an Honorary Fellow. Her work on issues affecting Gypsies and Travellers includes a review of inequalities for the Equality and Human Rights Commission, and a UK country study for a European Parliament funded project.

Patrice Van Cleemput has a background in nursing and health visiting, with a specialist focus on the health of Gypsy and Traveller families. Her previous work includes a Department of Health Inequalities Programme study of the health status of Gypsies and Travellers in England and she has recently completed the evaluation of Gypsy and Traveller core projects in the Department of Health Pacesetter Programme aimed at reducing health inequalities.

Brian Foster has been involved in the education of Gypsies, Roma and Travellers for 30 years, including work for the Greater London Council, Camden Traveller Education Service and the Inner London Traveller Education Consortia. He is a trustee of the Irish Traveller Movement in Britain and has advised the UK's Department for Education and education projects in Romania. Brian co-authored with Linda Walker *Traveller education in the mainstream: The litmus test* (Hopscotch Publishing, 2010).

Margaret Greenfields initially trained as a lawyer, with a special interest in family law and housing issues. She fairly rapidly moved into legal policy and has worked in the fields of child protection, domestic violence, 'looked-after' children living in 'kinship care' placements, and the health, education and social care needs of Gypsy Travellers. Margaret is Reader in the School of Social Sciences, Primary Care and Education at Buckinghamshire New University. A key research interest is Gypsy, Roma and Traveller communities.

Richard O'Neill was born into a large Gypsy/Travelling family in the North East of England and followed a traditional travelling lifestyle before settling in the North West in the mid-1980s, where he set up and ran successful construction and leisure companies. Having always had an interest in health, in 1992 Richard became a community volunteer and trained as a practitioner of clinical hypnotherapy, becoming a full-time therapist in 1995. In 1996, his interest in men's health led him to launch a local men's health day, which has since expanded into the National Men's Health Week, first launched in 2002. Richard is also a renowned children's story teller and is a frequent visitor to schools across Britain, where his stories raise insights and awareness among children about Gypsies and Travellers.

Joanna Richardson is Principal Lecturer in the Centre for Comparative Housing Research at De Montfort University, Leicester. She has written and edited several books, including *The Gypsy debate: Can discourse control?* (Imprint Academic, 2006), *Providing Gypsy and Traveller sites: Contentious spaces* (Joseph Rowntree Foundation, 2007), *From recession to renewal: the impact of the financial crisis on public services and local government* (The Policy Press, 2010) and *Housing and the customer* (Chartered Institute of Housing, 2010). Joanna has also recently worked on a project for the Arts and Humanities Research Council on co-production in research and has recently been awarded funding by the

Economic and Social Research Council to run a seminar series from 2012 to 2013 on Gypsy/Traveller issues and conflict.

Iulius Rostas is a doctoral candidate at Babes Bolyai University of Cluj, Romania, and a freelance researcher. Previously he had roles at the Open Society Institute and the European Roma Rights Centre and has been an expert consultant for the Government of Romania (Department for the Protection of National Minorities). Iulius has published several articles on educational policies, Roma movement and Romani identity. He recently edited a book for the CEU Press: *Ten years after: A history of Roma school desegregation in Central and Eastern Europe* (2012).

Andrew Ryder is a Fellow at Bristol University, Associate Fellow at the Third Sector Research Centre and a Visiting Professor at the Corvinus University, Budapest. Prior to this he was Policy Officer respectively to the Irish Traveller Movement in Britain and the Gypsy and Traveller Law Reform Coalition, and researcher for the All Party Parliamentary Group for Traveller Law Reform.

David Smith is Principal Lecturer in the School of Health and Social Care at Greenwich University. His key research interests are in the area of social exclusion, culture and poverty, social policy, changing industrial and class structure in London, benefit fraud, 'informal' working practices and immigrant labour. David is a member of and activist in the Gypsy Council, is the author of *On the margins of inclusion: Changing labour markets and social exclusion in London* (The Policy Press, 2005) and is writing with Margaret Greenfield a forthcoming volume on housed Gypsies and Travellers for The Policy Press.

Maggie Smith-Bendell was born to a Romani Gypsy family. Like most Gypsies at the time, her family travelled across the countryside, eking out a living from the woods and hedgerows, picking daffodils and snowdrops, catching rabbits, pheasants and wild duck, and collecting scrap metal and rags. Maggie advises on planning issues and is a tireless campaigner for Gypsy and Traveller rights. Her acclaimed memoir *Our forgotten years: A Gypsy woman's life on the road* (University of Hertfordshire Press, 2009) has been republished as *Rabbit stew and a penny or two* (Abacus, 2010).

Part One

Context, issues and policy responses

ONE

Setting the context: Gypsies and Travellers in British society

Joanna Richardson and Andrew Ryder

Introduction

The aim of this book is to examine issues that affect Gypsies and Travellers, including accommodation, health, education, social policy, employment and the European Roma framework. It seeks to explore cross-cutting themes of social inclusion, discursive control, media power, representation, empowerment, justice and contested spaces. The book also debates the place of the researcher and asks whether Gypsies and Travellers now have the chance to shape their own destiny according to their aspirations and cultural identity. These are fundamental questions of relevance to us all, for the outcomes will say much about the society we live in.

The book comes at a time of great political and economic change for Britain in the wake of a financial crisis in the banks and a sovereign debt crisis in Europe (Richardson, 2010a). The Conservative-led Coalition Government has been introducing changes to health and social care, and the planning framework, as well as the concepts of governance and delivery of public service through the Localism Act 2011. Many of the themes in the following chapters are affected by such changes, and their impact on the lives of Gypsies and Travellers is a concern to many. The book discusses these challenges that we face, but also tries to highlight the opportunities that the changing context might offer for the empowerment and inclusion of Gypsies and Travellers in British society.

The context

It is estimated that there are between 10 and 12 million Roma, Sinti, Gypsies and Travellers in Europe (Fundamental Rights Agency, 2010); they are Europe's largest minority ethnic group. The Council of Europe estimates that 300,000 Gypsies and Travellers reside in Britain, with one third living in caravan/mobile home accommodation (either on the roadside or on sites) and the remainder living in housing. Biannual count data collected in recent years (DCLG, 2010) show that of Gypsies and Travellers living in caravans, approximately a quarter live on unauthorised sites (on their own land without permission, on other land or on the roadside) – it would be difficult to find any other minority ethnic group with such large numbers that are effectively homeless. Gypsies and Travellers are some of the most excluded groups in British society, as reflected in low life expectancy (CRE, 2006; Cemlyn et al, 2009) and poor rates of educational achievement and participation (DCSF, 2009c). There are reports of growing unemployment and welfare dependency of members of these communities (CRE, 2004; Cemlyn et al, 2009).

Reports (eg, Briscoe, 2007) have suggested that 4,000 more pitches are required (although some Gypsy and Traveller representatives say that this is an underestimation of need, indicating instead that there are in fact more than 4,000 families with no official site to live on). One of the principal causes of the sites shortage and growth in unauthorised encampments and numbers in housing has been a failure of policy in the past. Legislation and policy under New Labour sought to address the shortfall in accommodation for Gypsies and Travellers primarily through a target-driven approach. However, progress on the actual provision of sites was slow and the Coalition Government has since revoked regional strategies and their targets for sites (this dilemma is discussed in more detail in Chapter Two).

A survey by MORI, commissioned by Stonewall in 2003, found Gypsies and Travellers to be one of the most reviled groups in society, alongside groups such as asylum seekers (Valentine and McDonald, 2004). This exclusion and vilification have been compounded by poor access to services, a lack of political power and exclusion from decision-making processes. A recent example demonstrates this. After a successful Irish Traveller Movement in Britain (ITMB) conference in November 2011, some of the delegates decided to go to the pub next door to carry on their debate. These delegates included Irish Travellers, the ITMB director, a police inspector, a solicitor and priest. They were barred from entering the pub, which was part of a large national chain. Inspector Watson confirmed the events in a newspaper headline for *The Irish Times* (Hennessy, 2011) and stated that he was going to report the matter to the Metropolitan Police as a racially motivated incident. It is difficult to imagine any other ethnic group being barred from entering a pub at 5pm after a conference debate; replace the word 'Irish Traveller' with any other race or ethnicity and there would be outrage. In spite of all the steps taken to increase equality for Gypsies and Travellers, incidents like this serve to illustrate that there is still a long way to go.

Who are Gypsies and Travellers?

Who are the people and communities being discussed in this book? This would appear to be a straightforward question but is one that has aroused strong passions and disagreements on the part of academics, policy makers and the communities themselves. Confusion and distortion often feature in the issue of identity, which Chapter Nine notes has been in part a product of unequal and hierarchical relations between 'researchers' and the 'researched'; a problem that, as noted in Chapter Ten, has been compounded through unbalanced media representation.

In legal terms, defining Roma, Gypsies and Travellers in Britain is difficult (this is partly because different definitions apply in equalities cases, in housing law and in planning law). In this book, the umbrella term 'Gypsies and Travellers' is generally used (although see more on this in the section 'Gypsy and Traveller identity' later in this chapter), but the authors recognise the problems of imposing a simplistic exonym on a wide range of differing travelling communities. The predominant travelling communities in Britain are Romany English Gypsies and Irish Travellers; plus also New Travellers, Welsh Gypsies and Scottish Gypsies, as well as new Roma migrants from the European accession countries. The size of Britain's Gypsy and Traveller population is an estimate, with Council of Europe figures putting it at about 300,000, with approximately 200,000 in settled housing (Liégeois, 2007). The courts have established that Gypsies, Scottish Gypsies and Irish Travellers are ethnic groups for the purposes of the Race Relations Act 1976 (as amended by the Race Relations [Amendment] Act 2000) (*Commission for Racial Equality v Dutton*, 1989 [Romany Gypsies]; *O'Leary and others v Punch Retail*, 2000 [Irish Travellers]; and the MacLennan case, 2008 [Scottish Gypsies]).

In this chapter, we give a very brief and simple history for context; however, readers will note that, as with many aspects of Gypsy and Traveller studies, terms are constructed and contested (see Chapter Eight). Gypsies or Romany (Romani) Gypsies, or Romanichal, as they are sometimes termed, were first recorded in British history in 1502 in Scotland and in England in 1514 (Bancroft, 2005). Roma populations across Europe are members of the same ethno-social group as British Gypsies, but their ancestors settled in other European countries (mainly in Central and Eastern Europe) earlier in the migration process, which started in India and culminated in this population reaching the UK 500 years ago (Kenrick, 2004). According to Kenrick and Clark's (1999) history, the Gypsies were welcomed by 'commoners' who had work that needed doing and who also wanted entertaining. However, the church objected to palmistry and fortune telling by the Gypsies and the authorities were concerned that because they did not live in a fixed abode they were not easy to 'register' for details such as name and date of birth. This lack of governmental control is possibly one of the reasons for the state's treatment of Gypsies and Travellers still today. This is one of the central tensions in the relationship both between the state and Gypsies, and between non-Gypsies ('Gaujos') and Gypsies.

By 1530, the first piece of legislation expelling Gypsies was introduced by Henry VIII. In 1540, Gypsies were allowed to live under their own laws in Scotland but by 1541 the first Scottish anti-Gypsy laws were introduced. In 1562, there was a further Act relating to 'vagabonds', which meant that they did not have to leave the country as long as they ceased their travelling lifestyle (Patrin, 2000).

Appleby Fair[1] was registered as a horse trading fair in 1685 and Gypsies from across the country continue to gather there every June to trade horses and meet socially. In this respect, Gypsy culture has been celebrated, but even in this context, to this day, there are debates on policing and crime, which detract from this historic cultural event. In 1780, some of the anti-Gypsy laws started to be repealed, although not all. In 1822, the Turnpike Act was introduced, which meant that Gypsies camping on the roadside were fined (Patrin, 2000). During the Victorian era, Gypsies and Travellers were certainly 'othered' in discourse (Holloway, 2002). The year 1908 saw the introduction of the Children's Act in England, which made education compulsory for Gypsy children for half of the year; this was continued in the Education Act 1944. During the Second World War, the Nazis drew up a list of English Gypsies for internment; and the holocaust of Gypsies in Europe is well documented (Kenrick, 1999). There are some good sociological, anthropological and historical studies of Romany Gypsies that go into the detail of lives lived that is not possible to achieve in the confines of this book. Examples include Okely (1983); Kenrick and Clark (1999) for a British history; and, for a history from a Romani Gypsy woman herself, Smith-Bendell (2009) is essential reading.

Another principal Traveller group in Britain are the Irish Travellers (*Pavees*). McVeigh (2007) has argued Irish Travellers have their origins in a Celtic (and possibly pre-Celtic) nomadic population in Ireland and are not Roma/Gypsies. Irish Travellers have travelled within the UK at least since the 19th century and possibly earlier (Niner, 2002). Here again there is controversy: in the past, tensions have arisen between different groups of Gypsies and Travellers, tensions often centred on competition for scarce resources between the groups, competing for employment activities or sites and spaces to live. In recent times, the shared cultural practices of both Gypsies and Irish Travellers, marital unions between the two groups but also coming together in campaigns and organisations such as the Gypsy Council and the Traveller Law Reform Coalition have created a momentum for a degree of cultural and political cohabitation.

Thus, Gypsies and Irish Travellers have differing origins and cultural traditions; despite this there are some striking similarities between the two populations. They have their own distinct community languages – Romanes (spoken by Gypsies) and Shelta/Gammon/Cant spoken by Irish Travellers – but the two groups operate within close-knit family structures, have strong nomadic traditions that are facing erosion as a result of sedentarist policies and hold a preference for working patterns organised around kin-groups and self-employment (see Chapter Six). The strong traditions of in-family socialisation and employment-related training preferred by both Gypsies and Irish Travellers have at times acted as a barrier to participation in formal education (Derrington and Kendall, 2004); both groups experience acute social exclusion (Cemlyn et al, 2009).

New Travellers (some of whom prefer to be termed 'Travellers'; Greenfields and Home, 2006) are not a distinct ethnic group recognised under race law, but struggle to get their culture, identity, values and needs recognised both in society generally and in the contentious debate on 'definition'. While the word 'New' denotes a community that has not got a history, it should be noted that there are second- and third-generation New Travellers. There has in fact been a long tradition of members of society taking up nomadic lifestyles but the New Traveller group took on a more identifiable form in the 'alternative' and 'festival' movements of the 1970s (Earle et al, 1994). The numbers who took up this lifestyle were swelled by the economic crisis of the 1980s and resulting urban decline and unemployment, which prompted some to experiment with new lifestyles (Earle, et al, 1994; Webster and Millar, 2001). In 1985, there was a crunch point between the police, the media and New Travellers at the 'Battle of the Beanfield' (Worthington, 2005), dubbed the 'Stonehenge Riots' by the press.

By the late 1980s, the popular press was orchestrating a media frenzy about festivals and unauthorised campaigning. Much of this was focused on the group they termed 'New Age' Travellers. In response, the Conservative government introduced new enforcement measures against nomadism in the Criminal Justice and Public Order Act 1994, which impinged on the nomadic practices of all nomadic groups. For some Gypsies and Travellers this was a cause of resentment as they felt that they were being punished for the transgressions of a group that was trying to usurp not only their lifestyle but also their identity (Hawes and Perez, 1996) – a point of conflict that continues to simmer over governmental planning definitions of 'Gypsies and Travellers' based on ethnicity and/or lifestyle. However, it should be noted that attempts have been made to create joint campaigning and broader political unity among travelling communities by including New Travellers in Traveller law reform, a process to lobby the government to implement accommodation measures to support and facilitate traditional and nomadic lifestyles for all travelling communities.

Roma

A new and important dimension to the character of Gypsy and Traveller communities in the UK is the arrival of Roma from Central and Eastern Europe. This process has in fact been occurring for centuries but accelerated with the collapse of the Soviet Bloc from 1989. Poverty, persecution, racism, going in search of a better life and a perception that the UK might offer greater economic and social benefit have driven their migration to the UK (Craig, 2007) where for many overcrowded housing and low-paid employment have awaited them (European Dialogue, 2009). Indeed, since the movement of Central and Eastern Europe towards a market society, the greatest victims of structural change and liberalisation have been Roma communities (Sigona and Trehan, 2009).

A8 Roma migrants come from the eight accession countries admitted to the European Union (EU) in 2004 such as the Czech Republic, Poland and Slovakia, while A2 Roma migrants are from Bulgaria and Romania, the two countries admitted to the EU in 2008. Roma are generally located in large urban centres throughout the UK, including Belfast, Cardiff, Glasgow, London and Manchester (Stevenson, 2007; Poole and Adamson, 2008; European Dialogue 2009). Despite claims by some UK politicians that their arrival would lead to an increase in the demand for sites, most are sedentary.

UK employment restrictions apply to Roma, in particular those coming from Bulgaria and Romania. These restrictions, combined with a lack of training, have forced some into the grey/informal economy

(European Dialogue, 2009). Media reporting on this topic reinforces negative stereotypes of Roma. European Dialogue (2009, p 59) found that the majority of its Roma interviewees were employed through private employment agencies in low-waged and menial work, some of whom were exploited by unscrupulous agencies.

Roma often live in overcrowded accommodation with multiple family occupation in units designed for one family (Fordham Research, 2008, p 73). A study on the Roma community living in the Govanhill area of Glasgow estimated that there are 2,000-3,000 Roma there, concentrated in four to five streets (Poole and Adamson, 2008). They are often dependent on the private sector, experiencing high rents, substandard conditions, no tenancy agreements and gross overcrowding (Poole and Adamson, 2008; European Dialogue, 2009). There is evidence among Roma that language and cultural issues impact on access to services, and that malnutrition and overcrowding contribute to ill-health (Poole and Adamson, 2008).

Ethnicity and race

Gypsies and Travellers are also highly visible as a racialised or 'pariah' group. While some may see ethnicity as primordial and unchanging, others see it as situational, that is, manipulable as circumstances demand or allow and acquiring importance in particular circumstances (Jenkins, 1996). Anthias and Yuval Davis (1992) argue that identity is not immutable but changes over time and in response to concrete economic, political or ideological conditions. Thus, ethnic groups are not static or rigid entities. The boundaries that separate them from outsiders and confirm identity for members are constantly being reinterpreted and remade. Interaction with 'others' is an important element in determining who and what group members are. As Barth (1969) observed, ethnic distinctions do not depend on the absence of social interaction and acceptance: on the contrary they are quite often the very foundations on which social systems are built. Interaction in such a social system does not lead to its liquidation, but through change and acculturation, cultural differences can persist despite inter-ethnic contact and interdependence. Therefore, the mistrust, fear and rejection of mainstream society have contributed to the formation of certain Gypsy and Traveller cultural identities. The external restraints placed on interaction with a 'pariah group' such as Gypsies and Travellers have helped to maintain the strong boundaries between Gypsies and Travellers and wider society (Barth, 1969).

While race relations legislation has prevented the public expression of hatred on grounds of race, asylum seekers have become increasingly racialised and the expression of hostile attitudes towards this group can give a wider legitimacy to racist expressions (Lewis, 2005). The 'riots' of 2001 in Northern English towns gave a major impetus to the integration agenda and called for the development of new forms of citizenship as expressed in the subsequent White Paper on immigration and asylum (Home Office, 2002). Bourne (2006, p 1) argues that prevailing philosophies on diversity have come full circle with this 'integration agenda' (the Coalition Government has reaffirmed support for this agenda), which is highly critical of multiculturalism and calls for all minorities to adhere to the central values and practices of British society. It is in this context that growing hostility to Gypsies and Travellers in the UK, and increasingly to Roma, must be viewed. Somehow these groups are envisioned as non-conforming and non-contributing outsiders to the interests of wider society.

This growing intolerance of those who are different – and who are seen as being legitimate targets not covered by anti-racist legislation – explains the increase in hostility towards Gypsies and Travellers. 'Moral panics' and a fear of 'folk devils' help to normalise mainstream institutions and values (Cohen, 1972; Jenkins, 1996). Dominant forces in society attempt to promote hegemony by looking for supposed opposites; this helps to define 'who' and 'what' they are. In contrast to 'law and order', Gypsies and Travellers are perceived to be lawless and antisocial (Richardson, 2006a). Thus, for Gypsies and Travellers, a growing mood of intolerance, and a debate that is veering ever closer to advocating assimilation, could influence policy agendas and pose serious difficulties. We can already see this in relation to changes in planning policy brought in by the Coalition Government in 2011, which were based on assumptions that everyone's needs are the same. Gypsies and Travellers have in part retained their strong identity by a system of cultural border guards that has maintained distance and carefully regulated relations between them and the wider society. This distance has preserved a set of life strategies and values that are different from those maintained by wider society. The space for maintaining that distance has become much reduced and this has major implications for the future of Gypsy and Traveller identity. Can new and inclusive partnerships be formed between Gypsies and Travellers and the state that herald not only new strategies but also genuine inclusion and intercultural dialogue and policy frameworks?

Gypsy and Traveller identity

The debate on defining Gypsies and Travellers is contentious and not at all simple. First, there are a number of different communities, as discussed in previous sections of this chapter, including Scottish and Welsh Gypsies and Travellers, and very many different groups of European Gypsies and Travellers. Second, there is also a view that Gypsies themselves have changed in composition, and perhaps may no longer be 'true' or 'real' (Richardson, 2006a). Some commentators have waded into this fraught debate asserting that there are now no real Romany Gypsies, claiming instead that this group have been fragmented and undermined by industrialisation and change. Such a view holds a very static and romanticised notion of what and who Gypsies and Travellers are and presupposes that minority groups are rigid and fixed entities that do not change and adapt with the passage of time. The danger of this definition is reflected by the then Labour Government Home Secretary Jack Straw's declaration:

> There are relatively few real Romany gypsies left, who seem to mind their own business and don't cause trouble to other people, and then there are a lot more people who masquerade as travellers or gypsies, who trade on the sentiment of people, but who seem to think because they label themselves as travellers that therefore they've got a licence to commit crimes and act in an unlawful way that other people don't have. (Millar, 1999)

The conclusion drawn from such sentiments is that what we have is a troubled and dysfunctional social group rather than a vibrant and proud minority ethnic group. Indeed, a continual theme throughout the history of Gypsies and Travellers has been the depiction of this group as criminally and socially deviant (Kenrick and Clark, 1999). Across Europe, policy makers, influenced by a culture of poverty theory, have advocated compensatory education and training to break the perceived culture of deprivation among Roma, Gypsies and Travellers. As a consequence of such assimilationist policies, some Gypsies and Travellers have found themselves in a more perilous situation with the fragmentation of traditional support networks and practices leading to isolation, cultural trauma and welfare dependency (Stewart, 1997; Arnstberg, 1998).

Although there is much debate over who is and who is not a Gypsy and Traveller, the state and social policy have often failed to make such differentiation or seek to understand their needs and aspirations. What all these groups have in common is the high level of exclusion they endure, exclusion that the state has actively contributed to through assimilationist and hegemonic discourse and policy. This book seeks to assess the effectiveness of social policy for these groups against the benchmarks of empowerment and social inclusion, which we interpret as freedom to choose and to lead the kind of lives that they value and equal access to services and life chances.

Readers will note that throughout the book there are differing terms used. The title of the book refers to Gypsies and Travellers, which encompasses most groups, including the diverse range of ethnic groups, as well as nomadic groups such as New Travellers; but the term 'Gypsies and Travellers' does not include Roma who have immigrated from Europe, or Showmen.[2] Sometimes, chapters will refer to the umbrella term 'Gypsies, Roma and Travellers'; this umbrella term tends to be used where the subject discussed (representation in the media, lack of access to services, hostility in public discourse) has an impact similarly across this wide range of groups.

There are a number of technically different definitions of Gypsies and Travellers in the law; for example in equalities legislation the focus is on 'race' and this means that no matter whether a Gypsy or Traveller lives on the roadside, on a site or in a house they have a distinct identity and it is protected by law. Definitions under housing law also retain this notion of a 'settled' Gypsy; however, in planning law, the definition of Gypsy and Traveller is linked to nomadism rather than race and as such there can be a big impact on planning decisions for those Gypsies and Travellers who have moved into bricks and mortar. Many Gypsies and Travellers have felt compelled to move into houses because of a lack of alternative suitable accommodation, and this has an impact on health (see Chapter Three, this volume) particularly with feelings of isolation from the community. The book does not have a separate chapter on housed Gypsies and Travellers, but for more information see Greenfields and Smith (2010); however, some of the issues discussed in the book (such as portrayal in the media) have an impact on Gypsies and Travellers in whatever form of accommodation they currently live.

We have included an explanation of Roma in Britain in the previous section of this chapter; some of the chapters focus their examination on Gypsies and Travellers who have been settled in Britain for centuries, but do also refer to the experiences of Roma alongside. Chapter Eleven focuses unapologetically on the European Framework for National Roma Integration Strategies, which clearly includes Roma at the heart of that debate. There is a need for a chapter on Europe, even in a book examining empowerment and inclusion of Gypsies and Travellers in British society. The chapter allows us to widen the horizons to provide a comparative approach on Gypsy, Roma and Traveller issues. While the relevance and sustainability of Europe has been much debated in the news following sovereign debt crises in Greece and Italy (both swiftly followed by elections in October and November 2011 in those countries), there is no doubt that for the purposes of a discussion of including and empowering Gypsies and Travellers in Britain, the wider European context must also inform the debate.

In introducing the notion of Gypsy and Traveller identity and the labels that are used about these groups, the editors of this book note that this can be an incredibly frustrating debate for Gypsies and Travellers themselves, who would rather academics and policy makers got on with solutions and ideas to policy problems such as the shortage of accommodation and access to healthcare. Readers who are interested in the issue of identity should turn to Acton (1997) (and particularly to McVeigh's and Ní Shuinéar's chapters in that volume). However, for now, we turn to Le Bas (2010, p 6) to make the point on the impossible circularity of discourse on the 'genuine' Gypsy identity:

> The cyclic-oxymoronic situation is that the Gypsy speaking to you cannot be trusted to tell the truth, even about the fact that they are a Gypsy, yet the only reason for this lack of trust is *that they are a Gypsy*. I do hope such Kafkaesque ludicrousness becomes recognised for the inanity it is as soon as humanly possible, as at present it remains a key component of many Gypsies' emerging diasporic experience, and it is boring and offensive. (emphasis in original)

From New Labour to the Big Society

The last decade proved to be an especially eventful one for Gypsy and Traveller communities in Britain. After a sustained period of policy neglect, the Labour government towards the end of its second term gave some thought to addressing what was considered to be the biggest obstacle to inclusion and community cohesion, namely the shortage of Traveller sites (Richardson and Ryder, 2009a). The shortage had increased following the abolition of the duty on local authorities to provide sites contained within the Criminal Justice and Public Order Act 1994 and the replacement of this duty with Planning Circular

01/94, which sought to privatise Traveller site provision; but the absence of a duty meant that many local authorities chose to ignore or thwart this guidance (Crawley, 2004). Labour's site delivery mechanism was to be delivered through regional spatial strategies and intense consultation on these processes meant that Gypsies and Travellers started to climb the policy agenda, a process facilitated by strong public declarations of support from the Commission for Racial Equality and the growing political mobilisation of Gypsy and Traveller communities themselves as evidenced by a new generation of activists coming forward and the establishment of new groups (Clark and Greenfields, 2006). These trends seemed to encourage a range of governmental agencies at local and national levels together with service providers seeking to explore new means to engage with and address the needs of Gypsies and Travellers.

These positive steps forward have to be contrasted with the fact that Gypsies and Travellers have also climbed the political and media agenda in a negative sense. In Parliament, frequent debates are held on this issue, the debates often being of an intemperate nature where politicians accuse this minority of not paying taxes, being law breakers and antisocial (Cemlyn et al, 2009). A similar negative narrative has been played out in the media, in particular the tabloid press (Richardson, 2006b). Gypsy and Traveller communities have also been traumatised by large-scale evictions of unauthorised Traveller sites where bailiffs and heavy machinery have evicted families with, it has been said, little regard for the health and safety of those residents being moved (Ryder and Greenfields, 2010). Equally prominent in the collective consciousness of Gypsies and Travellers have been the public outbursts of hostility towards them such as the violent attack on the Traveller boy, Johnny Delaney, which tragically led to his death (discussed further in Chapter Seven, this volume), public meetings where up to 1,000 local residents have attended to articulate their opposition to a small site development (Richardson, 2007a; Ryder et al, 2011) and the bullying of Gypsy and Traveller children in school (Foster and Walker, 2010).

This book seeks to review some of the events of the last decade in particular both under the New Labour Government, but also the changes under the Coalition Government, which form part of the Prime Minister David Cameron's mission for a Big Society. While many commentators have challenged the 'Big Society' and discourse analysts might examine its role as an 'empty signifier' with potential to mean many different things to different people, Cameron tried recently to be more specific on what the Big Society meant to him. He identified three key parts (Cameron, 2011):

- devolving more power to local government, and beyond local government;
- opening up public services, making them less monolithic (cooperatives and mutuals);
- more charity and philanthropy.

Put like that, the Big Society is difficult to argue with as a concept. However, as critical thinkers we must examine the impact and practical implications of the Big Society. Who can argue with the concept of empowering local people? However, go beyond the abstract and we can see that decisions taken by local people, without a wider framework, can exclude marginalised communities and unpopular developments. On a positive level, policy initiatives, such as opening up services and provision through cooperatives and mutuals, could hold the potential to give groups such as Gypsies and Travellers a greater say in the policies that affect them and a greater opportunity to help themselves (Ryder, 2011). However, there are implications for this 'opening up', most notably in the localism policy, which scrapped regional strategies for site provision, replaced Planning Circular 01/06 with the National Planning Policy Framework and reduced funding. It is all very well suggesting people should be empowered to help themselves, but then to take away the planning and financial framework to help deliver this means that the 'Big Society' in this context is different for Gypsies and Travellers. There is a cumulative effect too: other policy initiatives to assist Gypsies and Travellers in health, education, culture and empowerment, as examined in this book, also appear to be at risk.

Two years into the life of the Coalition Government came the progress report by the ministerial working group on tackling inequalities experienced by Gypsies and Travellers, which was chaired by the cabinet minister Eric Pickles MP (CLG, 2012c). As a result of being excluded from the process of the ministerial working group, UK Gypsy and Traveller representative groups have formed policy hubs on accommodation, education, health and employment. Through these deliberative hubs views will be collected from activists and communities producing a 'snapshot' of community aspirations that can be compared and contrasted to the outcomes of the inter-ministerial committee and relayed to the European Commission (Ryder et al, 2012). On a broader point the inter-ministerial report reflects Coalition Government thinking on localism but critics would respond that equality requires state action, underpinned by a commitment to social justice (Kisby, 2010) and should ideally be mediated and delivered through community representation. Such inclusivity will ensure change is relevant and tailored to the needs of excluded people (Fung and Wright, 2001), but also there are times when the state has to enforce equality and not merely be a spectator: this is a central theme in this book.

Structure of the book

The content of this book is wide ranging. It attempts to cover many aspects of Gypsies' and Travellers' lives and is divided into policy areas such as accommodation, health, education, social policy and economic inclusion. It also examines cross-cutting issues such as representation in the media and political debate, contestations of space, justice and empowerment. The focus of the book is on Britain, but there is one chapter that looks specifically at the wider contextual European and global framework (Chapter Eleven).

This book is divided into three main parts:

• Part One: Context, issues and policy responses;
• Part Two: Empowering Gypsies and Travellers;
• Part Three: Conclusions.

There is a common thread running through the book, which analyses the involvement and empowerment of Gypsies and Travellers. To this end it is important to include the voices of Gypsy and Traveller people who are themselves respected scholars and experts in their field, for example in Chapters Two and Ten. However, the concept of empowerment is debated in more of a theoretical framework in Part Two where we critically analyse attempts to devolve power to communities, challenges in representation within community groups and the recognition of culture, and reflect on research methodologies and media representation of Gypsies and Travellers.

The longstanding shortage of sites is a central contributory factor to the acute exclusion of Gypsies and Travellers. Chapter Two – *Accommodation needs and planning issues* (Richardson and Smith-Bendell) – draws on ongoing research into planning decisions on Gypsy and Traveller sites and numerous cases championing planning issues for travelling communities. The chapter outlines the current shortage in accommodation for Gypsies and Travellers, the legislation and policy that was introduced in 2004 to attempt to address the issue, the impact that has had and the changes for strategic planning for sites under the Coalition Government. The chapter explores the potential for the community to play an active role in site delivery and it uses a theoretical framework of power and control to explain the challenges of planning for sites in contested space.

One of the strongest indicators of Gypsy and Traveller exclusion has been the poor health status of this minority, ill-health often compounded by poor access to services but also poor relationships with health service providers where inflexibility and a lack of understanding of their cultural and health needs have acted as a barrier to the delivery of effective healthcare. Chapter Three – *Gypsy and Traveller health* (Van Cleemput) – follows a range of studies, including more recent research on health issues that outlines where Gypsies and Travellers have been effectively involved in the design of new models of inclusive health practice for this community through dialogue with the National Health Service and project design and 'personalisation' of services, primarily through the Pacesetters programme. Van Cleemput reviews the legacy of Pacesetters and the impact of Coalition Government reforms.

Education has often been perceived as a central tool in facilitating the inclusion and empowerment of Gypsies and Travellers but in the past schools have been the scene of persistent bullying and racism and a clash of cultures where education has been viewed as an agent of assimilation. However, in the UK in particular, with the development of a national network of Traveller Education Services and pioneering work by some schools, important progress has been made in raising Gypsy and Traveller educational achievement and attainment. Chapter Four – *Education, inclusion and government policy* (Foster and Cemlyn) – outlines some of the challenges for Gypsies and Travellers in having a say in the direction of their children's educational experiences. The chapter assesses the potential of the personalisation agenda as envisaged by the previous Labour government, but also the scope of Coalition Government policies.

One of the most emotive aspects of assimilatory and racist social policy has been the forced sterilisation of Roma women and the seizure of Gypsy, Roma and Traveller children and their placement in care or an adoptive family, experiences that have left a profound legacy of mistrust towards social services. Chapter Five – *Gypsies, Travellers and social policy: marginality and insignificance. A case study of Gypsy and Traveller children in care* (Allen) – explores social policy and work for the young and vulnerable in the UK. The chapter is based on new and ongoing research on Travellers who have been in care and examines the struggle that some people go through in search of an understanding of identity and belonging.

The 'Traveller Economy' has traditionally been at the heart of Gypsy and Traveller bonding social capital and self-help networks based on self-employment, entrepreneurialism and in-family training. However, it has been deemed by some commentators to be undergoing decline and stagnation yet has been neglected in terms of public debates. Chapter Six – *Gypsies and Travellers: economic practices, social capital and embeddedness* (Greenfields, Ryder and Smith) – examines the potential of the Traveller Economy but also the potential of new innovations including mutualism and social enterprise preserving the core features of Gypsy and Traveller economic practices in a modern context that can reverse economic and social exclusion.

Part Two of the book – Empowering Gypsies and Travellers – focuses on trends and initiatives to promote empowerment and involvement in measures to tackle exclusion. Chapter Seven – *Justice and empowerment* (Richardson and Ryder) – examines the notions of 'justice' and 'empowerment' as they relate to Gypsies and Travellers. In a time when the Conservative-led Coalition Government aims to empower everyone to take part in a 'Big Society', it is important to assess the extent to which Gypsies and Travellers will be included in this aim. The chapter also looks at the relationship between the police force and travelling communities, examining notions of justice in how police treat victimisation and discrimination against Gypsies and Travellers. Theories of power provide a framework and include the notion of discourse as control (Richardson, 2006a).

For centuries, Gypsy, Roma and Traveller communities have been bedevilled by negative and racist stereotypes, which still hold great currency today in the tabloid press and within popular opinion. One means to overcome this and to help facilitate new understanding particularly in the context of school has been through the promotion of Gypsy and Traveller culture and has featured in a number of initiatives over the past 40 years, which culminated in Gypsy Roma Traveller History Month (GRTHM). Chapter Eight – *Recognising Gypsy, Roma and Traveller history and culture* (Acton and Ryder) – provides an overview of GRTHM, providing insights into how this month has allowed Gypsies, Roma and Travellers to promote and develop their history, language and culture in communities and schools.

As part of the challenge to racist and ill-conceived stereotypes of this minority some forms of academic writing and practice are being challenged and instead new forms of research are being promoted that seek to move Gypsies and Travellers from the place of passive research subjects to partners in the research process. Chapter Nine – *Research with and for Gypsies, Roma and Travellers: combining policy, practice and community in action research* (Greenfields and Ryder) – reviews the potential for inclusive research approaches, the possibilities for empowering community members through the co-production of research methodologies and refers to participatory research projects that the authors have been involved with.

Gypsies and Travellers have high 'news value' and this can explain why they are used in election campaigns as 'scapegoats' and targets, or the topics of lurid media reporting. Chapter Ten – *'Stamp on the Camps': the social construction of Gypsies and Travellers in media and political debate* (Richardson and O'Neill) – examines the circular nature of anti-Gypsy discourse, that it allegedly reflects popular opinion, but also creates folk devils and moral panics (Cohen, 1972), which feed the negative discourse even further. The 'Stamp on the Camps' campaign and the television series Big Fat Gypsy Weddings are moments in media and public discourse that provide useful case studies to illustrate conceptual theories on discourse, racism and control.

The focus of the book in its examination of policy and practice is mostly located in Britain; however, this is achieved within a framework of understanding wider European and global issues for Roma, Gypsies and Travellers. Xenophobia against Roma appears to be on the rise, but there may be potential for European-wide social policy to address these issues in the form of the European Framework for National Roma Integration Strategies, discussed in Chapter Eleven – *The EU Framework for National Roma Strategies: insights into empowerment and inclusive policy development* (Rostas and Ryder). This book argues that such an initiative could give impetus to new forms of empowerment and social policy models that avoid the failed paternalistic welfarism of the past.

The threads of earlier discussion in the book are drawn together in Chapter Twelve – *Conclusion and next steps: inclusion, space and empowerment for Gypsies, Roma and Travellers?* – where Richardson and Ryder assess critically the future of community development and empowerment in the present policy context and explore what social inclusion and the Big Society actually mean for Gypsies and Travellers and whether social policy is set to merely repeat past mistakes and failures or whether there might be a more positive opportunity to improve the inclusion and empowerment of Gypsies and Travellers in British society.

Notes

[1] This is not the only horse fair: there are others, for example in Horsemonden, Hull and Stowe.

[2] Showmen are British citizens who are seen as distinct from Gypsies and Travellers, they travel around the country with fairs and other shows, their accommodation is on 'yards' and they have different needs from Gypsies and Travellers because of the imperative to accommodate their show equipment. Where there are similarities, however, these centre on the shortage of suitable accommodation.

TWO

Accommodation needs and planning issues

Joanna Richardson and Maggie Smith-Bendell

Introduction

In the previous context-setting chapter, the issue of accommodation was a focal point. Without access to accommodation, it has been argued, it is extremely difficult for Gypsies and Travellers to access healthcare, employment and education. There are also ramifications for community cohesion and social inclusion of groups that traditionally have been marginalised in society, if they cannot find a settled place to live.

This chapter takes the issue of accommodation and planning and examines the recent history of planning for sites today, particularly the recent changes in light of Coalition Government planning guidance for Travellers sites, and the raft of measures brought in under the 'localism' agenda. Research undertaken by Richardson will be used as an evidence base for the impact of strategic planning changes (particularly Circular 01/06: ODPM, 2006). A first-hand account of the effect of the planning system, and the lack of accommodation, is given by Maggie Smith-Bendell in this chapter. The authors then conclude with an examination of alternative solutions to the planning and accommodation problem. The contrasting perspectives and styles of writing are important in this chapter as they replicate to an extent what happens in planning in practice. There is a policy/academic debate that takes place in strategic planning; and then there is the personal lived experience of Gypsies and Travellers seeking permission to make their home. While the planning system may try to engage with the personal voice, so far it has failed to achieve this properly. In presenting the academic and personal perspectives alongside one another in this chapter, we hope to emphasise this point and to give the personal voice more prominence.

Planning, by its very nature, seeks to control. Planners control who can build what and where, effectively rationing housing and site development to designated areas, and imposing restrictions and conditions on any new build. While planning development control is the ultimate form of planning control, the parameters for setting the debate in planning policy can also control outcomes. Control comes from implementing policy, but also in setting the agenda. Just because planning policy is universal – it applies to us all – does not mean that the effects of its implementation are felt equally. It is well documented, for example, that planning applications from Gypsies and Travellers are refused in proportionately far greater numbers than applications from the settled population. In spite of this, the Coalition Government in its consultation on the changes to Planning Circular 01/06 sought to redress a perception of unfairness that Gypsies and Travellers had undue advantage in the planning system. Not only was there no evidence to support this claim of unfair advantage, it was also acknowledged that the changes to planning guidance were to deal with a perception rather than a reality. This is an example of just one policy that, when implemented, has an unduly negative impact on a marginalised group. Planning policy has the power to control; the discourse surrounding planning debate also controls (see Chapter Ten). It is for this reason that we seek, in this chapter, to debate the theoretical framework of power and control that shapes the system, but also to examine the recent changes in planning policy, and the impact that will be felt by Gypsy and Traveller communities.

Theoretical framework

Discursive practices of planners and wider society impact on outcomes for Gypsies and Travellers. Foucault (1969) makes clear the power of language. Discourse in planning appeal inspections both reflect and construct understanding on the definition of 'Gypsy' and on the perceived need for more sites to be provided. Porter (2010, p 11) refers to 'the culture of the practice of planning' and this needs more investigation and future research in the area of planning for Gypsy and Traveller sites.

Concepts for investigating space could help with the understanding of planning for places. Lefebvre (1991) suggests a 'conceptual triad', as presented in Figure 2.1.

Figure 2.1: Conceptual triad of space

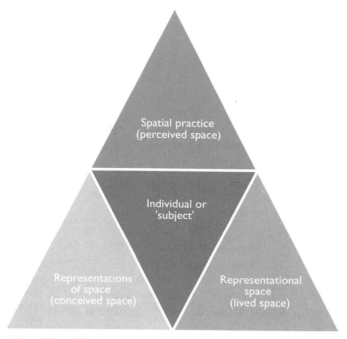

Source: Adapted from Lefebvre (1991, pp 38-9)

Lefebvre (1991) makes very clear that this concept should not be viewed in the abstract, if its importance is to be retained:

> That the lived, conceived and perceived realms should be interconnected, so that the 'subject', the individual member of a given social group, may move from one to another without confusion – so much is a logical necessity. Whether they constitute a coherent whole is another matter. *They probably do in favourable circumstances, when a common language, a consensus and a code can be established.* (1991, p 40, emphasis added)

Favourable circumstances certainly do not exist when we think about the process and debate surrounding planning policy for Gypsy and Traveller sites. One cannot see evidence of a common language, code or consensus and therefore it is unlikely that Lefebvre's conceptual triad can be anything but abstract in the realm of planning policy and decision making for the use of space in relation to Gypsy and Traveller site provision.

These different aspects of space are the source of conflict in the planning system on any planning applications, whether for new homes, wind farms or indeed Gypsy and Traveller sites. Fragmented societies create challenges for planning (Healey, 2005) and there is a need to recognise difference, understand past trauma and engage in participatory planning processes so that communities get to know each other better (Forester, 1999, 2009). Indeed, Forester (2009) makes the point that planning education and training have traditionally neglected skills to tackle conflict and tension in the planning process. Space is contested and it is represented and perceived in different ways – the construction of 'Green Belt' in the mind's eye of wider society, for example, is particularly interesting in the examination and consideration of planning inspectors' language in their decision making.

Porter (2010, p 16) states:

> [T]he structures of meaning and authorities of truth that give planning agency in the world are drenched in the colonial historiographies, and so the colonial relations of domination and oppression are ever present.
> ... If planning is a producer of place, what does it claim is worth producing and how is this particular view of the world continually mediated and reconstituted?

There may be an additional consideration that needs to be given particularly to planning in rural areas because of the romanticisation in discourse of 'Green Belt' and the effect that has on those who need to build homes in rural areas. Sturzaker and Shucksmith (2011) also examine planning for housing in rural areas and they argue that vested powers and interests can have an effect that increases exclusion: 'an 'unholy alliance' of rural elites and urban interests have wielded discursive power to define 'sustainability' on their own terms, which exacerbates the unaffordability of rural housing, leading to social injustice and spatial exclusion' (2011, p 169).

Planning for 'affordable' housing is challenging enough in rural areas. When one considers Sturzaker and Shucksmith's comments in light of the difficulties in planning for Gypsy and Traveller sites in areas particularly where the only available land is in the Green Belt, we can consider that Gypsies and Travellers are under a regime of some sort of spatial apartheid.

There is a need to look further at how the English planning system may have this dominance and oppression embedded in its policies and practices to establish whether there is perhaps a disproportionately negative impact on groups seen to be unpopular in media and social discourse – such as Gypsies and Travellers.

Within the context of a changing policy context of revoking the regional strategies and Circular 01/06 and within a wider framework of the Localism Act and the Big Society, what can we learn from the planning system and its impact on Gypsies and Travellers?

A brief history of Gypsy and Traveller planning policy

The post-war period witnessed major and often centrally driven programmes to create social housing but these approaches were not applied to Gypsy and Traveller sites. In 1960, the Caravan Sites (Control of Development) Act caused the closure of many stopping places used by Gypsies and Travellers as they moved around the country. Harold Wilson's Labour Government later supported Lord Avebury's Private Member's Bill, which resulted in the Caravan Sites Act 1968 and required local authorities to provide sites for Gypsies in England. However, the Act was never fully enforced and the envisaged post-war network of sites did not come to fruition. By 1972, some local authorities were already exempt from building sites for caravans. Nevertheless, the Caravan Sites Act 1968 later created the statutory duty for local authorities 'to provide accommodation on caravan sites for gypsies residing in or resorting to their areas'. This effectively created a duty for councils to design, build and manage sites. There was also recognition at this time that it may be necessary to accept the establishment of sites in protected areas, such as the Green Belt. Unfortunately, there was a severe policy implementation gap, which meant that sites were not delivered as the Act intended. The Cripps report of 1977 – *Accommodation for Gypsies: A report on the workings of the Caravan Sites Act 1968* (Cripps, 1977) – identified a number of obstacles to new site provision; key among these was the importance of public opinion.

In 1993, the Conservative Government announced its intention to introduce legislation to reform the Caravan Sites Act 1968. In 1994, the Criminal Justice and Public Order Act repealed many of the legal duties to provide sites. Circular 01/94 (DoE, 1994) was introduced with a purpose to facilitate Gypsies and Travellers to provide their own private sites. The circular based its rationale on the '[recognition] that many gypsies would prefer to find and buy their own sites to develop and manage. More private sites should release pitches on local authority sites for gypsies most in need of public provision (para 4)'.

Circular 01/94 also reversed previous guidance that in some cases development would need to be on open land. Section 13 states that 'as a rule it will not be appropriate to make provision for gypsy sites in areas of open land'. Looking back at the aims of Circular 01/94 against the actual outcomes of meeting need for sites, this was clearly a policy failure – new sites were not built in any great number.

Political and legislative debate over the Criminal Justice and Public Order Act 1994, which took away the duty from local authorities to provide sites, continues. The former Office of the Deputy Prime Minister's (ODPM) Planning, Local Government and the Regions Select Committee published a report in November 2004, calling for a duty to provide sites to be reinstated (ODPM, 2004). The government response in early 2005 was that it did not feel that a duty was needed, but it set up a Gypsy and Traveller Task Group on Site Provision and Enforcement. The Task Group's report (Briscoe, 2007) supported the legislative framework of the time; however, it was suggested that more momentum was needed around delivering site provision.

Two pieces of legislation in 2004 effectively placed duties on local authorities to assess needs and include sites in development plan documents – this should have resulted in the provision of more Gypsy and Traveller sites. The Housing Act 2004 and the Planning and Compulsory Purchase Act 2004 effectively required local authorities to assess the needs of Gypsies and Travellers and, via the Regional Planning Body, to include how this need would be met in local development plans. Section 225 of the Housing Act 2004 stated: 'Every local housing authority must, when undertaking a review of housing needs in their district under section 8 of the Housing Act 1985 (c. 68), carry out an assessment of the accommodation needs of gypsies and travellers residing in or resorting to their district.'

Two years later, Circular 01/06 (ODPM) was published to replace Circular 01/94 (ODPM, 2006). It provided fresh guidance for deciding on planning permission for new sites and it allowed the potential for considering Green Belt with the insertion of the word 'normally'. Paragraph 49 of Circular 01/06 states: 'There is a general presumption against inappropriate development within Green Belts. New gypsy and traveller sites in the Green Belt are normally inappropriate development, as defined in Planning Policy Guidance 2'. Evidence from research later in this chapter shows that in some cases planning inspectors did find cases that were not 'normal' and where other factors outweighed the protection of Green Belt.

Figure 2.2 presents a diagram from Circular 1/06, which shows that the first step in the planning process for Gypsy and Traveller sites was to undertake a Gypsy and Traveller Accommodation Assessment (GTAA) as required by the Housing Act 2004. The next step was then for the regional planning bodies to discuss the individual GTAA findings in their area, to evaluate, check and modify from a regional perspective and then to give specific pitch numbers for new site delivery, per local authority. These numbers would then, in the third and final stage, be incorporated into development plan documents.

Figure 2.2: Planning process under Circular 01/06

PLANNING PROCESS

Overview

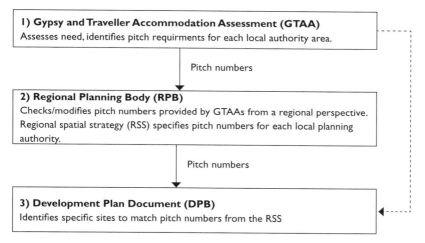

Source: ODPM (2006, p 7)

Step two was an important aspect of the process and allowed for a regional perspective. The examinations in public that happened during stage two also allowed for a wide range of people across district boundaries to openly discuss outcomes of GTAAs and the relationship between pitch requirements across borders for a whole region and picture of need. For Gypsy and Traveller sites, a regional approach is perhaps more appropriate for another reason too. There can be a large amount of objection to local sites, and taking a step back to a regional level can help mitigate some of the objection. While the localism agenda has laudable aims to empower local communities, there are some instances in planning where very local decision-making processes can marginalise disadvantaged groups.

Planning changes introduced by the Coalition Government from 2010 onwards

There was a great deal of change in the planning policy context for Gypsy and Traveller site provision from 2010. Very soon after the Conservative-led Coalition Government came to power, announcements were made by Secretary of State Eric Pickles that the regional strategies would be revoked, changing the landscape of planning policy-making processes. There was a legal challenge to the announcement brought by Cala Homes in 2011, but the government included provisions to revoke regional strategies in the Localism Bill 2010. As was noted in the previous section of this chapter, a regional approach seemed to be an appropriate and sensible context for considering Gypsy and Traveller site provision, and the loss of regional spatial strategies will have an impact on the deliverability of new sites. The Bill was enacted in November 2011, and while there had been consultation on a number of concerns, the key changes it proposed (namely the revocation of regional spatial strategies) remained in the Localism Act 2011.

There is much in the Localism Act 2011 which attempts to positively empower local communities. Central to the Act are the 'community rights', which include:

1. the Right to Challenge – for example where a local community thinks it can deliver a public service better than the existing provider;
2. the Right to Bid, which is additional to, but linked with, the asset transfer agenda and allows communities to bid for spaces that have a strong community value;
3. the Right to Build, which relates to small-scale development and means that traditional planning permission may not be required. There may also be the possibility to develop in the Green Belt, where there is strong local support;
4. Neighbourhood Planning – which the government feels empowers local communities to take more control over what should be developed in their area.

It is difficult to argue against 'community rights' as such, and these may be popular policy changes in many communities. However, there is a danger that Gypsies and Travellers are forgotten in a 'community' and that such rights as are included in the Localism Act may serve to further marginalise them in accommodation and planning policy and practice.

A further compounding factor to the revocation of regional strategies in the Localism Act was the National Planning Policy Framework, which replaced Circular 01/06 with 'light-touch' regulation. A number of detailed implications came out of the new framework, including removal of the word 'normally' from guidance on Green Belt, effectively implementing a blanket ban on development in the Green Belt; however there are wider community rights within the Localism Act which could provide powers to develop in the Green Belt if there is local support. It was suggested that GTAAs were not necessarily the most appropriate evidence base of need, and that planning authorities should 'plan for local need in the context of historic demand'. This is not how planning policy is made for the rest of society, where need is based on current not historic demand and on the most recent and robust technical evidence base; and in the final guidance there was less emphasis on 'historic demand'. The new planning framework (2011) also placed an overly strong emphasis on the use of temporary permissions to meet need, but it did state that planning authorities must set out a plan for a five-year supply of Gypsy and Traveller pitches. The National Planning Policy Framework also moved from a presumption against development generally to a presumption in favour, where appropriate. This new approach could result in more affordable homes being built to meet growing need; but there are still likely to be huge challenges where developments are unpopular in wider society, such as with proposed Gypsy and Traveller sites. Another recent change in the planning framework is the introduction of neighbourhood plans (set out as one of the key community rights in the Localism Act), which are voluntary and will add another tier below local authority plans. It is possible that not all areas will wish to have a neighbourhood plan, but where these exist it is important to have a dialogue on the need for Gypsy and Traveller sites. Neighbourhood plans will be able to state where residents think homes and commercial premises should be built and where community spaces should be protected; so it will be necessary for those writing neighbourhood plans to understand better the local need for sites too.

The Localism Act 2011 (revocation of regional strategies and targets) and the replacement National Planning Policy Framework (replacement of Circular 01/06 with a light-touch approach) caused concern for Gypsies and Travellers who saw the potential negative impact. There was also a third concern: the announcement of reduced capital grant funding from government for sites, which while unsurprising in the economic climate, will have an impact on the delivery of sites. Additionally, there were at this time some concerns that government announcements to criminalise squatting would have a disproportionate effect on Gypsies and Travellers; however, the representative groups lobbied hard and there were changes made to the detail of these plans, which meant that the offence of squatting would be limited to buildings rather than extend to ancillary land; this largely took on board the concerns of Traveller representatives. Included with the recent changes are also opportunities for the planning framework to include the need for Gypsy and Traveller sites and there may be a number of incentive levers including the New Homes Bonus and Community Infrastructure Levy, as well as a shift in presumption in favour of sustainable, appropriate development. The Homes and Communities Agency also announced in 2011 a reserved fund of £25m in the Affordable Housing Programme scheme for community-led development. There may also be funding in future to support an increased government focus on self-build (or 'custom-build', as it is sometimes referred to in policy debate). What is needed alongside structural changes to frameworks and strategies, however, is a concerted effort to provide persuasive information to the communities who have the ability to accept or reject proposals for new homes and new sites, so that they understand the Gypsy and Traveller communities better and consider their need for accommodation along with the rest of their community.

Research on the impact of Planning Circular 01/06

The research on the impact of Circular 01/06 (Richardson, 2011a) involved examination of planning appeal cases – it did not include planning cases resolved at council level. Over the entire research process, a total of 405 planning cases were analysed:

- Period 1: 1 November 2005 – 31 January 2006 (tranche one – pre Circular 01/06), 75 cases;
- Period 2: 1 February – 30 April 2006 (tranche one – post Circular 01/06), 54 cases;
- Period 3: 1 February 2007 – 20 January 2009 (tranche two – 'embedded Circular'), 231 cases;
- Period 4: 27 May – 31 December 2010 (tranche three – post revocation announcement), 45 cases.

The research was a cumulative process and so tranches of research were added when there were changes in planning policy and process. The time periods chosen transpired in response to opportunity to carry out the research, or in response to a request to analyse the impact of a particular issue. For example, periods one and two were taken together as one piece of research (tranche one) to examine the impact of the implementation of Circular 01/06, so appeals pre and post the February 2006 implementation date of the Circular were examined. An opportunity arose to take time to study a two-year period from 2007 to 2009 to see how the circular was being interpreted in appeals and to examine the decisions and outcomes (tranche two). May 2010 is clearly a key date, because of the election of the new Conservative-led Coalition Government and the announcement by Secretary of State, Eric Pickles, that the circular would be revoked. It is anticipated that further research will be undertaken in the future to see how the new National Planning Policy Framework, combined with the effects of the Localism Act, will impact on planning decision making.

The percentage of cases that were allowed and which gave planning permission in each period started from a position of 40% before Circular 01/06 rising to a peak of 70% in period 3 (the embedded phase of implementation of Circular 01/06). Period 4 showed a slight tailing off (the period after the Secretary of State's announcement on the circular and on the revocation of regional strategies) but there now needs to be more research following the implementation of the Coalition Government's new National Planning Policy Framework and the planning guidance for traveller sites, in 2011 (CLG, 2012a; 2012b) to determine the full effect.

Most of the cases examined over the five-year total period of the study were in rural areas – either in the Green Belt or in an Area of Outstanding Natural Beauty (AONB). There was a minority of instances of applications in non Green Belt land, but by the nature of Gypsy and Traveller site planning applications, the availability, suitability and affordability of land, the majority of cases were in Green Belt or similar type of land. The words 'Green Belt' can be hugely evocative and can provoke extreme responses during consultation exercises and in media reporting of cases; for example the unauthorised part of the Dale Farm site was on Green Belt land, but far from being lush and verdant countryside, this piece of land was a scrap yard before it was bought by the Travellers and turned into a site. The reality and the popular perception of Green Belt are not always the same, but nonetheless it is an issue that dominates not just the political and media discourse, but also planning appeal decisions.

Figure 2.3 shows the trend changes across the four periods. In periods 1, 2 and 4, the dominant type of permissions being allowed were permanent. However, during period 3 (which we can consider as the 'embedded' period of Circular 01/06) there were more temporary

Figure 2.3: Percentage of permanent/temporary planning permissions

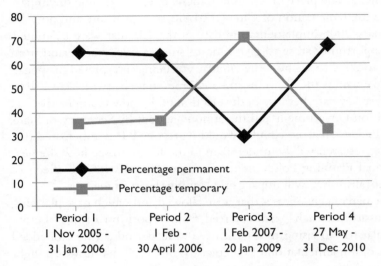

permissions, proportionate to the total number of permissions in the period, being allowed. Looking at Circular 01/06 in isolation may lead one up the wrong path of analysis – this trend reversal makes more sense when considering the regional strategy targets for new pitches to meet evidenced need and the anticipation of planning inspectors that temporary permissions could act to fill a gap until the development plan documents incorporate pitch requirements and ultimately lead to more sites being developed by councils. Regional strategy targets were revoked in the Localism Act before their true effectiveness in the delivery of new sites could have been measured. The announcement of their revocation may, in part, account for the return to permanent permissions as the dominant mode of appeals being allowed in the most recent period of study.

A number of themes came out of the planning inspectors' decision-making process. The key themes in decision rationale across the 405 cases were:

• impact on Green Belt or AONB;
• unmet need for sites in the area (evidenced by GTAA or regional strategy target figures);
• health needs (and the imperative to be settled in a place to access medical care);
• education needs (of children who wanted to access school);

- Gypsy and Traveller status (in some cases this was considered in great detail and there were examples where the planning inspector found that the appellant did not meet the definition under planning guidance);
- other personal circumstances (including aversion to bricks and mortar);
- highway safety (access from the site onto the road and the potential increase in vehicles);
- sustainability (whether the site was close enough to school, doctor and shops and whether excessive personal car use in remote areas would impact on environmental sustainability);
- human rights (if permission for the site was not given, would this interfere with the appellant's human rights, in particular Article 8 of the Human Rights Act 1998);
- Secretary of State to revoke regional strategies and to replace Circular 01/06.

Although a wide range of factors was considered across all cases, which were decided on by a number of different planning inspectors, three key areas seemed to be discussed most (see Figure 2.4).

Figure 2.4: Key factors in assessing planning appeal cases

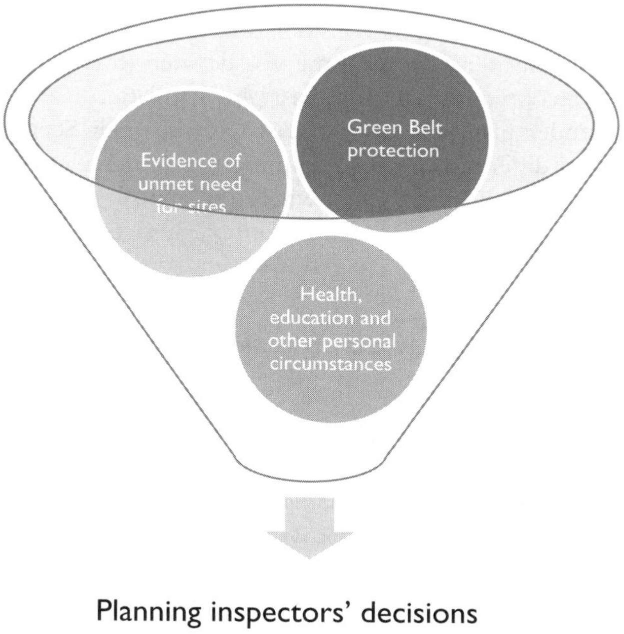

Evidence of unmet need for sites

Green Belt protection

Health, education and other personal circumstances

Planning inspectors' decisions

In each case, different aspects of the site and the circumstances were considered and in most cases a clear rationale for decisions given. However, it was not clear from the analysis across all of the cases, at what point personal circumstances, for example, would surely outweigh protection of the Green Belt. For some planning inspectors in some cases, protection of the Green Belt seemed sacrosanct, and for other cases there did seem to be a 'tipping point' at which the personal circumstances outweighed any harm to the Green Belt in granting temporary permission. Because each case is different, each must be judged on individual issues – but there is merit in further research, such as this, which has an overview of decisions across all planning inspectors to see whether interpretation of the guidance is largely consistent and reasonable.

Human rights

The majority of appeal decisions considered the impact of the appeal decision on the human rights of the Gypsies and Travellers seeking planning permission. There is a duty to undertake such considerations, and in Gypsy and Traveller planning permission cases this often links to Article 8 of the Human Rights Act 1998, which refers to the right to respect for private and family life and home. There were no cases in the primary research where an appeal was allowed and planning permission given, based on human rights considerations. There were individual cases where the recognition of home was debated (for example was 'home' only recognised under human rights legislation if it was also recognised under planning law?) and where the-then Secretary of State's opinion differed from one planning inspector's view. Overall, however, in nearly all of the cases, where the appeal was disallowed and planning permission refused, the planning inspector judged that any interference with human rights was 'necessary and proportionate'.

A place to stay – too much to ask?

My travelling days – Maggie Smith-Bendell

I well remember my travelling days in the 1940s and 1950s, when we thought we Romanies were free; and in a way I suppose we were. We had heritage stopping places, which our families had been using for generations; we could stop in the green lanes and the extensive common lands, which could be found in most counties. Our only drawback was having to stop on the roadside, where the police would move us on – much like they do today. Lives were made a misery by the constant pressure of being hunted on; tempers flared on many occasion and our men-folk would end up in the courts of law, being sent to prison or heavily fined.

But once on the common land, the police could not touch us. This land was shared by one and all; farmers sometimes grazed their animals on it: pigs, cattle and sheep, all for free. Alas, the common could not sustain us for long; we had to move in order to earn our living by hawking or scrap-collecting by horse and cart. Farm work was our main source of income, stopping in one place for up to six weeks or more at one time: working the land by hop picking, and picking fruit and vegetables. Here on the farms the horses could rest up from continuous driving up and down the country, and the families earned decent wages. Even though the work could be back-breakingly hard, it was work and we were glad of it.

Our road-side stopping places were picked out because each one afforded us with fresh spring water and nearby dwellings to hawk our wares, be they pegs or flowers, or dropping the old rag bills. All over England there are freshwater running springs; these had been marked out within our travelling pattern, by our forefathers. This was vital, because most house-dwellers did not like supplying us with cans of their water; we would make for the springs whenever possible and fast-flowing shallow brooks would be used. Rivers were considered unclean by my people, only good enough to wash the horses in or the wagons; if it was a shallow brook – and we knew them all – we made full use of them.

In the winters our men would get jobs on farms so that the horses would be fed on hay (keeping in mind we really did have the four seasons back then, and the hard snowy winters could be very cruel to man and beast). To get farm work such as stone-walling, logging or hedge-laying meant we were able to provide feed for our horses, because unless you worked for farmers, very few would want to sell us any hay. Of course the men earned a few shillings, apart from when the police were moving us on. Life back then was very pleasant. We had so many stopping places dotted within our travelling pattern, that we were more or less contented with our lifestyle – and this is how all the families lived country-wide.

Keeping in mind this was 70 years ago, there were not as many families on the roads as there are today: over the years these have grown, from hundreds to thousands, and include not just Romany Gypsies, but also Irish Travellers, New Travellers and other cultural and ethnic travelling communities, all travelling and seeking their living. All of these groups need somewhere to make a base. At the rate sites are being built, which is almost nil, Gypsies and other travelling communities will always be in need of and outnumber the pitches as they become available unless proper provision is made in planning and housing strategies and policies.

In the old days we had adequate stopping places – farms, common lands and green lanes – which today are inaccessible. Machines have taken over the farm and land work, common lands have either been sold or made inaccessible by ditches or huge boulders put in place to stop any access – roadside stopping places are now no-go areas. This is of big concern to me, because the Gypsy and Traveller population is growing by the week and will always outnumber the government's feeble action to build enough sites and pitches. A lot of our Gypsy sites have been bought up by private owners and landlords, who turn them in to mobile-home parks for the settled community; hence, there are more families seeking pitches this year in my county. Four permanent local authority sites and one council transit site have been sold off to a private buyer. There are well in access of 50 families residing on these sites. Who knows what the future holds for them.

When will the government wake up to these practices and realise that for each lost site, a new one has to be found and built?

Gypsies and Travellers have huge difficulty in finding and buying land on which to build sites. This can be due to a number of factors.

Maggie Smith-Bendell reflected on her many years' experience as a planning expert and adviser to Gypsy families, and as a representative for Gypsy people, and concluded that the following list presents the most oft-cited difficulties in getting sites built:

- lack of suitable affordable land;
- covenants put on land – 'no caravans or mobile homes';
- Green Belt protection;
- AONB;
- wildlife – newts, bats, birds, badgers;
- heathland;
- contaminated land;
- highways objection;
- sustainability criterion;
- open countryside;
- local objection;
- authorities taking a personal/prejudiced interest to stop permission being granted;
- local communities attending sales of land and buying it up at double the value to keep Gypsies and Travellers out the area;

- Members of Parliament against Gypsy/Traveller applications;
- development control committees taking prejudiced views on applications;
- racial prejudice thrown at Gypsy/Traveller families from all sides.

Maggie Smith-Bendell's list of factors above details a number of barriers to providing new sites. One stands out particularly – local objection. In previous research for the Joseph Rowntree Foundation (Richardson, 2007a), this was a key factor and, indeed, it was also identified prominently back in 1977 in the Cripps report as the dominant barrier to site provision. Smith-Bendell herself says of this local objection:

> 'There are very few, if any, local communities that welcome a proposed Gypsy site within their area, however small in number that site may be. The very word 'Gypsy' breeds fear, distrust and suspicion. People worry that a Gypsy/Traveller site will devalue their property, they think Gypsies and Travellers are dirty and are thieves, they don't want Gypsy–Traveller children in local schools and don't want their GP [general practitioner] to register Gypsy–Traveller families for healthcare.'

These objections are often founded on fear and on media representation, rather than on fact (see Chapter Ten, this volume). For example, the concern that the presence of a Travellers' site will devalue property prices is not backed up by evidence. Research for the Planning Exchange and Joseph Rowntree Foundation (Duncan, 1996) found that neighbours' concerns prior to a new site were very often allayed once the site was in place. Nevertheless, the fears of people can lead to extreme and hostile objections to new sites. One such example is in Meriden, Solihull.

An unauthorised development in Meriden, on land designated as Green Belt, provoked an immediate and sustained response from residents. An opposition group was set up: Residents Against Inappropriate Development (RAID). Eighty residents took it in turns to keep a 24/7 vigil at a camp set up to protest against the site (Greatrex, 2011). There were consultation meetings for local residents including local MP Caroline Spelman (also Secretary of State for the Department of Environment, Food and Rural Affairs) but excluding the Gypsy residents on the site. It was claimed by the appellants that the existence of RAID, camped out opposite the site, prevented meaningful communication between the residents on the site and the local people. Communication and balanced consultation meetings are vital to successful site outcomes (Richardson, 2007a) and media representation is key to the debate (a concept that will be discussed in more detail in Chapter Ten, this volume). A retrospective planning application was heard at a planning inquiry, and the decision at the end of October 2011 dismissed the appeal and refused planning permission. The primary considerations given in the decision by the Secretary of State echoed those of the planning inspector – namely that there was harm to the Green Belt and that the openness of the countryside was affected. The appeal considered the personal circumstances of the appellants and the recognised and acknowledged shortage of alternative sites; but it was found that the harm to the Green Belt outweighed these considerations. While the human rights of the appellants were also considered, the Secretary of State decided that the decision on the appeal was proportionate and necessary and therefore did not contravene the Human Rights Act.

As highlighted at the beginning of this chapter, lack of accommodation is not a problem in isolation; it links to a range of other health, education and employment issues. When asked to reflect again on her experience, Maggie Smith-Bendell suggested that there were many consequences of a lack of accommodation, but key among these were:

- Without an address and postcode, people cannot gain access to sustainable healthcare such as with a general practitioner. Some can only access healthcare through the Accident & Emergency Department at a hospital.
- People cannot gain access to education.
- There are epidemics of measles and whooping cough due to the difficulty of infants gaining access to immunisation.
- There is an increase in suicides.
- There is an increase in depression and other mental health problems.
- The lack of fresh running water impacts on people's health and standard of living.

Understanding different cultural needs in planning

All too often, the debate over new sites becomes an ideological battle over land use and who has the traditional right to access land. There are some sacred cows – such as Green Belt – which seem to be viewed as needing protecting, even from transitory use where the land is returned to its former state. Something that can help here is a method of seeing the value of land to a range of different cultures and viewpoints.

Cultural heritage assessments may be a useful approach for planners to take so that they can ascertain the importance of certain pieces of land and areas from a Gypsy and Traveller community point of view. The importance of Gypsy and Traveller culture is recognised in certain ways – for example, the Gypsy Roma Traveller History Month in June each year (on which there is more debate in Chapter Eight, this volume). However, this culture can be forgotten in strategic planning and housing systems. In examining the meaning of areas to Gypsy and Traveller culture, it may be possible to find appropriate places for site development and at the same time embed cultural lessons in the communication of ideas to the wider public. Cultural landscape assessments have been an important part in heritage planning practice in Australia, particularly in understanding the value of spaces to Aboriginal communities in consultation on new planning such as for wind turbines (Auswind, 2007). Although cultural assessments in the Australian context are being used to consult with communities on the impact of new development in their area, the premise of understanding cultural values could be translated, as appropriate, to better understand the need to be near certain spaces and areas for communities, such as Gypsies and Travellers.

Commons sharing and emerging initiatives to provide sites

Commons sharing is a very informal approach to sharing resources such as community commons in villages, wooded areas and so on. During a piece of research assessing accommodation needs in 2010, New Travellers were asked about commons sharing. Some of the responses to this question in the accommodation needs survey showed the exasperation in being asked a question that relates to an ideal that many feel they are trying to achieve anyway but are being stopped from doing so by planning and antisocial behaviour laws. One respondent replied 'Duh!' to the question on whether commons sharing was a good idea, thus demonstrating that it was not exactly a new idea to the travelling communities. However, it is not something that every single Traveller would want to be involved in, particularly if it was made official and prescribed through the council and various agencies, rather than arrangements being fluid and informal. Equally, for some Romany Gypsies, the notion of commons sharing is not necessarily an ideal scenario when security and stability, and family-only sites, are required.

There is a range of models that can be examined for common land sharing, and indeed decision making and power sharing. Ostrom (1990) pays attention to traditional models[1] and potential but unsatisfactory alternatives[2] before debating other methods, such as the Turkish fishing sites rota, which draws on collective action to share common pool resources. Buck (1998, p 35) provides some design principles for sustainable commons–sharing regimes:

- clearly defined boundaries;
- operational rules congruent with local conditions;
- collective choice arrangements;
- monitoring;
- graduated sanctions;
- conflict resolution mechanisms;
- rights to organise regimes;
- nested enterprises.

For multiple-use commons (which may be the case for some informal arrangements on common land that could be used by Travellers for a brief period for stopping and for grazing, but then used by other communities locally for other purposes at other times):

- Resource domain must be able to support all uses.
- All users must be represented.
- Knowledge of operational rules must be shared.

In some areas, community land trusts are being considered as an option for providing Gypsy and Traveller sites. A pilot in the South West of England uses recyclable grant funding (the money is repaid by members of the community land trust within a fixed period and so it can be used again to fund more provision) to help develop sites for Gypsies and Travellers. Development funding is important in supporting and facilitating the writing of a business plan, an application for planning permission, an application for a loan, rules of governance and site plans. While this may not be an appropriate model in all circumstances, community land trusts could be seen as an innovative alternative that may help to meet evidenced need for Traveller site accommodation.

Funding for new sites is also a problematic issue: government capital grant funding for new sites has dropped by more than half since 2011. Innovation is needed not just in the models for planning and managing sites, but also for financing them. However, there is also still a need for some form of affordable accommodation provision for those members of the travelling communities with insufficient funds or access to land. Local authorities and councils should still meet the need for affordable accommodation for those Gypsies and Travellers who need it. In other areas of public service provision, the idea of social investment bonds is being tested; this approach levers in private finance to help pay for a solution to a problem (a cost – both financial and social) and investors share in a proportion of the longer-term savings. The lack of accommodation for Gypsies and Travellers is a social cost to the travelling communities and wider society, and it results in a lack of community cohesion. There is also a financial cost to the policy of evicting rather than providing (Morris and Clements, 2002; Briscoe, 2007). Perhaps social investment bonds, or other alternative innovative models, could be considered to meet the challenges of funding affordable site provision.

Conclusion

Maggie Smith-Bendell reminds us of the human cost of past policy failure:

> 'Since the 14th century, the Gypsies of this country have been held in suspicion, put to death for being Gypsies. For hundreds of years this community has been harassed: moved on continuously. Sites which were built in previous decades, on bogs and landfill, are no longer in use for Gypsy sites. There have been very few local authority sites built in recent decades, but families have continued to grow with no additional provision to take account of site closures and changing accommodation needs. In the meantime, strategies for developing housing for the settled community have continued to attempt to align itself with evidenced current need through these years. Private site provision has been fought and won on appeals (sometimes two or three appeals before permission has been granted) and we must remember that private sites are self-funded with no burden on the taxpayer. There was some, limited, progress in planning for sites with Planning Circular 01/06, and yet this is under threat from the Coalition Government now. This circular had a better understanding of Gypsy/Traveller needs; we should keep it and allow it time to produce the long-aimed-for objectives – more site provision to meet need.'

This chapter has outlined the context and history of planning and accommodation provision for Gypsies and Travellers. The Localism Act

2011 and the changes to the planning guidance will have a cumulative effect on Gypsies and Travellers, and there is a fear that the new political agenda will not result in the identified need for appropriate accommodation being met. We have already outlined the impact of lack of accommodation on health, education and employment. In the next chapter, Patrice Van Cleemput examines health issues for travelling communities in more detail.

Notes

[1] The Tragedy of the Commons, The Prisoner's Dilemma and the Logic of Collective Action.

[2] Leviathan as the only way, Privatisation as the only way and 'the only way'.

THREE

Gypsy and Traveller health

Patrice Van Cleemput

Introduction: health inequalities experienced by Gypsies and Travellers

Previous dearth of research evidence

The lack of reliable research evidence on the health of Gypsies and Travellers in the United Kingdom (UK) prior to 2004 had been widely acknowledged in reviews (Hajioff and McKee, 2000; Doyal et al, 2002; Smart et al, 2003; Zeman, 2003). In 2002, Doyal et al's comprehensive review of studies concerning the health of Gypsies and Travellers in the UK and Ireland reported that there had been no studies that had attempted any systematic comparison of the health status of Gypsies and Travellers with the wider population and that most studies in the review were small scale and anecdotal.

The focus of the studies was virtually limited to the area of maternal and child health, with a particular emphasis on immunisation, consanguinity and congenital anomalies. As Atkin and Chattoo (2006) observe, this particular limited health focus can be problematic, particularly if prior causal assumptions are made, and if the minority ethnic health experience is misrepresented by use of stereotypical myths to explain beliefs and behaviour: 'this results in research often blaming ethnic minority communities for the problems they experience, because of their deviant, unsatisfactory and pathological lifestyles' (2006, p 102).

Behavioural and cultural explanations for health inequalities can be used to avoid contextualised examination of structural explanations. Ahmad (2000) reviewed evidence of health and social care problems among minority ethnic communities that are identified as arising from cultural practices. By reifying and essentialising ethnic categories, such research suggests that ethnicity is a cause of health differences. This pathologisation of culture is an example of the risk of poorly designed and poorly interpreted research that fails to contextualise the broader issues. However, there are notable exceptions. For example, in studies of Gypsy and Traveller healthcare (Pahl and Vaile, 1986; Feder, 1989), the authors demonstrated high perinatal and infant mortality rates as important areas of health inequality, and they reported an association with poor environmental conditions and with the experience of oppression; they also focused on inequity in access to healthcare.

However, it is over 20 years since those studies and there had been scarce attention paid to the findings in respect of either further research or policy measures. There may be various reasons for a dearth of subsequent reliable research evidence. These may include the difficulties and costs of conducting reliable research with marginalised and mobile groups who are understandably suspicious of the motives. It may also reflect the lack of any baseline data due to the relative invisibility of Gypsies and Travellers in health monitoring. Crucially, until recently, I would argue that the most likely relevant factors have been the lack of political awareness or will and the consequent low priority given to the health of Gypsies and Travellers by research funders.

Current evidence

The low priority referred to above has changed since the publication of the 2004 report 'The health status of Gypsies and Travellers in England' (Parry et al, 2004). By using reliable standardised measures as indicators of health and age–sex matched comparators, this study showed that Gypsies and Travellers have significantly poorer health than other UK-resident, English-speaking minority ethnic groups and economically disadvantaged white UK residents, with an inverse relationship between health needs and service use. The aspects of Gypsy and Traveller health that show the most marked inequalities are self-reported anxiety, respiratory problems including asthma and bronchitis, and chest pain. The excess prevalence of miscarriages, stillbirths, neonatal deaths and premature death of older offspring is also conspicuous.

The scale of health inequality between the Gypsy and Traveller study population and the UK general population is even larger. In the 2001 Census, the proportion of the population overall (all ages) reporting limiting long-term illness is 18.2% compared with 41.9% in the Gypsy and Traveller group in this study.

From the study results, and from comparison with UK normative data, it is clear that the scale of health inequality between the Gypsy and Traveller study population and the UK general population is large, with reported health problems being between two and five times more prevalent. Health status in the Gypsy and Traveller group was correlated with those factors that are recognised as influential on health: age, education and smoking. However, the poorer health status of Gypsies and Travellers could not be accounted for by these factors alone: 'The roles played by environmental hardship, social exclusion and cultural attitudes emerge from the qualitative study, and are consistent with the finding there is a health impact of being a Gypsy Traveller over and above other socio-demographic variables' (Parry et al, 2004, p 76). Nettleton (2001) points to a wealth of other evidence that shows that social factors have a persistent impact on health after control for smoking and other behavioural factors. This reveals the weakness of the behavioural argument as an explanation.

Social determinants of health and health equity: the causes of the causes

It is now well accepted that health inequalities are not inevitable: 'a burgeoning volume of research identifies social factors at the root of much of these inequalities in health' (Marmot, 2005, p 1099). The Commission on Social Determinants of Health 2005–08, chaired by Marmot, focused on the 'the causes of causes' in describing the social determinants of health as:

> the conditions in which people are born, grow, live, work and age…. These conditions or circumstances are shaped by the distribution of money, power and resources at global, national and local levels, which are themselves influenced by policy choices. The social determinants of health are mostly responsible for health inequities – the unfair and avoidable differences in health status seen within and between countries. (WHO CSDH, 2007, p 17)

Social exclusion

Social exclusion is one of the major 'causes of causes', and is identified as one of the 'solid facts' in the evidence on the social determinants of health (Wilkinson and Marmot, 2003). For many Gypsies and Travellers, Wilkinson's (1996, p 215) description encapsulates their experience of social exclusion:

> To feel depressed, cheated, bitter, desperate, vulnerable, frightened, angry and worried about debts or job or housing insecurity; to feel devalued, useless, helpless, uncared for, hopeless, isolated, anxious and a failure: these feelings can

dominate people's whole experience of life, colouring their experience of everything else.

A review on inequalities experienced by Gypsy and Traveller communities identified overwhelming evidence of persistent racism from the public, from services and sometimes from politicians (Cemlyn et al, 2009).

Prejudice and racism

A survey on attitudes to minority ethnic groups showed that the extent to which prejudices were expressed or manifested depended on the degree to which they were viewed as socially acceptable (Valentine and McDonald, 2004). It was perceived as more socially acceptable to hold negative views against particular groups if those views were felt to be rationally justified. Different types of prejudice were identified, which ranged in severity of outcome from unintentional prejudice to aggressive prejudice and which varied according to perceived level of threat or justification, as well as perceived levels of social acceptability. Common justifications were based on perceptions of economic threat, that is, that the minority ethnic groups in question were depriving others by gaining preferential access to resources such as housing or benefits. Other justifications were based on perceptions of cultural threat of difference, that is, that certain minority ethnic groups do not conform to 'traditional values' and that the majority culture may be undermined as a result. Gypsies and Travellers were one of the few groups in the survey who were subjects of aggressive prejudice (see Chapter Seven for a fuller discussion of racism).

Racialisation

It is the racialisation of Gypsies and Travellers, based on their supposed 'undesirable characteristics', that has led to their exclusion, and in reinforcing it, has such a profound impact on many levels. 'Racialisation' is a preferred term for the process of ranking people on the basis of their presumed 'race' and is described as being at the heart of a system of inequality and social exclusion (Macionis and Plummer, 2002). External influences such as a common experience of stigmatisation, prejudice and discrimination, resulting in exclusion, lead people from minority ethnic groups to recognise their ethnic status as one that has been racialised by the ethnic majority (Karlsen and Nazroo, 2000). The features, or cultural attributes, of Gypsy and Traveller ethnicity are identifiers of the social status that they are accorded by such racialisation. It is this racialisation with its accompanying stigmatisation, prejudice and discrimination that affects health. While Richardson and Ryder discussed the importance of recognising 'race' in Chapter One of this volume, it is clear that discrimination based on race has severe impacts on health. There is now a body of evidence to show that health outcomes of some minority ethnic groups are worse than would be expected solely on the basis of their socioeconomic circumstances and that their direct and indirect experience of racism is a key factor (Salway et al, 2010).

Social status and devalued identity

Gypsies and Travellers interviewed for the health status study (Van Cleemput, 2008a) attributed many of their bad experiences of healthcare or apparent clinical incompetence to prejudice and discrimination:

> They don't properly look at you, do they, the doctors, when they find you're a Traveller? (2004, p 230)

> You can feel the vibe. You can feel that … their attitude, towards you. (2004, p 239)

This felt lack of respect leads to Gypsies and Travellers feeling that they are worthless in the eyes of health staff, reinforcing a heightened sensitivity and low expectations. The feeling of being unvalued appears to be internalised as part of the experience of having a Gypsy or Traveller identity. As Goffman (1968) argues, those who are stigmatised can come to see themselves through the eyes of those who stigmatise them, and accept their devalued or inferior social identity. It is this sense of internalised shame that results from disrespectful attitudes and/or discriminatory behaviour that was a key finding in a study on access to primary healthcare by Gypsies and Travellers and interactions with health staff (Van Cleemput, 2008a).

The social environment resulting from a person's social position produces direct psychological effects that influence wellbeing and are implicated in other causes of morbidity and mortality. The ill-health effects and physiological mechanisms for these effects are well documented (Brunner, 1997; Taylor et al, 1997; Brunner and Marmot, 1999). It is the long-term stress caused by various psychosocial factors that affects health. Negative emotions, including depression, anxiety and hostility, which can result from low social status and related psychosocial factors, may lead not only to clinical mental ill-health but also to cardiovascular disease, diabetes and chronic inflammatory conditions such as asthma and rheumatoid arthritis and suppressed immunity (Wilkinson, 1999, 2005).

Accommodation and the physical environment

Accommodation and environmental living conditions are another major health determinant. For Gypsies and Travellers participating in the health status study (Parry et al, 2004), the focus on accommodation and associated threat to their travelling lifestyle was closely linked to their health experience and this was a dominant theme and the overriding factor mentioned by all respondents in the context of factors affecting their health. A review on housing and public health carried out by the National Institute for Health and Clinical Excellence categorised various specific direct and indirect elements of housing into three broad groups that can affect health, with evidence for each of the associations and impact on health cited (Taske et al, 2005). The elements in each of these groups are particularly pertinent to the accommodation experiences of Gypsies and Travellers:

- internal conditions on many Traveller sites;
- external social environments where sites are located;
- factors relating to macro policy such as Gypsy site policies that determine where and how they should live (Van Cleemput, 2008b).

However, one of the crucial factors related to accommodation for Gypsies and Travellers is the degree of control that they have over where and how they live. Lack of control over one's circumstances is in turn one of the health-damaging effects of low social status. So the psychosocial effects of a racialised Gypsy or Traveller identity can be seen to be pervasive factors implicated in the health inequalities that they experience.

Health damaging responses and consequences

The various reactions to manifestations of the marginalised status can also be health damaging. For example, different stress coping strategies such as smoking, alcohol or drug use in response to psychosocial stresses are also associated with indirect effects of physical health-harming behaviours (Wilkinson and Marmot, 2003). But to focus on these behaviours at the expense of tackling the underlying wider determinants would not be beneficial. Blaxter (1990) points out that harmful health behaviours have greatest impact on those already most at risk from other environmental factors, and therefore the relative impact on health outcomes of abandoning behaviours, such as smoking, is more limited. However, healthcare experiences of Gypsies and Travellers, which they perceive to be a result of their low worth in the eyes of health staff, result in various reactions to manifestations of their devalued identity and social status that have marked effects on their access to healthcare.

Gypsy and Traveller access to healthcare

Poor access to healthcare for Gypsies and Travellers was evident in the health status study (Parry et al, 2004) by the inverse relationship between health needs and use of health and related services. Poor access to services was also specifically implicated as a factor in a high maternal death rate (Lewis and Drife, 2001).

Reluctance to access healthcare

For Gypsies and Travellers there are many barriers to accessing healthcare. These include reluctance of many general practitioners to register Gypsies and Travellers who live on sites and have practical problems of access while travelling. However, mutual mistrust and poor relations between staff and Gypsy and Traveller patients are the major barriers for a greater number of Gypsies and Travellers, including those who are housed (Van Cleemput et al, 2007, 2010). The mistrust on their part is fuelled by their sense of devalued identity, and characterised by feelings of shame and humiliation. Any adverse experiences such as any errors experienced, past or present, are often attributed to discriminatory lack of care based on their identity. In turn, this leads to low expectations and to the adoption of various strategies to manage health for as long as possible without recourse to health services. Lack of confidence or trust in the doctor's ability, combined with fear of difficulty in communication, in addition to fears about the potential diagnosis, are common factors in this reticence in seeking healthcare. By the time a Gypsy or Traveller has decided to attend a doctor's appointment, the underlying fear that finally triggered the delayed consultation, and a lack of trust that they will be taken seriously, compound a sense of urgency.

Experience of healthcare services

The felt urgency to be seen and treated can then lead to a situation where any refusal of an early appointment can precipitate an angry encounter and fuel the mistrust of health staff towards Gypsies and Travellers who they stereotypically perceive as demanding and challenging. Health staff in the health study (Parry et al, 2004) reported that they rarely had any contact with Gypsies and Travellers outside of their work setting and several said that their views about them were influenced by the media and/or past negative experiences in the workplace.

The experience of Gypsies and Travellers accessing healthcare and strategies to deal with their cultural needs and potential conflict are similar elsewhere outside of the British Isles; for example the need for groups of women to support each other by attending healthcare appointments together and having the support of many relatives visiting when in hospital (Thomas, 1985; Sutherland, 1992; Neff-Smith et al, 1996; Lehti and Mattson, 2001). What is particularly striking is the common contextual fear and mistrust of healthcare and communication conflict with staff.

Gropper and Miller (2001, p 104) illustrated such potential for conflict: 'Fear of mistreatment and a scapegoat mentality underlie the people's reluctance to admit they are a Gypsy.... A visit to a doctor with a brusque no-nonsense manner can make them suspect that "he wouldn't give me a pill; he doesn't want me to get well".'

Cultural competence in health staff

For Gypsies and Travellers who have found a general practitioner who they are comfortable seeing or a practice that they are comfortable attending, one of the most frequently cited reasons for satisfaction is that they 'understand Travellers' or know their personal or family history (Van Cleemput et al, 2007). This knowledge and understanding from the health worker instils confidence that they do not need to explain who they are or their situation. Above all they feel accepted. However, this remains a minority experience and explains why so many Gypsies and Travellers still prefer to travel miles to a culturally competent and trusted doctor or practice rather than be seen locally.

In addition to the need to understand and address the barriers to provision of culturally sensitive healthcare at an interpersonal level, it is also important to tackle the broader political and structural factors that cause inequity of access.

Addressing Gypsy and Traveller health inequalities and access to healthcare

Determinants of health inequalities refer to the unequal distribution of health determinants. The distinction has relevance for policies, as it is quite possible to tackle health determinants without tackling determinants of health inequalities. For example, policies aimed at raising educational standards or reducing smoking will focus on overall exposure to health-damaging factors. The real need is to tackle those social health determinants that are responsible for such wide differences in people's life chances and social positions, and to provide additional services for those in greatest need.

As stated by the Commission on Social Determinants of Health (WHO CSDH, 2007, p 1155):

> To make a fundamental improvement in health equity, technical and medical solutions such as disease control and medical care are, without doubt, necessary – but they are insufficient. There will need to be empowerment of individuals, communities, and whole countries. We see empowerment operating along three interconnected dimensions: material, psychosocial, and political. People need the basic material requisites for a decent life, they need to have control over their lives, and they need political voice and participation in decision-making processes.

This requires policy measures to tackle the racialised nature of the social exclusion of Gypsies and Travellers and must involve joint working across sectors. There are various definitions of social exclusion and debate about the causes and meaning, but definition is important if the question of equity is to be achieved. An appropriate definition is that used by the Centre for Analysis of Social Exclusion: 'An individual is socially excluded if a) he or she is geographically resident in a society but b) for reasons beyond his or her control, he or she cannot participate in the normal activities of citizens in that society, and he or she would like to so participate' (Burchardt et al, 1999, p 229). This definition does not just go beyond identifying the socially excluded as merely those who lack material resources, it also allows for a focus on the wider social divisions and multiple causes of deprivation that can contribute to exclusion.

Health provision at the local level

The roles of other sectors in addressing multiple causes, such as accommodation, education and social participation, are covered in other chapters of this volume, particularly those in Part One, but the health sector also has a key wider role to play than solely being concerned with health provision. Health visitors have always had a wider public health role to influence policies that may have adverse effects on health. Dedicated health visitors for Gypsy and Traveller communities have a long history of emphasis on this aspect of their remit through engagement in local strategic partnerships and multi-agency forums, as well as advocacy at different levels within the health sector to highlight the specific cultural needs of these marginalised communities. At a fundamental level this has often included advocacy to ensure that a Gypsy or Traveller is able to access a general practitioner or other health services.

However, areas where there are dedicated services for Gypsies and Travellers, in the form of either health visitors or other roles such as health inclusion workers, are still too few in number. There is a debate about whether services for Gypsies and Travellers should be separate or mainstreamed, and this debate takes place among Gypsies and Travellers themselves as well as service providers. However, for participants in the health status study (Parry et al, 2004) where there were such posts they featured positively and prominently, particularly with regard to advocacy in raising awareness of health provision and facilitating access to health services. Other important aspects of the role of dedicated health workers are to improve capacity building, to use a community development approach and to conduct health needs assessments with a focus on outcomes.

Outreach and peer support

Some National Health Service (NHS) trusts and local authorities employ outreach workers to fulfil some or all of these roles. In other areas, Gypsy and Traveller support organisations employ outreach workers from the Gypsy and Traveller community. One example is Friends, Families and Travellers in Sussex, which employs up to six outreach workers with different remits, including mental health and adult social care. Friends, Families and Travellers, along with other such organisations such as the Irish Traveller Movement in Britain, acts as an intermediary to statutory services that do not provide outreach.

There is a variety of job titles and remits that fall into the category of outreach worker and a range of backgrounds, lay and professional, from which post holders are recruited. However, as also noted in a report on early years outreach practice (Riches, 2007), managers of outreach workers need to clarify expected outcomes and to support practitioners in their role, enabling them to respond appropriately to the needs identified in their work with families.

Ethnic monitoring and the need for data

One of the reasons why the needs of Gypsies, Roma and Travellers are unidentified, understood or unmet is the absence of adequate data. Ethnic monitoring is still not mandatory at a primary care level, and even where this is required, Gypsies, Roma and Travellers have rarely been included. It is to be hoped that this invisibility may change in the future with their inclusion as separate ethnic groups in the 2011 Census (as many organisations utilise the Census categories for local use) so that commissioners do develop services that are specific to their needs.

Health policy measures

Joint Strategic Needs Assessments (JSNAs) are a critical part of the commissioning process to ensure that services are provided on the basis of determined local need. However, although there has been a mandatory requirement for local authorities and primary care trusts to undertake regular JSNAs since 2007, many JSNA datasets do not always effectively capture the needs of socially excluded groups such as Gypsies, Roma and Travellers. There are exceptions in areas of good practice, such as Cambridgeshire, where separate JSNAs are conducted for different population groups, including Gypsies and Travellers, and key findings and recommendations of each of the separate JSNAs are then brought together into a summary document. However, as noted in a review of race equality and JSNA practice, '[a]lthough separate assessments provided much richer data and improved analysis of need, they did not always appear to influence the wider JSNA' (Local Government Improvement and Development, 2011, p 34).

This awareness of continued experience of health inequalities by socially excluded groups forms the background to the Inclusion Health initiative (DH, 2010). The document Inclusion Health: Improving the way we meet the primary health care needs of the socially excluded was launched in April 2010, and in its guidance to support commissioners in improving primary care services for socially excluded groups such as Gypsies and Travellers, by developing specific targeted services, it addresses the issue of paucity of data: 'Assessing the needs of those experiencing multiple disadvantage, however, requires commissioners to go beyond the routinely available local data and work creatively with partners to identify the pattern of needs and experiences of socially excluded people in the local community' (DH, 2010, p 20). This initiative has laudable aims and provides examples of good practice in its guide, not dissimilar to the aims of Primary Care Service Framework: Gypsy & Traveller communities (NHS PCC, 2009), which preceded it. The specific purpose of the Primary Care Service Framework for Gypsies and Travellers is to:

> equip PCT [primary care trust] commissioners with the necessary background knowledge, service and implementation details to work with providers and practitioners to deliver accessible primary care services, over and above mainstream services, for Gypsy and Traveller communities and to improve Gypsy and Traveller health and quality of life by providing effective, appropriate, ongoing support. (NHS PCC, 2009, p 3)

However, the framework is all too easy to ignore, and remained on the shelves, with no perceptible changes in service provision as a result. Negative and inaccurate publicity in various newspapers and other forms of media in the form of criticism about the launch of the framework gave a further indication of the pathologisation of Gypsies and Travellers in society. For example, a Member of Parliament said 'No one should get priority treatment in the NHS ... Decisions about who should be treated first should be based on a patient's medical needs not their ethnic group' (Andrews, 2009). In the same newspaper article, a spokesman from the TaxPayers' Alliance infers that Gypsies and Travellers are outsiders who do not pay tax, and are not entitled to equitable provision: 'This will be incredibly frustrating for people who have paid tax all their lives to fund the NHS and are left struggling to get a doctor's appointment and prompt treatment. Hardworking people will be outraged at this double standard' (Andrews, 2009).

Provision of equitable healthcare to Gypsies and Travellers, as to other socially excluded groups, does inevitably require extra cost. However, there has been an opportunity for practices to make use of support in the past through the local Enhanced Services scheme. One notable example, used in the evidence pack to support Inclusion Health (DH, 2010) as evidence of inclusive practice (Cabinet Office, 2010), was a practice in Market Harborough, Leicestershire. Aspects of its enhanced service included:

- registering as many Gypsies and Travellers as possible and not deregistering those away for over six months;
- no clients to be turned away without consultation or an agreed appointment;
- family consultations when requested;
- identifying (ethnic coding) Gypsy and Traveller patients on its records to enable health monitoring;
- outreach in the form of a practice nurse appointed and trained to visit Traveller sites twice a week;
- male doctors prepared to visit sites to encourage older men to attend surgery for screening and diagnosis;
- Gypsy and Traveller forums to monitor users' views of the services provided.

At present, such wide-ranging provision at general practice level to improve access to and provision of healthcare for Gypsies and Travellers is rare, and it is hard to envisage how this will improve in light of current cost savings that are required by primary care services and the forthcoming changes in commissioning arrangements.

Inclusion Health (DH, 2010) aimed to improve primary care provision for all socially excluded groups, but local impact is questionable as primary care trusts struggled to meet the needs of such groups in the face of uncertainty over implications of the health and social care reforms. Until regional or local leads are appointed to lead on this agenda it seems unlikely that commissioning bodies will have the necessary information, knowledge and persuasion to commission appropriate services. The question is posed in the document: 'Who will be the champion for this issue within the PCT? Is there a named Director with responsibility?' (DH, 2010, p 55). However, the answer at present appears to be 'Don't know'.

Three of the recommendations in Inclusion Health – to work with partners including the third sector to identify need better, to employ methods of 'outreach' including the use of advocates/support workers and to involve clients from start to finish – are essential to ensuring relevant and adequate health service provision. These priorities were also central features of the Gypsy, Roma and Traveller core strand of the Pacesetters programme (DH, 2009). However, the Department of Health and most NHS trusts have had a poor history of engagement with Gypsy and Traveller communities and, despite notable successes, many faced particular challenges (Van Cleemput et al, 2010).

Inclusive practice in improving Gypsy and Traveller health and healthcare experience

The Pacesetters programme (DH, 2009) was groundbreaking in its commitment to inclusion and genuine involvement of Gypsies and Travellers at a collaborative level at the design stages. By seeking out and inviting a small number of Gypsies and Travellers who were known to have a keen interest in health and were known to the health professionals who also attended, the Department of Health demonstrated its commitment to inclusion at the preliminary meetings. However, despite the continued commitment in having a Gypsy and Traveller Quality Assurance Group comprised of community members from participating regions, the absence of a clear mandate and remit for the group and lack of continuity in keeping the group engaged during the programme resulted in those members feeling unable to achieve their desired level of involvement. It became clear that the resources required to facilitate community engagement at a truly collaborative level had been underestimated. This is an all too common obstacle and one that was replicated in many of the local Pacesetters projects. The most successful projects were in primary care trusts where either there was already prior engagement with the local Gypsy and Travellers communities, usually with a key link person who was known and trusted for their cultural competence and participatory ways of working, or where trusts worked closely with a Gypsy and Traveller support organisation to ensure relevant community involvement. Commissioners of services need to be aware of the lessons learned from this programme; crucially that community members should be fully consulted and involved at the outset and that genuine involvement requires resourced time and sustained effort.

Working in partnership

One of the voluntary organisations that worked well in partnership with the local East London Foundation Trust and NHS Newham Trust on Pacesetters projects was the Roma Support Group in Newham, London. It worked in partnership with the key link person – the Patient Advice and Liaison Service manager – to deliver cultural awareness training to primary care trust staff and this resulted in some of those staff then volunteering to be involved in raising awareness about health needs in a culturally sensitive manner and performing health checks at a jointly organised health day for Roma. Both these initiatives were evaluated very well, with several Roma having health needs identified and being referred on to relevant healthcare services (Van Cleemput et al, 2010). The Roma Support Group's own model for engagement was a key factor in the success of these projects (Roma Support Group, 2010). The first step in its model is involvement in community consultation events to ascertain needs and to develop a suitable plan of action. The second step – community representation – is one that can be a stumbling block, unless community representatives are elected or chosen by other members on the basis of their ability to voice their community's concerns. In the case of the Roma Support Group, this model was relatively easy to achieve as it had a 10-year history of capacity building and previous experience of working in partnership with statutory organisations.

Staff cultural awareness raising

Raising cultural awareness of healthcare staff was one of three key themes that Pacesetters projects could choose to focus on. A few primary care trusts struggled to engage with community members and some of these failed to deliver projects as a result.

Many trusts, in consultation with community members, chose to deliver cultural awareness training, either solely, or initially, as part of a wider project. Leicester City Primary Care Trust was one of the flagship projects initiated by the Travelling Families Health Service after community consultation at an open exploratory meeting. It decided to use the opportunity as a capacity-building initiative whereby community members were recruited to train as health ambassadors and enabled to deliver outreach training. Leicestershire has provided dedicated healthcare to this community since 1995 through its Travelling Families Service. A strong mutual trust had been established between the health visitor for travelling families, Lynne Hartwell, and the Gypsies and Travellers in Leicestershire over the previous 15-year period that she had worked with them and this trust meant that she would consult them fully and involve them completely in the process, which was one of the crucial factors that motivated the initial 30 community members to participate: 'she came up with different ideas and then we suggested and came up with different ideas ourselves' (Van Cleemput et al, 2010, p 45).

Between them they identified aims that went beyond raising awareness among healthcare staff of the culture and health needs of Gypsy and

Traveller patients and to train people from Gypsy and Traveller communities to deliver training. They also aimed to encourage trust and dialogue between Gypsy and Traveller and healthcare communities and to enable each group to develop a genuine understanding and appreciation of the cultural and organisational constraints that impinge on each other. One of the key aims of the project was to break down barriers, and the ambassadors acknowledged from the start that this needed to happen on both sides. It was evident in the evaluation that this objective was achieved, and that access to and provision of culturally sensitive healthcare in places where training had been delivered improved. This is illustrated in the following quotes, respectively from a health ambassador and a health worker who attended a training session:

> 'At first there was some [health staff attending training] that was a bit funny, and then perhaps we were a bit funny to them, but then when we all started talking, different questions started coming out and answers, and we got to understand each other and it was better, and we thought they are not as bad as we thought and they were probably thinking the same about us; because at first there's a barrier – "oh Gypsies/Gorgers" but it come down and you could sit and chat with them.'

> 'The few [Gypsy and Traveller patients] I have met since seem more relaxed and confident. I am not sure if this is because I am better equipped to help them, or they understand my service; I guess it's both.'

There are many barriers for Gypsies and Travellers in accessing healthcare, but good communication built on mutual understanding is key to improving the awareness of and access to healthcare services and improving the healthcare experience. Success is most evident where Gypsies and Travellers are involved and engaged in outreach, as health ambassadors, as community development workers or in other outreach roles, and where there is genuine partnership work.

Health reform agenda

Key proposals

In 2011, the Coalition Government introduced arguably the most wide-ranging proposals of any incoming government for the reorganisation of the NHS since its inception in 1948, in the form of the Health and Social Care Bill 2011. The core principles of the NHS – meeting the needs of everyone, free at the point of delivery and based on clinical need, not the ability to pay – are now threatened. The Health and Social Care Bill finally became law on 27 March 2012 after prolonged debate and opposition resulting in at least 40 key amendments from its original form during its 14-month passage through Parliament.

During this process, some minor concessions to the most controversial proposals were achieved as a result of public pressure that forced the government to announce a two-month 'pause' in the Bill to review concerns in a 'listening exercise', but the health and social care legislation still signals a substantial move away from a 'national' health service to a system of healthcare based on market forces that is in line with the government's localism agenda.

The key proposals that remain in the 2012 Act include:

- *Clinical commissioning groups (CCGs)*. All primary care trusts will be abolished in April 2013 and will be replaced by a number of new CCGs. These will be responsible for spending around £80 billion of NHS funds on treatments for their patients. It is not known how many general practitioner consortiums there will be; however, they may have different boundaries to those of local authorities, or cover several local authority areas.
- *NHS Commissioning Board*. CCGs will be responsible to a new independent NHS Commissioning Board. This quango (quasi-autonomous non-governmental organisation) will hold them to account for the quality of health outcomes they help to produce and their financial performance.
- *Health and wellbeing boards.* In order to promote greater democracy and accountability in the NHS, each local authority will have to set up a health and wellbeing board to oversee the quality of local services, present local people's views and draw up a health and wellbeing strategy for the area.
- *Public Health England*. A new, integrated, national public health service – Public Health England – will be created and there will be a return to local authorities for local public health teams.
- *Monitor.* Monitor was created as the regulator of foundation trusts (hospitals that have opted out of direct governmental control). Monitor says that its core duty will be to:

> ...protect and promote patients' interests... In carrying out
> our sector regulator role, Monitor will license providers of
> NHS services in England and exercise functions in three
> areas:
> 1. regulating prices
> 2. enabling integrated care and preventing anti-competitive
>   behaviour; and
> 3. supporting service continuity.
> (www.monitor-nhsft.gov.uk/monitors-new-role/
> overview)

There are a vast number of concerns and fears in relation to the impact
of key components of the Act for the public as a whole, but there are
both crucial threats and potential opportunities with regard to the Act's
potential impact on the health of Gypsies and Travellers.

NHS reform implications for Gypsies and Travellers

Some of the wider general concerns about the impact of the reforms,
such as the pressures on general practitioners to reduce referrals to
secondary hospital care, are likely to intensify the mistrust between
Gypsies and Travellers and health staff.

However, the government is committed to placing a legal duty
on the Secretary of State for Health to reduce health inequalities
and implement the Equality Act 2010. With this focus, the Health
Inequalities Unit in the Department of Health, despite a greatly
decreased budget and staffing, is retaining Inclusion Health, set up by
the previous government. Gypsies and Travellers are one of the core
vulnerable groups on which it is focusing (by aiming to 'improve the
health of the poorest, fastest'). It remains to be seen, however, whether
these competing priorities of the government's health reform agenda
do succeed in reducing health inequalities for Gypsies and Travellers.

FOUR

Education, inclusion and government policy

Brian Foster and Sarah Cemlyn

Introduction

In this chapter we first outline a model of inclusive practice and the issues and tensions that affect the education of Gypsy, Roma and Traveller pupils. We then review the policies of the previous Labour government towards the education of these communities, and the current policies of the Coalition Government. Our conclusion draws some hope and some trepidation from this review.

Inclusion

> Education either functions as an instrument which is used to facilitate the integration of the younger generation into the logic of the present system and bring about conformity or it becomes the practice of freedom, the means by which men and women deal critically and creatively with reality and discover how to participate in the transformation of their world. (Shaull, 1970, p 16)

The capacity of education to oppress or to empower, articulated by Shaull (above) in his foreword to Freire's (1970) *Pedagogy of the oppressed*, persists in the dialogue between Gypsies, Roma and Travellers and those who support their educational inclusion. Freire (1970, p 95) himself states: 'One cannot expect positive results from an educational or political action program which fails to respect the particular view of the world held by the people. Such a program constitutes cultural invasion, good intentions notwithstanding.'

'Inclusion' tends to be the term that educationalists in the UK prefer to use because it implies adjustments to policies and practice to take account of community needs and aspirations. Alternative terms 'integration' and 'assimilation' suggest greater degrees of cultural modification and suppression. If the square-peg-in-a-round-hole analogy were to be used, assimilation suggests that the child is reshaped, whereas inclusion implies an adjustment to the system. In reality, schools, particularly secondary schools, are large institutions that change with difficulty; and although the least culturally repressive term is preferred, the practice described may require significant adjustment by the child. Furthermore, it is the case not just that secondary schools are large and difficult to change because of their institutional structure, but also that in the case of responding to the needs of Gypsy, Roma and Traveller pupils, there is frequently a misunderstanding surrounding the legitimacy of the very cultural status of these communities. The compassionate aim of some schools is one that perceives their mission to rescue these children from a threatening, debased and under-class existence. Such schools rationalise their task as compensating for deprivation. However, in this process the school does not develop more nuanced insights into the needs of these children and thus fails to devise relevant and effective strategies.

The experiences of Gypsies, Roma and Travellers in secondary schools may be different from the inclusive ideal. Derrington (2007) identified several push-and-pull factors that affect engagement and retention in secondary school. Of these, cultural dissonance (a result of conflicting expectations between home and school) and social exclusion featured strongly. Of a sample of 44 pupils, only 13 remained in school to the age of 16, and they displayed more adaptive strategies such as cognitive reframing, developing social support networks and adopting a bicultural identity. Those who dropped out of school adopted strategies described as 'maladaptive', referred to as fight (physical and verbal retaliation and non-compliance), flight (self-imposed exclusion and non-attendance) and playing white (passing their identity by concealing or denying their heritage).

Teaching staff interviewed by Wilkin et al (2010) identified a tension between family aspirations and those of the school, with pupils sometimes caught in the middle. Most schools suggested that the attainment outcomes for Gypsy, Roma and Traveller pupils were low because of parental and community attitudes. Parents' aspirations were influenced by cultural expectations and their own limited educational opportunities. But a Children's Society report, based on interviews with pupils about their experiences, identified more factors pushing pupils away from school, than ones pulling them back to their communities

(Ureche and Franks, 2007). Pupils gave the following reasons why they did not attend school regularly:

- travelling (pull);
- non-relevant curriculum (push);
- bullying (push);
- failure to deal with bullying (push);
- other children's behaviour that was inhibiting learning (push);
- difficulty understanding the work (push);
- parents wanting girls to stay at home after puberty (pull).

Roma appear to be more comfortable with education as a tool for empowerment and, despite problems of access and of segregation in special schools (UNICEF, 2007; ERRC, 2008a; Roma Education Fund, 2009) in most Eastern European countries, there is a small but growing educated minority among Roma who are influential within non-governmental organisations and in central government, particularly in the context of the 'Decade of Roma Inclusion 2005–2015'.[1] Most Roma in the UK do not regard education as a threat to their culture and identity, they are less likely to drop out of secondary education and more likely to continue in further education or training post 16.

Gypsies and Irish Travellers, however, can feel that education has the potential to alienate their children from their culture. People who have been marginalised and subjected to prejudice for generations, look to their own communities to equip children with the skills they will need as adults, learning those skills by working alongside their relatives. There is an emphasis on being quick-witted and taking opportunities, on living for the moment in the face of future uncertainty (Ní Shuínéar, 1994). The world in which education takes place over two decades, student debt and no guaranteed employment prospects can be alien to communities, in particular those with more traditional views, who generally expect their young people to marry early and be able to support their family from the outset. An increasing minority of Gypsies, Roma and Travellers are seeing the value of formal education (ITMB, 2010), but if genuine inclusion is to take place, the education system needs to recognise and respect the values of these communities and work in partnership with them to ensure that education helps enrich culture, not undermine it.

The education of Gypsies, Roma and Travellers under the Labour government

Before 1999, many Traveller Education Support Services (TESSs) suffered a marginalisation parallel to that experienced by the families whose inclusion they supported; it seemed that although the work of practitioners in the field was recognised and respected, it was not seen as important or relevant to mainstream, local authority practice (Ofsted, 1999, p 22; Foster and Walker, 2010, p 64), despite the positive praise that TESSs received in a number of Department for Education and Skills and Ofsted reports (Ofsted, 1996, 1999, 2003; DfES, 2003). However, the network of TESSs that had been developed and their ability to lobby and promote Traveller education, together with the influence and support of Her Majesty's (HM) Inspectors of Schools and sympathetic civil servants, created a growing body of pressure on Conservative and then Labour governments to be more proactive in the sphere of Gypsy, Roma and Traveller education. Such overtures were in tune with strands of policy that characterised the Labour administration post 1997, specifically 'education, education, education' (Blair, 1996) and 'joined-up government' (Bentley and Gurumurthy, 1999), both of which had a significant impact on education provision for Gypsies, Roma and Travellers.

Recognising the issues

Labour politicians were quick to engage with the issues. Months after the General Election, the then Education Minister Estelle Morris made a keynote speech to the Advisory Council for the Education of Romany and other Travellers (ACERT) conference 'Beyond Reading and Writing'. She stated: 'The problems of racism, social exclusion and educational failure are particularly acute for gipsy and traveller [sic] children. Only 5 per cent are still registered or regularly attend school by key stage 4....The reasons for this are complex and deep-rooted and cannot be solved overnight' (Morris, 1997). She recognised the progress made in primary education and the work of TESSs, but concluded that much still needed to be done. Charles Clarke, her successor, addressed the National Association of Teachers of Travellers + Other Professionals' (NATT+) conference in 1998, stating: 'We want to commit ourselves to working with you to continue that process and to achieve a "step change" in the whole way in which we can improve the education and life circumstances of the children of Travellers' (DfEE, 1998).

Evidence of this commitment emerged when the Office for Standards in Education, Children's Services and Skills (Ofsted) decided to add Gypsy Travellers to three other underachieving groups in a thematic review entitled 'Raising the attainment of minority ethnic pupils' (Ofsted, 1999). African Caribbean, Bangladeshi and Pakistani pupils had been identified previously by national data and a research review on minority ethnic achievement (Gillborn and Gipps, 1996) but Gypsy Travellers were not then included in ethnic monitoring categories and therefore did not figure in the review.

Ofsted (1999, p 11) made the following stark conclusion:

> Of the four focus groups in this survey, Gypsy Traveller children are the most at risk in the education system. Although some make a reasonably promising start in primary school, by the time they reach secondary school their levels of attainment are almost always a matter for concern. Many, especially boys, opt out of education by Year 9 and very few go on to achieve success at GCSE [General Certificate in Secondary Education level] or beyond.

Ofsted's report also drew attention to the high proportions of Gypsy Travellers on the Special Education Needs register, low teacher expectations and Gypsy Travellers' vulnerability to hostility and prejudice. It highlighted the broad job description of TESSs and the risk of their work being marginalised '[u]nless the school as a whole addresses the needs of Gypsy Traveller pupils' (1999, p 22).

In February 1999, the Department for Education and Employment invited tenders for a small-scale research project into the issue of low attainment of Gypsy Traveller children and to identify the effective practice thought best to improve attendance and to raise attainment (Bhopal, 2000). Recommendations from this study and the DfES (2003a) follow-up report were incorporated into good-practice guidance to schools (DfES, 2003b), which was published with a powerful introductory message by the Parliamentary Under-Secretary of State for Schools, Stephen Twigg:

> All children and young people should be able to achieve their potential, whatever their ethnic and cultural background and whichever school they attend. Working towards and achieving good practice in the education of Gypsy Traveller pupils is the responsibility of everyone within the education

system – DfES [Department for Education and Skills – formerly the DfEE], LEAs [local education authorities], schools, teachers, governors, the Traveller Education Support Services, parents and pupils. (DfES, 2003b, p 1)

The guidance emphasised the following points:

- informed leadership and an ethos of respect;
- training, which raises expectations and enhances all staffs' knowledge and understanding;
- a culturally relevant and affirming curriculum;
- an approach to induction for newly arrived pupils, addressing their social and academic needs;
- ethnic monitoring and data collection;
- raising the profile of race equality in schools;
- providing equal educational opportunities;
- involving Traveller parents and the wider community.

To some extent, policy, provision and practice were shaped by these principles for the rest of the 2000s.

Ethnic monitoring

Target setting and monitoring were central to the Labour government's programme of raising standards and accountability. HM Inspectorate, practitioners and the voluntary sector recognised that Gypsy, Roma and Traveller pupils needed to be identified within national statistics if the effectiveness of measures to raise their achievement were to be evaluated. In this endeavour they were able to overcome the initial reluctance of officials.

In 2003, the government, encouraged by ACERT and NATT+, introduced new ethnic categories into the Annual School Census, which added Gypsy/Roma and Traveller of Irish Heritage to school admission forms. The first analysis of data including these categories appeared in 2005, providing statistical support for the inspection evidence of earlier reports:

Although numbers recorded in these ethnic categories are small, it is clear that Gypsy/Roma and Travellers of Irish Heritage pupils have very low attainment throughout Key Stage assessments and also have much higher identification of special educational needs.... Permanent exclusion rates are higher than average for Travellers of Irish Heritage, Gypsy/Roma, Black Caribbean, Black Other and White/Black Caribbean pupils. (DCSF, 2006, p 2)

The report also noted that only a third of the number of Gypsy/Roma and less than half of Travellers of Irish Heritage were registered on the Annual School Census at Key Stage 4 compared to Key Stage 1. It found that fewer than 4,000 pupils identified as Travellers of Irish Heritage and 6,500 as Gypsy/Roma, significantly below Ofsted's (1996) earlier estimate. TESS staff, who had detailed knowledge of families and schools, realised that many families had chosen not to ascribe their children to the two categories, fearing exposure to further discrimination, opting instead for the more neutral and equally accurate White British, White Irish or White Eastern European categories. The report also found that schools had not always made the options explicit to parents. The Department for Children, Schools and Families (DCSF) (created following the demerger of the Department for Education and Skills) responded by publishing guidance on strategies to persuade children, families, schools and local authorities of the benefits of accurate voluntary self-ascription (DCSF, 2008b).

The national strategies

'Excellence for the many, not just the few: raising standards and extending opportunities in our schools', the title of the then Secretary of State for Education and Employment David Blunkett's speech to the Confederation of British Industry in 1999 (Blunkett, 1999), summed up the government's philosophy. The previous year he offered to resign in 2002 if his department failed to reach the targets of 80% of pupils achieving the expected Level 4 at Key Stage 2 in English and 75% in Maths (rising from 63% and 62% respectively in 1998)[2] and, although these targets were not met (75% and 73% respectively), the government remained committed to raising the proportion of pupils achieving the level required to provide a firm foundation for a successful secondary experience.

The National Primary Strategy, which provided a mix of guidance, training and resources to support improvements in the quality of learning and teaching, was the vehicle through which this improvement was to be achieved. The strategy involved a broad range of interventions, including whole-school approaches, good classroom practice, catch-up and personalisation of the curriculum to reflect individual needs.

'Quality first teaching' as set out in the National Primary Strategy aimed to differentiate class teaching to meet the needs of at least three groups of children: those at, those above and those below age-related expectations. The literacy and numeracy hours set aside dedicated time each day for teaching core skills. Targeted interventions were offered to children who fell behind, often delivered to small groups, to boost learning and facilitate full participation in class. For a further minority of children, particularly those with special educational needs, there was a range of wave 3 interventions often delivered one to one. The model was extended from the primary phase into early years and secondary education, embracing attendance, behaviour, inclusion, leadership and governance, pupil progress, transition, school improvement and initial teacher training.

Many of the strategy interventions replaced and systematised the inputs previously made by TESS staff, and were generally effective in enabling those Gypsy, Roma and Traveller children who were able to attend school regularly to make progress and access the curriculum.

The Gypsy Roma Traveller Achievement Programme (GRTAP) was initiated in 2007 to improve outcomes, meet educational aspirations through personalised learning, develop inclusive schools and race equality, improve cultural understanding of local authorities and schools, and tailor mainstream resources. It comprised three overlapping phases of two years, each funding 12 selected local authorities and six schools or settings from each authority. Case studies and guidance were published in newsletters, on CD-ROM, online and as hard copies. The GRTAP did much to develop good practice and disseminate it to schools nationally. The high-quality resources it produced represented an effective partnership between regional advisers, local authority strategy teams, TESSs, schools and communities. However, Gypsies, Roma and Travellers were one of the last strategy focuses and in 2009 the Education Secretary, Ed Balls, announced that the contract with Capita, the strategy's provider, would not be renewed. The recession had begun to bite, the contract was expensive and there was a growing backlash among schools against prescriptive, top-down initiatives (Webb and Vulliamy, 2006). This sentiment was reflected in the recognition by the Labour leadership that the government needed to move away from top-down targets and embrace greater decentralisation in education (Kelly, 2009).

Target setting

A majority of Gypsy, Roma and Traveller pupils have much in common with other pupils within the resistant 'long tail of underachievement', predominantly poorer, White British pupils (Strand, 2008; NatCen, 2009). In the latter part of the 2000s, there was a growing recognition that socioeconomic factors had a much greater effect on achievement than ethnicity, particularly at Key Stage 4. In 2009, the regulations on statutory local authority targets were changed to focus more sharply on underperforming groups. Local authorities were required to set targets for Key Stage 2, Key Stage 4 and Early Years outcomes for just eight groups of pupils where underperformance remained a problem: Black Caribbean, White/Black Caribbean, Black African and White/Black African, Black Other, Pakistani, White Other, Gypsies/Roma and Travellers of Irish heritage, and children eligible for free school meals.

Local authorities had to set targets where there were 30 or more pupils from each group in the age cohort, local authority-wide, except in the case of Gypsy/Roma and Traveller of Irish heritage pupils where there were three or more such pupils in the combined age cohort, local authority-wide. The relatively small population size and wide distribution of Gypsy/Roma and Traveller communities, low levels of ascription and high proportions of pupils missing education created a target-setting dilemma, addressed by the conflation of the two ethnic categories into a single-target setting group and the setting of the lower numerical threshold. Target setting showed the government's commitment to raising attainment for these groups but created problems of statistical validity and loss of anonymity.

Gypsy Roma Traveller History Month

Possibly the most radical of the Labour government's support for inclusion of Gypsies, Roma and Travellers through cultural recognition was their endorsement and financial support for Gypsy Roma Traveller History Month (described in much more detail in Chapter Eight, this volume). The fact that this was a government- rather than community-led initiative is regrettable but, in educational terms, it suggests that the DCSF took a wider view of ways to promote inclusion and raise achievement. The department also showed a degree of flexibility when the communities sought to take ownership of the event and develop it beyond the educational context.

E-Learning and Mobility Project (E-LAMP)

The E-Learning and Mobility Project (E-LAMP) (Marks, 2004) used information and communications technology (ICT) to provide enhanced independent and distance learning support for Traveller children. This action research, funded by the Nuffield Foundation, prompted a series of pilot projects, funded by the DCSF and coordinated by NATT+. The initial pilots focused on providing ICT-enhanced distance learning support for pupils travelling away from their winter base-school, so that they could use the internet to keep in contact with school and to receive and submit assignments. From 2006, the project explored the potential of ICT to re-engage secondary school-age Traveller pupils who had left school or were on the fringes of schooling. In 2008, in the run-up to the Home Access programme to promote the home-use of ICT by all school-age children, the scheme was extended to non-mobile Gypsy, Roma and Traveller pupils who would benefit from internet access to complete schoolwork. When Home Access went national, families experienced greater difficulties accessing national helplines from mobiles to troubleshoot and arrange repairs.

Elective home education

In 2004, the Department for Education and Skills commissioned a small-scale study (Ivatts, 2006) to respond to concerns expressed by TESSs and HMI about a significant increase in the number of Gypsy, Roma and Traveller children registered for home education, whose parents were themselves educationally disadvantaged and would find it difficult to offer a suitable curriculum. Questionnaires were sent to the TESS and the department/officer responsible for the approval and monitoring/inspection of elective home education provision, in each of 23 authorities identified by the Department for Education and Skills as models of good practice for the inclusion of Gypsy, Roma and Traveller children.

The report recommended legislation to apply to all home-educated children, requiring registration, monitoring and assessment to establish that the education they receive is suitable to their needs and wishes, and the curriculum is broad and balanced. A national review of elective home education (Badman, 2009) shared these concerns and recommended a national registration system, but also suggested that local authorities should provide more support for parents electing to home educate. These recommendations were incorporated into the

Education Act 2010, but the opposition parties found the proposals contentious and the relevant clauses were removed from the Bill passed by Parliament in the wash-up before the 2010 General Election.

Research

In 2007, the DCSF commissioned a major piece of research to explore the issues faced by Gypsy, Roma and Traveller pupils, especially those in secondary schools, and identify strategies found to be effective in improving their educational outcomes. It aimed to maximise the information to be derived from the National Pupil Dataset to identify and quantify the impact of issues affecting outcomes for Gypsy, Roma and Traveller pupils and separate the effects of social and economic factors from issues specifically relating to Gypsy, Roma and Traveller learners through comparison with a carefully matched sample from the National Pupil Dataset. The study, which took place over three years, involved four strands of research activity: national data analysis, progress mapping (through questionnaires to schools), a literature review (Wilkin et al, 2009a) and case studies. It concluded that schools were using six key approaches, all equally important and necessary to improve outcomes; the absence of any one would undermine the effectiveness of the others:

- safety and trust;
- flexibility;
- partnership (with families and other agencies);
- (mutual) respect;
- (additional support for) access and inclusion;
- high expectations (Wilkin et al, 2009b).

The study also provided hard data (based on all pupils identified to the ethnic categories in the cohort in Year 6 in 2004) to confirm that:

- 20% fail to transfer from primary to secondary school;
- half of Gypsy, Roma and Travellers drop out of secondary schools;
- only 37% appear in all six possible Annual School Censuses;
- Irish Travellers are most likely and Roma least likely to drop out;
- girls are more likely than boys to stay on except in the case of Roma (Wilkin et al, 2010).

Another important research project funded by the DCSF was undertaken by European Dialogue into Roma communities living in the UK, which drew greater focus to the experiences of Roma children in the education system as well as giving valuable background information on numbers and family circumstances (European Dialogue, 2009).

Both these pieces of research made recommendations for policy at national, local and school levels, as well as calling for additional monitoring and research into effective strategies. There is no evidence, however, that the previous government had, or the current government has, seriously considered the recommendations of either report.

The role of Traveller education support

The achievement of Gypsies, Roma and Travellers became a national priority, with increasing references in policy documents and incorporation into the national strategies. At local authority level, the report A new relationship with schools (DCSF, 2005a) redefined the role of centrally employed staff, working increasingly on a consultancy model where schools monitor their own provision, establish their areas of weakness and the School Improvement Partner brokers in appropriate support.

Before 1997, TESSs had developed a way of working that met the needs of families and schools. They took every opportunity to deliver training and build capacity, but there was little interest at local authority level, and TESSs rarely had an impact on policy development and planning. The introduction of the Gypsy/Roma and Traveller of Irish Heritage ethnic codes resulted from lobbying by professional and voluntary organisations, while significant documents such as *Aiming high* (DfES, 2003) represented strategic collaboration between central government and TESS professionals. TESS staff joined the national strategies as regional advisers and the strategies began to synchronise the work of TESS with broader initiatives through regional meetings.

Coalition government policies impacting on Gypsy, Roma and Traveller educational inclusion

In October 2010, representatives of ACERT and NATT+ met with Nick Gibb MP, the Minister for Schools. They sought to establish how previous key initiatives introduced by the Labour government were viewed by the new administration and how they might be built upon for the future of support for Traveller education.

It became clear that the Home Access scheme would no longer be available to support low-income or mobile pupils, only those with special educational needs. There was no plan to replace the national strategies and there was uncertainty about whether or not the Home Access website and downloadable resources would continue to be available. It was agreed that the research study (Wilkin et al, 2010) would be published online but there was no commitment made to consider the recommendations. Gypsy Roma Traveller History Month would continue to be endorsed by the renamed Department for Education (DfE) (which was formed by the Coalition Government, taking on the responsibilities and resources of the DCSF) but no funding would be provided. Target setting was to be abolished and there were no plans to incorporate the recommendations of the Badman (2009) report, which reviewed elective home education in England, in future legislation. The Gypsy, Roma and Traveller Education Stakeholder Group would continue to meet to advise the DfE, and an interdepartmental committee would develop Coalition policies on Gypsies and Travellers (not Roma), led by Eric Pickles, the Secretary of State for Communities and Local Government.

The DfE has continued to consult with the Gypsy, Roma and Traveller Education Stakeholder Group and voluntary organisations about a number of initiatives specifically targeting Gypsy, Roma and Traveller pupils. Although ministers have agreed none of these proposals at the time of writing, they do suggest some developing commitment from the Coalition Government.

Among the ideas currently under consideration, and on which the DfE is seeking feedback from community members, practitioners and voluntary groups, are the following:

> Seeing whether any of the lessons learnt from the Virtual Headteachers' pilot for Looked After Children could be applied to GRT [Gypsy, Roma and Traveller] pupils; looking at ways in which attendance among GRT pupils could be improved; identifying and sharing latest models of effective practice in schools in raising the attainment and attendance of GRT pupils; and exploring how GRT role models could be used to raise educational aspirations among GRT pupils. (ACERT, 2011, unpaginated)

There is too little detail in these proposals to attempt an objective assessment, but the impact of the broad sweep of Coalition policies is already being felt in local authorities, schools, and the homes of Gypsy, Roma and Traveller families, which allows us to make a preliminary appraisal.

Education funding

The Coalition Government has sought to preserve funding to schools at the expense of local authority services, and as a result the TESS network has suffered disproportionately (NUT, 2010). The Pupil Premium will take its place, with schools receiving extra funding for children eligible for free school meals and other groups such as children of parents serving in the armed forces. The Travellers Aid Trust panel review of Coalition Government policy with regard to Gypsies and Travellers (Ryder et al, 2011, p 46) included the government's response on funding:

> We know that there is a particularly strong link between deprivation and underachievement and in primary schools, 43.2% of all registered GRT pupils are currently eligible for Free School Meals; this figure rises to 45.3% in secondary schools and 57.5% in Special Schools. Those GRT pupils who are eligible for Free School Meals will benefit directly from the new pupil premium, which will provide an additional £430 per pupil from April 2011 to help raise their attainment. They will also qualify for additional support through the £110m Education Endowment Fund, which will fund bold and innovative approaches to raising the attainment of disadvantaged children in underperforming schools.

In practice, Gypsy, Roma and Traveller pupils will not 'benefit directly' since the Pupil Premium can be used however schools see fit, with schools being held accountable by Ofsted, applying a more 'focused' approach, mainly concerned with attainment. The change of name of the Department from Children, Schools and Families to Education and the title of the White Paper *The importance of teaching* (DfE, 2010a) signalled the narrowed focus. The Education Endowment Fund (DfE, 2010b), with a budget of £110 million, will distribute money to local authorities, academy sponsors, charities and other groups that bring forward innovative proposals to improve performance in underperforming schools; Gypsy, Roma and Traveller pupils, if they benefit at all, will only do so through the general improvement in the schools they attend.

The government response to the panel review also suggested that schools and local authorities could agree to use part of the £208 million Ethnic Minority Achievement grant to maintain Traveller education support but '[w]e believe that schools and Local Authorities are best placed to decide how support services should be organised in their areas and we are confident that they will make the right decisions as to the most appropriate local provision' (Ryder et al, 2011, p 48). The response also claimed that as 'more and more schools have successfully taken on their own outreach work within these communities, there has been a reduced need for LAs [local authorities] to provide specialised support services' (Ryder et al, 2011, p 48).

This view seems over optimistic, not to say complacent. The national strategies and research from the National Foundation for Educational Research (Wilkin et al, 2010) identified schools that take their duty of care to children from these communities very seriously, going the extra mile to engage parents, celebrating and respecting identity and culture and personalising the curriculum; but those schools were examples of best practice, which was, in most cases, the result of ongoing partnership work with TESSs. It is difficult to see how the government's vision will address the needs of the most vulnerable children and young people, those who are highly mobile, excluded or disengaged from school.

The White Paper and the Education Act 2011

The educational philosophy of the Coalition Government explicitly focuses on the quality of teaching and discipline in schools (DfE, 2010a). Wilkin et al (2010) found that good-quality, personalised teaching and learning, and clear behaviour policies, made an important contribution to the school experiences of Gypsy, Roma and Traveller pupils. However, high levels of permanent and fixed-term exclusions among Gypsy/Roma and Traveller of Irish heritage pupils (DCSF, 2006) have been confirmed by the most recent data (DfE, 2010c), and it will be important to monitor the effect of the additional powers granted to schools in the Education Act 2011. Unfortunately, the Act also limits the remit of Ofsted to: pupils' achievement; quality of teaching; quality of leadership and management; and pupils' behaviour and safety – removing the responsibility to report on equalities or community cohesion.

The 'schools know best' ethos, which parallels the localism agenda, has some validity, but requires close monitoring with regard to its impact on marginalised groups who are vulnerable to prejudice. There is a presumption that all new schools will be either academies or free schools, both being highly autonomous of local authority control (speech by the Secretary of State, Michael Gove, 20 June 2011). Hence, there are likely to be few mechanisms whereby central or local government will monitor the educational experiences of Gypsy, Roma and Traveller pupils, or for TESSs (where they still exist) to advocate on behalf of pupils.

The Education Act abolishes various current duties on schools to cooperate with local authorities, to improve children's wellbeing and be represented on local Children's Trust Boards. These are key elements of the Every Child Matters philosophy developed through the Children Act 2004, which has supported the inter-agency approach appropriate to some of the most vulnerable families. The abolition of schools' duties to cooperate is likely to mark increased separation of education and social care responsibilities.

The White Paper *The importance of teaching* (DfE, 2010a) envisaged a strategic role for local authorities in supporting vulnerable pupils, including 'looked-after' children, those with special educational needs and those outside mainstream education. It would appear that this wording, which would have given authorities a duty to safeguard the education of Gypsy, Roma and Traveller families, has not found its way into the Education Act. The Coalition Government's emphasis on small government could undermine local authorities' ability to reach out proactively to excluded groups, which has resulted in the gradual improvement on secondary enrolment. The government lead on Gypsy, Roma and Traveller issues is to be taken by the Department for Communities and Local Government, which may mean that enforcement will take priority over inclusion. Localism is likely to reinforce the impact of local hostility to sites, but adequate culturally appropriate accommodation is key to inclusion (Brown and Niner, 2009; Cemlyn et al, 2009). The Act also removes support for vocational education by abolishing Connexions and privatising careers advice, abolishing the Young People's Learning Agency for England, repealing the duty to secure sufficient number of apprenticeship places for all suitably qualified young people and repealing the diploma entitlement for 16- to 18-year-olds. These changes, reinforced by the withdrawal of the Education Maintenance Allowance, are likely to undermine much of the progress that has been made towards continuing participation in education and training post 16.

Vocational education

In Wilkin et al's (2010) study, vocational training figured significantly in the views of schools and parents and it was clear that it played an important part in personalising the curriculum and encouraging pupil retention. There was frustration that courses continued to be theoretical and learning-by-doing remained rare. A report on economic inclusion for Travellers (ITMB, 2010, p 41) found that younger Gypsies, Roma and Travellers had a strong interest in vocational skills, and favoured experiential styles of learning. The survey found that 35% of the sample of 95 interviewees had experience of further or vocational education, and that the learning styles supported in post-school education were more acceptable to young people from these communities.

In September 2010, Michael Gove, the Secretary of State for Education, commissioned Professor Alison Wolf to lead a review into pre-19 vocational education. His speech to the Edge Foundation illustrates Coalition Government thinking (Gove, 2010). No previous administration had, in his view, got to grips with the issue, with the possible exception of Margaret Thatcher's modern apprenticeship scheme, and under the last government practical and technical education had lost its way.

> One of the unhappy trends which actually grew in force over the past 13 years was the assumption that the purely academic route was really always the preferred one – and unless you'd secured a place on leaving school to study at university for three years you were somehow a failure. (Gove, 2010)

His view of proper vocational education is one that would find resonance in the homes of many Gypsies, Roma and Travellers: '[P]roper vocational education also needs to provide us with the courses and qualifications to underpin the future success of chefs and childcare workers, beauticians and care assistants, landscape gardeners and fashion photographers.' He also mentioned European countries where children can opt for a technical route from the age of 12.

The Wolf report, published in March 2010, is understandably less rhetorical and more focused (Wolf, 2010), but makes a number of recommendations that might improve vocational education for pupils 'whose aptitudes and talents are practical' and for whom 'expectations are too often limited and opportunities restricted' (Hayes, 2010, p 6).

While some of the changes in the Education Act will impact negatively on vocational education, there appears to be some commitment from the Coalition Government to develop this area of learning in a way that could benefit Gypsy, Roma and Traveller young people.

The impact of change

The New Labour Government significantly promoted the inclusion of Gypsy, Roma and Traveller children in the education system, through interventions, monitoring and research, and the dissemination of good practice nationally. Although not always attentive to the complexity of the challenges facing Gypsy, Roma and Traveller pupils and schools, ministers were prepared to grasp the nettle, and were generally responsive when civil servants and HMI brought forward proposals to create positive change. The initiatives of committed and proactive officials, working in close partnership with practitioners, produced grounded and practical guidance, resources and reports that were of high quality, with powerful, consistent and realistic messages. Although none of these initiatives created the 'step-change' originally sought by ministers, they supported the search for appropriate solutions. There was an impatience about the approach that generated a succession of initiatives and looked for instant results, focusing particularly on those pupils capable of reaching the expected levels in SATs tests rather than ensuring all children reached their full potential. The commissioned research told a more nuanced story about how inclusion of marginal communities might be achieved. Joined-up solutions, such as the Every Child Matters agenda, gave more meaning to the approaches used by Traveller education practitioners, but data-driven approaches constrained the work to narrowly defined attainment rather than family and community support. The Academies Programme, initiated by Blunkett but embraced by Gove, increased the problems encountered by local authority staff monitoring and supporting pupils. The strategies approach reduced the amount of poor teaching, although in some cases it stifled good teaching, and by the time the Gypsy Roma Traveller Achievement Programme came on-stream, teachers were suffering initiative fatigue, the national strategies were increasingly discredited and the resources probably received less attention in schools than they merited.

It is likely that Gypsy, Roma and Traveller pupils have benefited from the more focused and consistent teaching of basic skills, the monitoring of pupil progress and the range of interventions to address specific learning difficulties. The role of TESSs has changed, becoming focused more on training and school improvement than on pupils and families. The mainstreaming agenda has given some authorities the opportunity to impose a way of working on TESSs that does not address the challenges they face; outreach to families and cross-borough working have in some cases been regarded as peripheral to the core objective of school improvement. Local authority staff tend to focus on schools in danger of falling below floor targets or attracting the attention of Ofsted; they are less likely to be concerned about schools in which a small number of pupils are struggling because they are experiencing prejudice or teachers are not effectively personalising the curriculum.

Arguably, the writing had been on the wall for Every Child Matters for some time, as huge structural changes in children's services had failed to percolate to the grassroots. Ironically, Traveller education services worked in ways consistent with the Every Child Matters philosophy long before the Children Act 2004. Foster and Walker (2010, pp 50-9) found that TESSs performed well against the criteria for Every Child Matters good practice developed by the Local Government Association (2008). Joint Area Review inspections, which focused on the needs of the most vulnerable children, have commented positively on the work of Traveller education support: 'There are examples of excellent support services to specific groups, such as young Travellers where the good work with families has resulted in significantly increased attendance at secondary school and raised ambitions for further and higher education' (Ofsted, 2006, p 21).

Foster and Walker (2010) recognise the need for mainstreaming but argue for a clear focus on these groups across all aspects of the Every Child Matters agenda, drawing parallels to the virtual schools established within local authorities to respond to the complex needs of looked-after children.

With the financial cutbacks in the public sector (see further Richardson, 2010a), it is estimated that around one third of local authorities will have no identified support for the education of Gypsies, Roma and Travellers and in most other areas staff numbers have been reduced and roles have been restricted and/or extended to other areas of support (NUT, 2010). There may be an increased role for community and voluntary organisations, but these groups are finding it difficult to secure funding in the current climate and may find that taking on some functions of TESSs compromises their roles as advocates.

The Coalition Government plans to take the Academies Programme established by the previous Labour Government to the next level. The government is inviting all schools in England to become academies and encouraging parents to set up their own schools, called 'free schools'. Academies are funded directly by central government and have more freedom over their finances, the curriculum and teachers' pay and conditions. They receive additional funding that would previously have been held back by the local authority to provide extra services available to all schools, such as Traveller education services. Local authority staff have little influence over these schools and their ability to monitor and challenge provision for Gypsies, Roma and Travellers is significantly diminished. There is, however, evidence from voluntary organisations that some academies are taking their responsibilities seriously and are requesting, and are prepared to pay for, training and consultancy support.

'Free schools' are schools set up by groups of parents, teachers, charities, trusts, religious groups and voluntary groups funded, like academies, directly from central government. The Free Schools Programme has attracted some interest from community groups as a means of enabling Gypsy, Roma and Traveller children to attend schools where they might access a more relevant curriculum based on appropriate learning styles without being vulnerable to racist bullying or moral and cultural threats. The positive examples from a programme in the United States of underachieving schools in predominantly black communities being turned around, were based in communities that already had strong community organisations, enough families in a locality to support the schools, and a sense of claiming their full educational entitlement. Traveller communities are quite dispersed, and generally not well organised; they are clearer about what they do not want from education than what they do. Unlike many other minority communities, who see good-quality education and qualifications as the way to economic advancement, they have not taken the opportunity to set up supplementary schools to perpetuate their culture and values and improve their children's chances in mainstream education; most Gypsy and Traveller communities (less so Roma) still feel that education does not provide the skills they need for life and hence are inclined to avoid rather than embrace it.

The idea of a free school only for Gypsy, Roma and Traveller pupils would be regarded as discriminatory, but a free school providing the values and curriculum that those communities want might attract sufficient numbers of a local population to make it viable. The previous incarnation of government-funded independent education – direct grant schools – located themselves between grammar schools and private schools. They did not provide a different kind of education, but the same education to a selected group of pupils. It would be interesting to see how the DfE would respond to an application from Gypsy, Roma and Traveller families to set up a free school or how enthusiastic groups planning free schools would be to including them.

The Labour administration made a significant effort to include the education of Gypsies, Roma and Travellers within their ambitious programme of educational reform. The Coalition Government does not, as yet, appear to have the same commitment to this area of educational practice. Their priorities on Gypsies and Travellers (Roma not included) are being led by the Communities and Local Government Secretary, with an emphasis on fairness as a means of balancing their needs against those of other local community members. The policies they have are reducing central funding, leaving decision making to local authorities and schools with an emphasis on fair treatment for all.

The partnerships and relationships built between schools, families and TESSs will ensure that a fair proportion of Gypsy, Roma and Traveller pupils continue to enjoy an education that meets their needs, is affirming, relevant and creates opportunities. But there are others, and they may be in the majority, who do not have contact with Traveller education support, who attend schools that are hostile or indifferent to their identity, culture and aspirations, and who experience hardship in other areas of their life, who will be excluded or become disengaged. Their safety net will have been dismantled and the progress made over the past decade to make the education system more inclusive will go into reverse. It is to be hoped that, as under the previous Labour government, practitioners, community members and sympathetic civil servants may yet prevail and catch the ear of ministers, leading to inclusive and resolute action for one of the most at-risk and disadvantaged groups in the education system.

Notes

[1] For a discussion of the 'Decade of Roma Inclusion 2005–2015', see www.romadecade.org/about and Chapter Eleven, this volume.

[2] The targets were not met; David Blunkett had moved to the Home Office by 2002 and his successor, Estelle Morris, fell on her sword.

FIVE

Gypsies and Travellers and social policy: marginality and insignificance. A case study of Gypsy and Traveller children in care

Dan Allen

Introduction

The empowerment and inclusion of Gypsies and Travellers presents a challenge for the implementation of social policy in the pursuit of social equality. While social policy is orientated towards the pursuit of social justice, we know that the discrimination and injustices experienced by many Gypsies and Travellers are socially constructed. Yet, if we emphasise the nature and potential impact of them, we create a discursive conundrum in which the challenges faced by Gypsy and Traveller communities might (incorrectly) be attributed to individual lifestyle choices, rather than to the structural forces that exist around them (this was discussed by Richardson and Ryder in Chapter One, and will be revisited in Chapter Seven). This position, in the face of a commitment to empower those who are marginalised through institutional oppression, fails Gypsy and Traveller communities as well as Gypsies and Travellers themselves.

This chapter attempts to discuss this challenge by examining the position of social policy, highlighting the importance of its interpretation in practice. It starts with a brief outline of social policy and considers the way in which it can simultaneously signify the competing demands between social equality and social capital. It will then reflect on these issues by introducing the preliminary findings of ongoing research being conducted by the author, a higher degree research student at De Montfort University, which aims to develop a more critical sociological understanding of the experiences of Gypsies and Travellers who have lived in local authority care as children in England, Scotland and Ireland. For this section, specific abstracts are taken from the study and actual commentaries are used. As these commentaries are based on reflections and consequences of real lived experiences, some are sensitive and harsh in content and the reader is invited to reflect on their own reactions to them, including their own perceptions and prejudices, in order to fully understand and appreciate the messages behind them. The penultimate section reflects on the role of social policy with Traveller and Gypsy children living in care and makes a series of considered recommendations in relation to the empowerment and inclusion of those who are marginalised or viewed as insignificant. The final section concludes the chapter.

Social policy: a brief discussion

Social policy refers to guidelines and interventions for the changing, maintenance or creation of living conditions that are conducive to social wellbeing (Titmuss, 1974; Donzelot and Hurley, 1997). This includes the pursuit of social equality for those disenfranchised by unequal opportunity, which in turn permeates the design and implementation of the driving principles in health, education and social care. Together, they encapsulate the ideal moral foundations of contemporary society to reinforce the normalised principle that no individual, no matter how disenfranchised, or for whatever reason, should be further disadvantaged by unequal access to health, education or social care (Blakemore and Giggs, 2007). This intention, particularly in relation to more recent social history, aims to realign a Victorian division between the 'deserving' and 'undeserving' poor in a move motivated by principles of egalitarianism, literally the creation and conservation of universal social equality.

Although the ambition of social policy might attract support from the majority, the pragmatic determination of the constituent parts of social equality remains highly contested. Social divisions, created through structural inequality, the Left–Right political divide and cultural prejudice, often position single and teenage parents, those dependent on substances, 'hoodie' youth, unemployed people and those travelling communities who are seen to live beyond sedentarised social convention, as less deserving of social support than those disadvantaged by ageism, disability discrimination, homophobia, racism and sexism. If we consider the universal commitment to social wellbeing, most people would agree that society should protect young, older and vulnerable people from exploitation and abuse, and because of this, social policies to this end are generally uncontroversial. However, as seen by the recent Dale Farm evictions, the idea that society should protect Gypsies and Travellers in their pursuit of traditional mores that may enable social wellbeing is far more controversial.

Sociologists such as Bentham (1987) have endeavoured to theorise the controversial nature of social policy. Based on the overarching concerns of structural inequality, he suggests that the social policies that societies produce can be understood as the way in which any particular society recognises, and gives expression to, the autonomy and ultimately the importance of its members. Although the underlying ideology of social policy aims to restore social equality, the continued presence of social prejudice towards Gypsy and Traveller groups continues to reinforce social stereotypes of those individuals, families and communities, which continue to compartmentalise them within relegated social categories.

The fact that social prejudice and discrimination play such a significant part in the value of social equality (one person is entitled to equality while another is not) reveals that, as standalone documents, social policies have no real significant value in the world. For Smith (2010), social policies are nothing more than an aide memoire, or a series of recommendations, for social intervention. Their power, he argues, only becomes manifest when their words and recommendations are observed and interpreted in the conscious mind of a social policy consumer. If we take this point on board and consider, for illustration, the politically advocated nimbyism that represents a significant threat to the provision of sustainable accommodation for travelling communities, it is possible to argue that these resistant actions are supported under the auspices of anti-Traveller interpretations of sedentarised and articulated social policy. In the case of the frequent enforced evictions of Gypsies and Travellers from land and property, the potential influence of social policy in the equal provision of social accommodation does not rest within the pages on which it is written, but within the subjective social bureaucracies that interpret it under the jurisdiction of overarching socioeconomic and political structures (Bellamy, 1993). Local authorities will build, or procure, social housing, but they are less likely to build, or procure, social campsites. As in this stark example, much subjective interpretation of housing and accommodation policy is based on the divisional power inequalities that have positioned travelling communities as undeserving of equality in the provision and maintenance of social accommodation. Here the apparent decision not to live in a house is perceived by the majority to represent a lifestyle choice that subverts social convention and compounds the undeserving anti-Traveller stereotype. This consequently negates the requirement for specialist services based on cultural need.

Additional examples of social inequality are not difficult to locate. As we have seen, the rhetoric of social policy declares a universal commitment to the improvement of health and social care. As Gypsies and Travellers are reported to experience inequalities in health and social care (Van Cleemput, 2004), a series of detailed recommendations have been made that call for the development of specialist and localised health and social care teams (Cemlyn et al, 2009). Yet, as with the call for sustainable accommodation, the vast majority of local authorities and primary care trusts continue to overlook the unique needs of travelling communities by providing services, instead, within the mainstream (Cemlyn et al, 2009). The truth of this matter rests on the fact that the creation of such specialist health and social care provision would require the allocation of additional economical resources, which may be seen by the majority as being disproportionally unjust. Notwithstanding the inclusion of equality legislation and duty, anti-Travellerism determines the argument that specialist resources would be incorrectly allocated to a travelling person who experiences inequality in health because of their own lifestyle choice, rather than by the consequence of structural inequality. (If they want the same access to health as everyone else, why do they not just move into a house?) However, this example shows that although social policy may 'recommend' the development of such community-based services, the pragmatic actualisation depends entirely on an accurate, unbiased and inclusive understanding of the unique challenges faced by Gypsy and Traveller people by the mainstream. Where this consideration is misplaced, the value of social policy in terms of health and social care equity can only really apply, and in many respects be justified, to those people who are publicly perceived to be deserving of health and social care support. Accordingly, these groups tend to include, and are limited to, older people, people with physical, sensory or multiple impairments and young people who live according to sedentarised social convention.

As the meanings attributed to social policy can often contain a high degree of prejudicial value distortion, Bentham's (1987) proposition that the implementation of social policy reflects the importance placed on individuals by society is crucial to understanding its potentially detrimental role in relation to Gypsies and Travellers. The fact that there is potential for the (mis)interpretation and implementation of social policy for Gypsies and Travellers to be contaminated by personal, cultural and structural prejudice (Garrett, 2004, 2005) highlights a crucial point of unequal social power. Underlying the universal ambition of social policy is the critical social theory that inequality is inevitably bound up within unequal relations, which in turn makes the implementation of social provision for people experiencing social inequality inevitably contested (Foucault, 1979). While social policy aims to promote the theoretical concept of 'social wellbeing', the pragmatic attainment of it remains a highly complex process. For this reason, not only can the users of social policy fail to achieve the ideological underpinnings of social equality, they can also seriously undermine them, as we shall now see.

Undermining social policy

The Care Matters (DfES, 2006, 2007) agenda includes the most significant social policy in terms of looked-after children and recommends, as a prerequisite, putting the individual needs of children living in care at the heart of childcare reform. The introduction to the Green Paper *Care matters: Transforming the lives of children and young people in care* (DfES, 2006, p 4) emphasised the 'importance' that social care departments should place on the centrality of children welfare and rights:

> The Green Paper aims to transform both the way in which the care system works for children and the quality of experience they and others on the edge of entering or leaving care actually receive. And in doing this, we are determined to put the voice of the child in care at the centre both of our reforms and of day-to-day practice. It is only by listening to these children that we can understand their concerns and know whether or not we are meeting their needs.

The principles enshrined in the Care Matters programme formed part of the Children and Young Persons Act, which received Royal Assent in November 2008. Building on the recommendations of the Care Matters social policy, the Act emphasises the statutory duty to consult children living in care and act on their views and wishes. The focus on consultation has been welcomed by service providers. The Children, Schools and Families Committee (2009, p 15), for example, declared that 'only by setting more store by children's satisfaction with their care will we get closer to finding out how cared about they really feel, how stable and secure their lives seem'. Also included in the Children and Young Persons Act 2008 is an extension to the statutory framework for children in care in England and Wales, ensuring that all young people living in care receive high-quality care and services that are focused on and tailored to their needs.

The ideologies supporting the Care Matters agenda and the Children and Young Persons Act 2008 are certainly 'progressive' and universalistic in nature. Both the Care Matters social policy and the Act identify the unmet needs of a number of hitherto hidden and marginalised groups. However, reference to the welfare needs of Gypsy and Traveller children has been omitted, which undermines the social policy's otherwise universalistic rhetoric. Because the words Gypsy and Traveller are absent, their position in care is either not fully understood, or simply ignored by the majority. With the notable exceptions of Cemlyn (2000a, 2000b), Cemlyn and Briskman (2002), Greenfields (2002, 2006), Fisher (2003), Garrett (2004, 2005) and Cemlyn et al (2009), few empirical studies have focused on their experiences, or the implementation of specific and tailored care services. For this reason, Garrett (2005) argues that social policy has failed Gypsy and Traveller children living in public care. A direct consequence of this is that Gypsy and Traveller children living in care are often thought to be placed outside of their own culture, cut off from both their community networks and support in relation to their cultural identity (Cemlyn, 2000a, 2000b). Supporting this, Father Gerard Barry, a chaplin at HM Prison Full Sutton, quoted in Cemlyn et al (2009, p 128) states:

> There is evidence that if a decision is made to have a Traveller child taken into care, then no effort is made to find a Traveller family to care for them – quite contrary to the normal practice of trying to find a family best suited to a child's cultural background.

The 'normal practice' referred to here is enshrined within the Children Act 1989 and the United Nations Convention on the Rights of the Child 2002. Both statutes clearly state that '[a]ny decisions concerning a child must take into account their religion, racial origin and their cultural and linguistic background' (Children Act 1989, section 17(4)).

While social policy has made enormous efforts to ensure that children in care are offered support in terms of their religion, racial origin and cultural and linguistic background, Cemlyn et al (2009) indicate that there is a desperate need for political recognition of the appropriate placement of Gypsy and Traveller children. In the absence of a more forceful legislation, and the lack of specific evidence-based practice in this area, there is a danger that the placement of Gypsy and Traveller children will compound the challenges that they face growing up in care in the first place (Cemlyn, 2000b). What is more, Fisher (2003) has said that the failure of social policy to acknowledge the presence of Gypsy and Traveller children in public care has led to a lack of understanding and validation of their culture and experience. She suggests that the cultural dominance exerted through hegemonic social policy means that Gypsy and Traveller children living in care may face more risk of cultural re-socialisation than any other child. The exclusion of the Gypsies and Travellers from the Care Matters agenda consolidates the lack of concern regarding understanding their personal lived experience. Thus, any understanding of their relatedness to or involvement in the care system compounds their position of disenfranchisement and marginalisation highlights the lack of social importance placed in them.

The study

Using interpretive phenomenological analysis, this study aimed to problematise contemporary discourse surrounding looked-after children by providing opportunities for seven Irish Travellers, one Romany Gypsy and one Showman to describe their experience of living in care as children in line with government policy (DfES, 2007).

The study included face-to-face and telephone semi-structured interviews, blogs, reflective letters, poems and song lyrics, all informed and guided by the same research schedule. The research used the same methods and research questions in England, the Republic of Ireland and Scotland. In addition to the barriers constructed through structural discrimination, such as the invisibility in social policy, there appeared to be an embargo by local authorities on permitting any kind of research with Traveller care leavers. The people who did contribute to this study became involved via referral from independent organisations and opportunities related to the researcher's own contacts. This process initially identified 17 people, however after an initial discussion about the aim of the project, eight people felt that they were not able to describe their experience as it made them remember parts of their life that they preferred to forget. The interviews were conducted in English at a location of the interviewee's choice.

Interpretive phenomenological analysis was used as a research strategy to provide opportunities for Gypsies and Travellers to describe their experience of living in care and away from their families as children. Developed by Jonathan Smith (see Smith et al, 2009), interpretive phenomenological analysis draws on phenomenological perception and includes the importance and relevance of discovering underlying aspects of experiential features, in this case features that may lie at the heart of the experience of living in care. The original analysis yielded five superordinate themes based on the experience of living in care as children, which were expressed across the group. It must be noted that the results presented in this chapter represent only a summary of the research findings.

In order to assist this process and the narrative coherence of quotations, any editorial elision by the author is indicated by an ellipsis. Repeated words and utterances such as 'erm' have also been omitted for the same reason. All information that could potentially identify the people who took part in the study has been omitted (all names have been changed), as have geographical locations and the names of children's homes, foster carers and social workers.

Social policy in practice: washing away my identity

All of the people who took part in the study described entering care between the ages of two and six. Sarah's description of this process provides a good representation of the whole. Sarah was four years old when her parents were told that she would have to go into care. She explained how social services insisted that her parents would not be able to meet her needs while living by the roadside. Rather than exploring the support resources available within the community as required by social policy, the authorities gave her parents no other option than to place her into care:

> 'The social workers would have said that living on the road was unsuitable. [Settled] families are given a house, but my mother and father were only given the choice to put me in a children's home. My parents were under enormous pressure, they were at the mercy of the system. They didn't know that they were able to make a choice; they didn't know that they could say no.'

The experience of being at the mercy of the system, described in this brief extract, was a significant factor for all of the people who spoke about social work intervention. For Louise, the presence of social services reinforced her family's isolation from the travelling community. She described how her family's experience of substance misuse and domestic violence had resulted in her family being shunned by the travelling community and, like the majority of people who spoke about social services, attributed the community ostracisation to the main reason why she went into care:

> Louise: 'Some families bring scandal on themselves by fighting, drinking or taking drugs. If this happens the community will turn its back on you. This is when the trouble starts and when "the social" become involved. Like when a baby animal is separated from the herd ... that's when the lions strike....'
>
> Interviewer: 'What do the lions do?'
>
> Louise: 'Take children into care....'

In this extract, Louise compared the travelling community's culture to a protective band that ensured the interests of its more vulnerable members. Using the analogy of a defensive herd and a predatory lion, she explained that it was not until helpless families lose this protection that they become susceptible to social care intervention. The perception of social services as being damaging and aggressive was shared across the whole group as they described their treatment in care. Mary recalled how she was told that she was going to be taken into care for her own protection, but described her treatment in care as being more abusive than it was at home:

> 'I remember as soon as they [my parents] were gone I was pushed into a bath and scrubbed because they told me I was dirty because I was from a Traveller family ... I had beautifully thick, long black hair. If you stood me in a line with the other girls you could tell that I was a Traveller because of my hair. The care workers cut it all off because they said it was dirty.'

Despite a duty to protect children (DCSF, 2010), the experience of being made to feel dirty and different from other children was a common memory for all. Peter remembered how he was taken from his parents because there had been reported incidents of substance misuse and domestic violence. Instead of experiencing care and empathy in line with social work ethical standards, he explained how he was made to sit in an office, to wait to find out where he would be living:

> 'When the police took me, I spent the day at "the social's" office. I remember being scared, hungry and thirsty. When they took me to the foster carers the foster carers cried and told me to get into the bath....To them I must have looked different, but to me they were washing away my Traveller identity.... They made you feel like they were doing you a favour, and that they were saving you from an awful life because you were a Traveller.'

Notwithstanding the recommendations in social policy to maintain inter-family contact and cultural identity (DH, 1998), all of the people who took part in this study described an experience of being cut off from their families and communities, and being immersed in a culture that was completely separate from their own. As Louise explained:

> 'The first memory I have of the foster home was how closed in it was. The house was dark and smelt of damp ... there were stairs ... I'd never seen stairs. I remember my bedroom being next to the toilet ... I remember thinking to myself how dirty that was. It wasn't anything that I was used to.... It was like unlearning what I knew was right ... unlearning the Traveller way of life.'

Here Louise described the shock of being sent to live in a house. For her the adjustment to having a bathroom next to her bedroom was important as it represented a move from one culture to another. In a similar way, Sarah felt compelled to adjust to her new life in care in order to survive, but reflected on the feelings of guilt that she had because this meant that she was becoming separated from her family:

Sarah: 'The kids at my new school picked on me because of my accent ... I told my foster family but they didn't care.... So I thought well, I won't speak with an accent anymore.'

Interviewer: 'Was that a difficult decision to make?'

Sarah: [Sobbing] 'Yes because I loved my mum and dad ... but it didn't work. The kids carried on picking on me anyway, saying I was just trying to be like them.'

Interviewer: 'How did it make you feel about being a Traveller?'

Sarah: 'Dirty.'

This description of being made to feel dirty indicates the impact of cultural severance on the emotional wellbeing of all of the people who took part in the study. For Sarah, she tried to distance herself from the travelling culture in order to feel 'normal' and fit in to her new life. However, over time, the impact of adopting certain settled mores begins to impact on the ability of Gypsies and Travellers to enjoy the contact that they have with their own families. As Rita explained:

> 'I had the smell of the institution on me. I was losing my accent. I wasn't allowed to wear Traveller clothes anymore and that I was losing my Traveller culture and identity.... You didn't understand when you went home. You didn't know your family. You had to re-learn the Traveller stuff. I was bringing home certain settled values and then was making a fool of myself in front of my family.'

Although social policy aims to promote the emotional and mental health of children living in care (Jackson, 2006), the impact of living in care, away from family and the Travelling community, can have a significant lifelong impact on all Gypsies and Travellers. Louise explained that as an adult she was unable to reintegrate back into the Traveller community because she had lived with settled carers. She described her Traveller community as being highly aware of women's reputations. She explained how, when looking for a husband for example, the family's reputation was vitally important, second only to the perceived reputation of the woman. Because she lived in care, Helen described how her family's and her own reputation meant that she would never be able to marry a Traveller man:

> 'Because of the drink and fighting that brought scandal on my family, a Traveller man would see me as dirty. What's worse ... because I lived with a settled family, everyone thinks that I went to discos and hung around with boys. They think that I am like a settled girl....That I drink, take drugs and sleep around....That I am half radge [half Gypsy].'

In terms of cultural identity and the collective responsibility within social care to promote it (Children Act 1989), the description of being 'half radge', or half settled, is very important to the perception of self within the travelling community. For Helen, being associated with a violent family and being known to have grown up in care within the Gypsy community created significant barriers to inclusion. She felt that her reputation as a girl who grew up in care would prevent her from marrying a Gypsy man because she had been socialised in a separate way.

For Mary, the experience of growing up in care had a significant and lifelong effect on her ability to come to terms with her own mental health:

> 'I'm an adult that is not able to have any intimate relationships or any physical ... and that I find very difficult to understand and to live with and to manage. I had to live in a psychiatric hospital at times. I have had an eating disorder – I could not eat in front of other people – I cut my breasts.'

In an attempt to regain a sense of identity, eight people had tried to integrate back into the Gypsy or Traveller culture. However, the experience of forced eviction, racism and lack of social support, coupled with a lack of socialisation in regard to survival, has had significant implications for people. Rita described that her search for identity had resulted in her own children being taken into care:

> 'I have had problems with emotional issues throughout my life and my relationships have suffered. Being an adopted Gypsy has affected me as an adult because I haven't had proper support to find my family ... I am finding it hard to communicate with a support network, or even find anyone to help me. I felt that I have been sheltered from the Gypsy world and now I've seen the outcome; I am quite shocked how it really is. I have been a Gypsy in my own right and now my children are gone into care and I am not allowed to see them. I now realise why I was attracted to the Traveller way of life ... I've grown up but there are pieces missing, aren't there? One of my main dreams is to find my dad and mum. It is part of my world of hope and future. I need this to settle the hole in my soul. Just a cuddle from Dad and Mum would help me cope with my future and bring

forgiveness and understanding. Maybe create emotional stability within myself and help me get my kids back.'

The description of the challenges faced by Rita summarise the difficulties faced by all. For Rita, her mother and father remained the single most important people in her life. Her quest to find them for her own sense of wellbeing had completely taken over her life. But for her, the opportunity to track down her parents had been taken away because no records were available of her life prior to going into care despite the recommendations that all records should be kept for 75 years (Data Protection Act 1998). This is central in understanding the potential impact that inter-familial severance can have on Gypsies and Travellers, particularly when it comes to leaving care. At a time when adulthood signifies inter-familial unity for many, for Gypsies and Travellers leaving care, the use of standardised leaving-care legislation can lead to feelings of social marginalisation and loneliness. As Mary remembered:

> 'When I left care they got me a flat. Now some do and some don't, I know that, but Travellers are never meant to live alone in a flat away from ... [sobbing] ... it's bad for the soul....'

Gypsy and Traveller voice: implications for social policy

Putting the voice of Gypsies and Travellers who have lived in care at the centre of this study has presented an important opening in the dialogue between evidence-based practice and the implementation of social policy proposals for day-to-day practice. By listening to their views, we can understand their concerns and also how a lack of cultural recognition and implementation of specifically tailored health and social care services have made them feel emotionally dirty, physically different and socially isolated.

The testimonies contained within this case study highlight the difficulty in achieving social equality for Gypsies and Travellers living in care. Although the experiences described in this chapter could echo across the whole looked-after system regardless of ethnicity, they also provide a number of additional examples that may be unique to Gypsy and Traveller children. Although social policy specifically designed for all children living in care focuses on the centrality of welfare, rights, consultation, culturally appropriate care and empowerment, this case study has shown that the realisation of these core principles depends entirely on an informed understanding of the unique challenges faced by Gypsy and Traveller children living in care. Where this understanding remains concealed within personal prejudice, the value of social policies such as the Care Matters agenda can only really apply through, and in many respects be justified by, the value judgement of social workers and foster carers who may see a sedentarised way of life as being more beneficial to a child than a travelling way of life. In these cases, Gypsy and Traveller children living in care could be seen as being in need of saving from an undeserving lifestyle choice that has led to their accommodation in care in the first place. The existence of disparate mores further compounds this sense of difference that sees the consumers of social policy sidestepping the focus on a child's individual needs as the principles of normalisation are often unwittingly applied. Once again, this case study has shown that the difficulty in achieving social equality for Gypsies and Travellers rests within the structural discriminations and the associated negative stereotypes that exist towards them. Unless these perceptions are reversed, and a more accurate understanding enabled, those directly responsible for implementing the recommendations of social policy will continue to overlook the serious challenges faced by Gypsy and Traveller children living in care, by attributing their pre-care experiences and difficulty in transitions to lifestyle choices. This study has shown that although the marginalisation of Gypsy and Traveller children living in care is socially constructed, this sociological understanding is not always factored into decisions about service provision. Similar to the recommendation for specialist health and social care provision, this is perhaps the reason why no specialist services have been created for Gypsies and Travellers living in care within the United Kingdom.

In order to acknowledge this disadvantage, we must reflect on and address this disparity and pay (more) attention to the empowerment of Gypsy and Traveller children. It is here that empowerment should be understood to refer not simply to what Gypsy and Traveller children living in care are able to do, but also to their freedom to choose and to lead the kind of lives that they value. A similar concept was vital to the development and success of the Shared Rearing Service, a specific fostering team for Irish Traveller children in Ireland (see O'Higgins, 1993), because it cuts through the debate about whether their social needs are absolute or culturally relative.

Reflecting on the findings of the study, it is clear that the ability of the care system to meet the needs of Gypsies and Travellers is relative and dependent on the social and economic context, which truly denies these children the freedom to live as members of Gypsy and Traveller society. Based on the principle of empowerment, this current structure should be reversed. Therefore, instead of being driven solely by the socioeconomic processes that construct inequality, it should be committed to the provision of certain universal preconditions of wellbeing and personal autonomy. Not only do Gypsies and Travellers living in care need to be healthy enough to physically survive the challenges associated with state care, they also need to be empowered to make informed choices about their own lives. Although these basic needs will be individual to each child, it is possible, based on the findings of this study, to define certain intermediate demands for personal practice. Although the following list is not exhaustive, these actions must include:

- the explicit inclusion of Gypsies and Travellers in social policy;
- active consultation and increased empowerment of Gypsy and Traveller children in all social interventions;
- an increased importance given to the voices of Gypsies and Travellers;
- the ability of Children and Young People's Services to conduct kinship carers' assessments of extended family members outside of local authority boundaries;
- the recruitment and training of Gypsy and Traveller foster carers and childcare practitioners;
- support of contact between family members and the wider community;
- wider community liaison and consultation;
- the promotion of customs and mores and their inclusion in review processes;
- the appointment of community advocates in decision-making processes;
- closer scrutiny of care plans;
- a heightened importance given to life story work by informed practitioners;
- specific preventative child and adolescent mental health intervention;
- the development of organisational structures that can provide accommodation that meets cultural mores for young people leaving care;
- specific inclusion in social research;
- personal motivation for social care and health workers to 'critically reflect' on the impact of their own value positions, in line with social policy and specific professional codes of practice;
- personal confidence to challenge the discriminatory work of others.

Conclusion

Reflecting on the position of social policy and the experiences of Gypsies and Travellers who have lived in care away from their families and communities as children, this chapter has identified significant deficits in meeting their health and social care needs. In the light of these findings, a series of recommendations has been made in regard to the way in which social policy, and those who deliver services, should begin to interrogate their structural ethos in order to achieve true empowerment. Nevertheless, like social policy, I understand that the power of these recommendations could only become manifest through interpretation and implementation, which of course may not come easily or quickly. The undermining principles of socially constructed inequality and economic austerity remain a significant barrier in terms of social equality. For this reason, it would be idealistic, and perhaps rather naive, to simply call for an increase in service funding. Although funding is important, it is equally vital that we continue to reflect critically on our own personal professional practice and go further still to fully balance our commitment to Gypsy and Traveller families, after all the responsibility to achieve empowerment rests with us. We must therefore value the intention of social policy, which aims to include marginalised groups, and place this central to policy making. We must be confident to reflect on our own practice and understand our own power in the interpretation of social policy and the implementation of procedure and protocols for service delivery. If achieved we may be enabled to play a more significant role in the way that social policy is meted out, and in turn reduce the risk of it being left open to misinterpretation. Most of all, we should be able to recognise that the challenges faced by Gypsies and Travellers are not attributed to a lifestyle choice, rather their disenfranchised position in all aspects of social inclusion and equity is attributable to those structural forces that create anti-Traveller values in the first place. It is crucial therefore that health and social care agencies across the country are not implicit within this and seek to establish more culturally responsive services for Gypsy and Traveller children, families and communities. Where this is achieved, emphasis should be placed on promoting and celebrating good practice so that comprehensive evidence-based practice frameworks can be established and developed. By taking these recommendations seriously and committing to our own rhetoric, we could use social policy in a more effective way to empower Gypsies and Travellers to choose and to lead the kind of lives that they value, while challenging the prejudicial dilutions of social policy that are so often simply resource led.

SIX

Gypsies and Travellers: economic practices, social capital and embeddedness

Margaret Greenfields, Andrew Ryder and David Smith

Introduction

As a number of chapters in this volume testify, Gypsies and Travellers are some of the most marginalised minorities in the UK, with an ever-increasing weight of evidence highlighting the extreme social exclusion and inequalities experienced by these groups in access to housing, health equity and educational attainment (Crawley, 2004; CRE, 2006; Cemlyn et al, 2009). However, other than a consideration of the impacts of changing employment opportunities on family life presented within Cemlyn et al (2009), Greenfields (2006) and research undertaken by the authors of this chapter (eg, Smith and Greenfields, 2012), the working practices and economic status of Gypsies and Travellers have been largely ignored in research focus and policy discourse. This chapter, in seeking to shed light on the changing face of Gypsy and Traveller economic practices and the impact of increasing bureaucratisation and mechanisation on traditional employment opportunities for these communities, draws on both findings from the Traveller Economic Inclusion Project[1] (Ryder and Greenfields, 2010) – to date the leading study into Gypsy and Traveller working life – and a series of projects that explored barriers to work with a focus on the housing experiences of this population (Greenfields and Smith, 2010b).

In order to understand the speed and scale of economic change experienced by Gypsies and Travellers in recent decades, it is necessary to consider their traditional modes of employment and the interplay between rapid social upheaval and economic exclusion. For several hundred years, up until the early to mid-20th century, most Gypsies and Travellers were nomadic, living in tents or wagons and travelling for seasonal work purposes, with the most important modes of economic engagement being trading (for example, via door-to-door sales or at markets and fairs), the provision of entertainment and seasonal agricultural work. Large-scale social and economic changes in the post-war period, which have made many itinerant jobs obsolete, have created profound cultural change for this group, impacting on them, we suggest, even more severely than on many other people working in semi-skilled manual trades. As discussed elsewhere in this volume, a number of factors have made a nomadic life increasingly difficult to maintain:

• urbanisation;
• an increasing demand for land;
• a decline in stopping places;
• planning laws and successive legislation that have sought to outlaw nomadism and settle the travelling population either on permanent sites or in housing (Belton, 2005).

Cemlyn et al (2009, pp 35-6) highlight the high levels of unemployment and economic inactivity among Gypsies and Travellers; although the authors note that there are significant variations by type of accommodation and British region in levels of economic activity and in the types of work undertaken.

Throughout history, adaptability and flexibility have been two key features of nomadic economic practices (Clark and Ó'hAodha, 2000), but, in the context of the large-scale social and economic changes of recent decades, it is arguable whether such centuries-old responses to fluctuating work opportunities provide adequate opportunity for members of the Gypsy and Traveller communities to continue working in opportunistic, casualised employment fields without suffering significant income insecurity, a point reiterated by interviewees in the 'housed Gypsies and Travellers' studies (Greenfields and Smith, 2010b), who felt that it was increasingly difficult to earn a living using traditional skill sets. Accordingly, the Traveller Economic Inclusion Project (see Chapter Nine for further information) explicitly sought to examine whether it is possible for Gypsy and Traveller cultural and economic practices to survive and flourish in contemporary society without completely changing employment preferences and approaches to training to the extent that sociocultural, ethnic and gender boundaries need to fundamentally shift to provide fiscal security for families.

Market societies and social capital

The economic status of any particular group (as opposed to individuals considered in isolation) is a reflection of power relations in society, and thus the economic practices and experiences of minority groups need to be located within wider structural environments and hierarchies of social relations. Classical political economy starts from the premise that economic processes consist of an independent, autonomous self-regulating system in which social relations have little relevance (Smith, 1776 [1980]), an approach critiqued by Polányi (1957 [1944]), who argued that pre-modern economic systems were 'embedded' in social relations and based on redistribution, reciprocity and household economic units, an approach that we argue does indeed bear resemblance to some Gypsy and Traveller economic practices as well as being common to many Southern hemisphere, non-Western societies. Further, it has been suggested that under modern capitalism, economic action is largely disengaged from social obligations and driven by individual gain in a depersonalised economic framework that creates both a loss of autonomy and a process of proletarianisation for large numbers of the populace (Gudeman, 2001). Granovetter and Swedberg (1992), however, argue that Polányi and his followers have 'over-sociologised' their analysis and that in fact interpersonal relations are embedded in the modern economy through social and professional networks, with personal reputation and trust holding currency in a range of situations so that they impact hugely on both self-employed individuals and big businesses' fiscal stability.

In essence, therefore, the quality and nature of networks available to an individual and their access to a range of 'capitals' (economic, social, cultural and symbolic; see Bourdieu and Wacquant, 1992) impact on all aspects of their working life and economic wellbeing. In a market-driven society, work-based relationships often revolve around short-term material networks that are forged to fulfil the aims of a particular project, rather than employment connections being but one element in a complex web of interconnected social and personal experience such as may be common in faith-based groups or where individuals reside in 'ethnic enclaves' (Batthu and Mwale, 2004). Where working relationships are merely a 'means to an end' (Collingwood, 1989), such connections inevitably lack the intensity, emotional reward and longevity of those associated with closely 'bonded' social networks as institutional arrangements act as a functional substitute for core values of trust and loyalty (Okun, 1981), rather than relying on social and community expectations and shared values to maintain a socioeconomic nexus.

In contrast, for individuals and communities where work is but one element of community membership, access to economic resources and opportunities are frequently centred on the 'quality of relations' (that is, access to social capital) and the resources that different networks provide. Putnam (2000), in an exploration of the impacts of network resources on life chances, broke down the concept of 'social capital' into two subtypes, namely 'bonding' and 'bridging' social capital, both offering significant social advantages and disadvantages to their possessors. 'Bonding' social capital within Putnam's typology is inward-looking and reinforces exclusive identities and homogeneous groups. When carried to the extreme, intense 'bonding capital' may be associated with suspicion and hostility towards 'outsiders' and enforce a lack of opportunity or incentive to engage in wider social patterns. Thus, Clark and Drinkwater (2002), when undertaking a secondary analysis of the Fourth National Survey of Ethnic Minorities (Economic and Social Data Service, 1997), found lower incidence of self-employment and higher rates of unemployment in ethnically concentrated areas (for example where particular migrant groups dwelt closely together for reasons associated with access to support, sociolinguistic reasons and to avoid experiencing discrimination) than those where populations were more diverse and new social connections were formed as a matter of necessity. Accordingly, they argued that residence in an ethnic enclave afforded few economic benefits to most residents.

In contrast, Putnam (2000, pp 22-3) discusses the value to social cohesion and socioeconomic integration of access to networks that are outward-looking, incorporate people from diverse backgrounds and can therefore be described as enabling the network member to possess 'bridging capital'. Too great a reliance on 'bridging' capital may, however, potentially damage close-knit intra-community ties, which like all social relationships require maintenance and adherence to certain shared norms. Moreover, Halpern (2005) notes that despite the value associated with bridging capital – which can often be moneterised in terms of access to work or associated opportunities – a rapid rate of 'decay' can occur in such networks, with many connections utilised merely for short-term gain, as theorised by Polányi (1957 [1944]) and Collingwood (1989).

In exploring issues pertaining to the value to individuals and groups of social networks that impact on economic access and modes of distribution, it is worthwhile to expand the concept of 'social capital' to include the (perhaps unduly undervalued) field of 'emotional capital'

– an element characteristic of giving and receiving support within the private sphere (as opposed to the public) and confined within the bounds of affective relationships between family and friends (Nowotny, 1981). For many Gypsies and Travellers (as well as for other groups operating within tightly 'bonded' networks), emotional capital may relate as much to employment availability, for example working with a relative in preference to an 'outsider' even though the relative may for some reason (age, disability and so on) not be as efficient a worker as non-kin; as to caring responsibilities and gendered expectations of economic activities (see Greenfields, 2008). Such awareness of the multiple levels on which closely bonded groups operate and through which differing forms of 'capital' (economic, social, cultural, symbolic and emotional) coalesce, assists in understanding the functioning of Gypsy and Traveller economies, and is discussed below.

Gypsy and Traveller economic cultures

Cossée (2005) identifies the 'Traveller Economy' as defined by:

- self-employment;
- flexibility in seasonal (and family-based) employment;
- informal family-based training and a lack of separation between the home and the workplace.

As Okely (1983) notes, income generation for Gypsies and Travellers has always relied primarily on the provision of goods and services to the wider society, creating a symbiotic relationship. We suggest that there is no self-contained, fully autonomous 'Traveller Economy', unlike some other forms of 'ethnic economies' where all goods and services are found among a single ethnic grouping or available within a small locale inside an ethnic enclave (Kloostermann and Rath, 2003; Khattab, 2009). However, the Traveller economy does display traits of intense social networking, which has ramifications for economic activity patterns. Gypsies and Travellers have been noted throughout history for the kin- and communal-based nature of their social structure (see Greenfields, 2006) and thus their primary social networks tend to be highly 'bonded', and cemented by the degree of importance attached to attendance at frequently occurring community social events such as fairs, weddings, baptisms and funerals as well as living, where possible, in extended family groupings (Crawley, 2004; CRE, 2006; Cemlyn et al, 2009; Greenfields and Smith, 2010a, 2010b). Attendance and involvement in such social arenas strengthen ties within the social network and are a means of collectively asserting identity and group membership as well as identifying sources of work or planning future economic activities (Okely, 1983; Ryder and Greenfields, 2010). Bourdieu (1986, p 250) proposes that the social capital that flows through such networks is the foundation of group solidarity and provides members with a 'collectively-owned capital, which entitles them to credit, in the various senses of the word'. This is a point taken up by Roberts (1991, p 93), who notes that within informal economic networks, '[t]he trust necessary to conduct business ... is mainly generated by kinship and community relationships, (including ethnic ones), while in the formal economy it is mainly generated by laws that guarantee contract and the operation of the free market'.

Within the Gypsy and Traveller communities explored in both the Greenfields and Smith (2010a, 2010b; Smith and Greenfields, 2012) and the Traveller Economic Inclusion Project (Ryder and Greenfields, 2010) studies, the opportunities for engaging in informal economic networks were overwhelming gendered, with men who worked in Gypsy/ Traveller economies (undertaking hybridised forms of 'traditional, Gypsy/Traveller work' such as gardening, vehicle sales and repair, construction work or market trading), having greater opportunities to operationalise their networks and use their social capital to gain financial benefit, than did women. In contrast, while women were found to maintain highly sophisticated social networks, which could be used to pass on information to their male relatives about potential opportunities, women who were wage-earners in their own right (rather than providing supporting services for their families while the men were in paid work) were overwhelmingly either involved in relatively mainstream employment (for example, working in offices, cleaning work or factory work, which were not dependent on 'informal networks') or were employed in specialist roles as community workers (Ryder and Greenfields, 2010) where their effectiveness was predicated on knowledge of their own community, but where access to work was not necessarily reliant on their kinship ties.

Thus, for men (or families) where a significant proportion of income is derived from 'traditional' economic activities, access to extensive social networks is critical to sourcing informal labour and commodity exchange and providing a conduit through which work can be derived, deals struck and components or machinery secured. As one (male) interviewee in Ryder and Greenfields' (2010, p 41) study declared: 'I can't do it all the time [construction projects], but I know where I can get a man to do it. Yes, we're logistics specialists. I haven't been in the army or anything, but it's just putting it together, isn't it?'

The above quotation typifies Halpern's (2005) identification of the fact that access to social-employment networks can reduce transaction costs and time, and increase profitability for members engaged in joint working. Indeed, many Gypsies and Travellers interviewed for the projects considered in this chapter highly prized their system of economic practices and informal exchange networks, which they considered enabled people in their social position and possessing relatively low levels of formal education to maximise the material assets to a greater extent than might be expected. The strong preference for family-based self-employment expressed by many respondents was reflected in contempt for the waged economy and the loss of agency that this can entail:

> [The Traveller Economy]... It's brilliant, I wouldn't swap it. It's a nightmare someone telling you what to do from 7 in the morning to 7 at night. I did that for 12 months and that was to avoid the dole. I've never been a scrounger and didn't want to go down that road. After a year though there was no one more relieved than me to finish the job and I threw their bleeper at them when I left. (Ryder and Greenfields, 2010, p 41)

> "I wouldn't want to be cooped up in no office nor inside all day – being told what to do all the time by someone – that's not what we do, we work for ourselves." (Focus group participant, interviewed in relation to Greenfields' 2008 study of Traveller youth employment aspirations – previously unused data)

> "If you're self-employed you can say I don't want to go in tomorrow 'cos like you can get to decide." (Focus group participant, interviewed in relation to Greenfields' 2008 study of Traveller youth employment aspirations – previously unused data)

Thus, for many Travellers, control over working environment (or conversely loss of autonomy) determines levels of symbolic capital (status) within their kin and community group.

Despite the sense of community and communality fostered by Gypsy and Traveller forms of socioeconomic organisation, in its most traditional form, such working practices are not completely egalitarian given the central role that male family elders have played in directing family economic activities and the heavily gendered nature of family work, which again, in its most traditional form, has confined women to domestic and secondary support work (Cemlyn et al, 2009). For some women, however, access to closed intra-community female networks can itself act as a source of income and financial independence: 'I sew all the old girls' clothes for them. When anyone needs something fixing they bring it to me and I'll do it' (Smith and Greenfields, 2012).

Skill sets within close-knit communities with high levels of bonding capital are frequently passed on in a manner that transcends the need for access to formal education or training. Formal education or training is increasingly demanded in post-modern society, but has the disadvantage of removing a member of the family workforce from the group and adds 'costs' in time and financial outlay. Thus, traditionally within the Traveller Economy, a strong emphasis has been placed on family-based training, where younger family members work within the family unit and learn their skills through experiential learning (Derrington and Kendall, 2004). Smith and Greenfields (2012) note, however, that changes in practice are beginning to occur, such that some families are 'encouraging young people who have attended school and are thus aware of educational opportunities to access training which will benefit the wider family group: "he is going to college to be a mechanic – then he will have the piece of paper even though he knows how to do it along of [taught by] his Daddy"'.

For those community members following 'traditional' employment practices, Gypsy and Traveller economic relations remain 'embedded' through systems of redistribution and reciprocity that reflect the social hierarchy of the kin group. Accordingly, not uncommonly the head of the household may collect and redistribute income to other family members and, in the case of children, social networks are often utilised to ensure the intergenerational transmission of economic, social and cultural capital to establish a young adult in business or to 'pass on' a family business when an older person retires or dies. The theme of reciprocity runs through such intra-familial economic systems with time-honoured exchanges of support, goods and services based on family and extended kin/ethnic networks,[2] providing a useful mechanism for generating labour, expertise and knowledge. Moreover, where family household production may not generate adequate surplus for its own consumption, the family unit is an important component of the internal economy, which can maximize profit by working as a collective unit. Thus, a close interrelationship between culture, work and bonding social capital forms a central part of Gypsy and Traveller identity and survival mechanisms. Such practices offer a level of autonomy, which we propose cannot be sustained easily within mainstream waged economic practices.

The decline of traditional employment practices

Despite the historical success of such models of kin-based economic practices, rapid societal change has in recent decades threatened this model of working. Findings from the Traveller Economic Inclusion Project indicate that 80% of the sample (approximately 90 interviewees) had fathers who had worked in 'traditional' Gypsy/Traveller pursuits compared to 40% of respondents who were now engaged in variants of such work (Ryder and Greenfields, 2010). Change had been most dramatic in the agricultural sector where only two interviewees were employed, whereas in contrast, the great majority of interviewees' parents had been engaged in seasonal farm labour, enjoying a symbiotic economic relationship with farmers who provided stopping places and short-term accommodation for family units. This reciprocal relationship has undergone a process of decline because of technological change and cheap labour arriving from Central and Eastern Europe (Cemlyn et al, 2009), a factor identified by some interviewees as breaking down understanding between travelling people and 'mainstream society' through diminishing opportunities for social contact: 'on the farms we [Gypsies and gorjes] were all the same, we were a big team and there were hardly any problems' (Smith and Greenfields, 2012).

Restrictions placed on doorstep trading have also impinged on some elements of 'traditional Traveller economies' as the establishment of 'No Cold Calling Zones' have led to fewer Gypsies and Travellers willing to go 'on the knock' to seek building and gardening work or to sell carpets, (a mainstay of modern economic practices increasingly confined to market stalls). In 2007, the consumer magazine *Which?* estimated that there were 1,000 such zones, covering 100,000 households in Britain, but it noted that '[t]hese zones have no legal authority and serve only to alarm and worry legitimate traders who call, like Avon ladies. These are totally unfair restrictions on human rights' (*Which?*, 2007, unpaginated). A number of Traveller Economic Inclusion Project interviewees claimed that the new restrictions had led to the police and trading standards officers relying on Gypsies' and Travellers' lack of understanding of the law to harass them and stop them securing work from doorstep calling. One third of interviewees voiced concerns about the 'cold calling' restrictions, with some regarding it as a direct attack on Gypsy and Traveller lifestyles:

'They put everything in their way to say these Travellers can't work. It is like they are trying their hardest to find ways to put Travellers out of business ... every time when you go out there and you are trying your hardest to get a job, someone brings a new law so you can't do this and you can't do that.' (Ryder and Greenfields, 2010, p 44)

The economic impact of site shortages

The national shortage of Traveller sites (Chapter Two) has also had negative economic impacts for Gypsies and Travellers. As far back as the 1970s, Acton (1974) noted a growing trend towards settlement when economic nomadism could no longer be sustained, a problem compounded by the decline of agricultural work. The accrued legislative impacts on travelling lifestyles and decline in sustainable economic nomadism (coupled with age-related settlement) have led to a situation where between one half and two thirds of the Gypsy and Traveller population reside in conventional housing (CRE, 2006). Evidence suggests that the settlement of these communities has resulted in an increasing economic bifurcation of the community between those who have successfully adapted elements of traditional economic practices by moving into construction work, trading and associated areas, and a significant population of long-term unemployed and economically inactive Gypsies and Travellers. For the latter group, close 'bonding' ties to those similarly unemployed and a lack of 'bridging' ties that transcend their own networks and circuits of social capital are key causal mechanisms in their continuing social and economic exclusion (Greenfields and Smith, 2010b).

The decline of the 'Traveller Economy' has probably been most acute on local authority sites. Multiple exclusion, including the location of many local authority sites in deprived areas, a lack of workspaces on or near sites, low levels of literacy and increasing welfare dependency are factors that have led to the rapid decline of traditional employment practices in localised and spatially isolated spaces of acute exclusion (ITMB, 2007; Ryder and Greenfields, 2010). By contrast, living on family-owned private sites enables extended families to live together and utilise family networks and the sites themselves as centres of economic activity (Cemlyn et al, 2009; Ryder and Greenfields, 2010).

Problematically, however, where families set up unauthorised developments as a way of seeking to establish an autonomous work–living space, legal and financial demands of lengthy and complex planning cases create a drain on financial resources and a distraction from the development of family businesses:

> 'They say they want more sites for Travellers, they are advising you to buy your own land ... but you can't really concentrate on your work while you have to fight for getting your site passed.... If you get peace and quiet to live and you get your own property you can do what you want to do eventually. I want to put an office on the site with my computers, phone line and fax machine. What people don't want to understand is that if my business is successful I'll be employing people and it means less people are going to be unemployed. I can employ somebody from the Traveller as well as from the housed community.' (Ryder and Greenfields, 2010, p 94)

Economic adaptability and post-industrial economies

Although a large number of Gypsies and Travellers feel that traditional work patterns are becoming harder to sustain, there appears to be an increasing trend (predominantly among men) to successfully fuse skilled and manual trades with mainstream economic practices. A number of younger interviewees had supplemented their in-family training through undertaking formal training, for example attending bricklaying courses and obtaining recognised trade qualifications. One Traveller Economic Inclusion Project respondent stated:

> 'The lads without any qualifications they've got no skills on paper; a lot of them can't read and write but are probably the best plasterers, the best roofers you'll ever see. They've got nothing on paper and I think they are beginning to realise if they don't do something to change they are not going to be able to earn a living. I speak from experience, that's what I found as well. I come from a building background again with no qualifications and I realised if I carried on doing it I'm not going to make a living so I went back to school, got some formal qualifications and that made a difference.' (Ryder and Greenfields, 2010, p 51)

For young women, training as a hairdresser, along with obtaining National Vocational Qualifications in the trade, seems to be an increasingly popular career choice, and one that can 'mean you can work when the chavvies are bigger ... and women on the site always need their hair doing" (unpublished data gathered by Greenfields, 2010). In addition, Greenfields (previously unpublished data) has interviewed several young Gypsy and Traveller mothers who are turning their sewing skills to good use through creating baby clothes and selling them on the internet to 'mainstream' clients as well as to community members at horse fairs such as the Appleby and Stow fairs.

Indeed, the Traveller Economic Inclusion Project identified an emerging trend among younger and/or more 'innovative' interviewees to formally register their businesses and become certified practitioners in their particular field. In a number of cases, Travellers had set up websites to promote their businesses: 'I have an e-mail address and I have my own website with pictures of my work. I'm registered and authorised by the Environment Agency. It is just the way forward' (Ryder and Greenfields, 2010, p 51).

In the main, traders who utilised new technologies were involved in relatively traditional forms of economic activity such as landscape gardening, construction or retail (for example, sale of baby clothes, refurbished wagons and so on). Such traders were overwhelmingly likely to have a stable residential home base, and to have benefited from formal education and/or formal training (Greenfields and Smith, 2010a).

Gendered 'waged' employment

Several of the studies considered above (Ryder and Greenfields, 2010; Smith and Greenfields, 2012) have found a trend towards a growing number of Gypsies and Travellers entering waged employment, with housed Gypsies and Travellers most likely to do so. Overall, one third of the Traveller Economic Inclusion Project interviewees in waged employment were women working in community projects as outreach staff and mediators. Satisfaction levels for women in this sector were high not least because they reported that their employment greatly enhanced community trust in services and involvement in projects as well as encouraged other Gypsy and Traveller women to consider work that was outside of mainstream career choices for many people who left school at a young age or with minimal qualifications (Ryder and Greenfields, 2010, chapter 7).

All of the studies considered above found evidence of growing female employment in low-skilled waged work such as cleaning, kitchen assistants and retail sales. The move to such work was predominantly driven by increasing employment of younger women with school-age children, a finding noted in some Gypsy and Traveller Accommodation

Needs Assessments and in the limited number of research studies that explore employment (Cemlyn et al, 2009).

Overall (as noted in the Traveller Economic Inclusion Project report: Ryder and Greenfields, 2010), it is anticipated that recent welfare reforms that place greater pressure on unemployed people to take any form of work, combined with increased fragmentation of the Traveller Economy and a growing shortage of sites, could increase Gypsy and Traveller employment in the waged sector. Moreover, it is expected that competition for such low-paid work will increase in the context of the recession, which is leading to job losses across many sectors.

Mutualism, social enterprise and the 'Big Society'

One key finding from the Traveller Economic Inclusion Project report (Ryder and Greenfields, 2010) (explored within an explicitly gendered context in a study by Greenfields, 2011, which considered women's employment opportunities within black and minority ethnic social enterprises) concerns the networking and training opportunities arising within the context of mutualism and social enterprise ventures. Such activities can be particularly successful among groups with bonding social capital and a strong sense of community identity, suggesting that Gypsies and Travellers may be well suited to working within these forms of organisation, which guarantee autonomy and environmental control, factors identified as central to employment aspirations for members of this group.

While there are a number of strong community projects and national charities (for example, the Irish Traveller Movement in Britain and Friends, Families and Travellers) that employ substantial numbers of Gypsy and Traveller staff, to date only a small number of social enterprises have been developed by Gypsies and Travellers. One example of such an agency is Homebase, a community interest company (a not-for-profit organisation) set up to build and manage sites while employing substantial numbers of community members as staff and subcontractors engaged in construction works. Other Gypsy and Traveller social entrepreneurs have, over a number of decades, established private residential sites on a commercial basis, which meet the needs of community members while acting as a beacon of good practice in terms of high-quality provision (EHRC, 2009). In addition, an increasing number of small community groups have been established by innovative individuals who have secured local service contracts and who employ staff to deliver diversity training on issues pertaining to Gypsy and Traveller issues.

The above examples, while relatively few in number (and in many cases threatened by the substantial loss of funding to community groups since the advent of the Coalition Government in 2010; see Greenfields, 2011), provide indications of the way in which social enterprise activities could take root and blossom within Gypsy and Traveller communities, potentially leading to significant employment opportunities and a growth in the 'ethnic economy' in a manner similar to that found within other minority populations.[3]

Bonding social capital has long been noted as being a valuable asset for successful social enterprise development (CONSCISE, 2003). The high levels of bonding capital and notions of reciprocity common to the Gypsy and Traveller communities, when coupled with a growth in 'Big Society' driven specialist service delivery targeted at populations recognised as at high risk of marginalisation, present an ideal forcing ground for fledgling social enterprises. Thus, opportunities exist, for example, for entrepreneurial Gypsy and Traveller groups to develop outreach and training services for unemployed community members in socially deprived locales. Indeed, it has been suggested that social enterprises located in disadvantaged areas have a potential competitive advantage over 'outsiders' due to their degree of embeddedness within the community (Peattie and Morley, 2008), a factor that should enhance the likelihood of community projects winning tenders to work with groups popularly seen as 'hard to reach'. In this way, while the (current at the time of writing) governmental conceptualisation of a 'Big Society', which removes the need for many public services as local populations are expected to step up to deliver services, may significantly damage the infrastructure of the welfare state, for innovative Gypsy 'bricoleurs' (Okely, 1983) who are able to take advantage of rapidly changing opportunities, mutualism and social enterprise might just offer a resurgence in new forms of economic activity. On the other hand, the Big Society may further marginalise Gypsies and Travellers as it is feared by some that only the most well-resourced and confident sections of the community will be able to mobilise to take on such roles (concerns discussed by Richardson and Ryder in Chapter Seven).

Conclusion

Within this chapter we have demonstrated the ways in which innovative 'Traveller economic practices' have evolved historically to become a dynamic instrument that enables community members to offset some of the most extreme forms of exclusion, while retaining a sense of autonomy and control in their working and cultural lives.

The erosion of many traditional employment opportunities therefore risks impoverishing large swathes of the community (as has happened in many Central European countries where Roma are frequently destitute) unless there is an increased focus on personalised and empowering policy responses, and individual entrepreneurs work in partnership with their communities to promote new business models based on mutualism, while exploiting new technologies and old skills. In the current economic climate, it is unlikely that government strategies will take particular account of the specialised needs of marginalised black and minority ethnic populations, preferring instead to 'mainstream' responses to unemployment. In times such as these, the determination and relentless drive to survive common to Gypsy and Traveller populations mean that innovative individuals will doubtless seek out and identify ways of 'turning a penny a new way' (Smith and Greenfields, 2012). For those unable to do so, it is to be hoped that close-knit community bonds will see the vulnerable through the hard economic times that lie ahead; a situation weathered so often before by a population comprised of the ultimate 'flexible workforce'.

Notes

[1] See Chapter Nine for a discussion of the background to, and research methods utilised in, the Traveller Economic Inclusion Project.

[2] See Finch and Mason (2000) for a discussion on the informal expectations and reciprocal exchanges within 'mainstream' households and families.

[3] See Sepulveda et al (2010) for a comprehensive review of black and minority ethnic social enterprise activities.

Part Two

Empowering Gypsies and Travellers

SEVEN

Justice and empowerment

Joanna Richardson and Andrew Ryder

Introduction

This chapter examines the notions of 'justice' and 'empowerment' as they relate to Gypsies and Travellers. It aims to provide a theoretical basis on which to understand the ideas. In a time when the Conservative-led Coalition Government aims to empower everyone to take part in a 'Big Society' (as discussed in Chapter One, this volume), it is important to assess the extent to which Gypsies and Travellers will be included in this aim.

Theories of power will provide a framework, and will include the notion of discourse as control (Richardson, 2006a). Within this debate we will examine the extent to which Gypsies and Travellers are marginalised by wider society, but also the resistance to control and discrimination by the travelling communities through different forms of representation. Hence, part of the chapter focuses on a process of ethnogenesis, namely the political and cultural mobilisation and growing sense of self-identification by Gypsies and Travellers.

The chapter's discussion on justice is centred on a brief debate on policing Gypsies and Travellers, in a wider societal sense, but also looks at the relationship between the police force and travelling communities. We do not propose to look at issues of crime and criminality here, but more to examine notions of justice in how police treat victimisation and discrimination against Gypsies and Travellers. We will ask, do the police, and local politicians, view the travelling communities as part of their constituency, and are they treated fairly?

Theories of power and empowerment

Traditional notions of power centre on one dimension: decision making (Dahl, 1961). Bachrach and Baratz (1970, p 24) further define power as follows:

> A power relationship exists when (a) there is a conflict over values or course of action between A and B; (b) B complies with A's wishes; and (c) B does so because he is fearful that A will deprive him of a value or values which he regards more highly than those which would have been achieved by non-compliance.

Power here seems to be simple and overt. B does something he would not otherwise do because he is fearful of what A might do to him otherwise. However, Bachrach and Baratz add a further second dimension to our understanding of power: non-decision making. There are more complex issues and relationships at play when considering power and empowerment. Lukes (1974) goes further still with three-dimensional definitions, explaining that power is where:

- there is an overt resolution of conflict between two or more conflicting positions (first dimension);
- there is a covert or hidden dimension that excludes issues from public decision making ('non-decision making') (second dimension);
- interests are institutionalised within society, and structures of power are accepted and internalised without question or even recognition (third dimension).

Those who hold that society is essentially cooperative (infinite, variable) maintain that the exercise of power is confined to decision making alone, in circumstances where there is an overt conflict (the first dimension), but as Lukes explains, power is also exercised by control of the political agenda – as much through keeping issues away from decision making as through dominating the decision-making process. His view of power:

> … allows for consideration of the many ways in which potential issues are kept out of politics, whether through the operation of social forces and institutional practices or through individuals' decisions. This, moreover, can occur in the absence of actual, observable conflict, which may have been successfully averted – though there remains here an implicit reference to potential conflict. (Lukes, 1974, p 24)

Developing thoughts on power and control further, Foucault (1980) also considered the concept of power to be more fluid, but thought about bases and targets of power, and he saw that there was not necessarily a central originator or target of power, as such. He saw instead a plurality of power and noted the flow and resistance in power.

> Power is employed and exercised through a net-like organisation. And not only do individuals circulate between its threads; they are always in the position of simultaneously undergoing and exercising this power. They are not only its inert or consenting target; they are always also the elements of its articulation. In other words, individuals are the vehicles of power, not its point of application. (Foucault, 1980, p 98)

Taking Foucault's ideas into a further dimension, Laclau and Mouffe (2001, p 135) discussed 'hegemonic articulations', which they suggested are based on two core aspects:

- articulatory moments;
- confrontational antagonistic practices.

It is not enough for just articulation or antagonism for hegemony to take place: the articulation must occur within antagonistic practices (see Figure 7.1). The antagonistic forces are fluid and not fixed; differences can be constructed and reconstructed. If we think about the social construction of Gypsies and Travellers in the social space, we can see the construction of identity that creates antagonistic communities, and yet the identity is not fixed but constantly changing. Think of the example of the public, press and politicians blaming Gypsies and Travellers for their own lack of accommodation and place in the community because of an 'unwillingness' to settle and live as the rest of society in houses. However, when talking about Gypsies and Travellers who have bought a plot of land and applied for planning permission to allow them to live the settled life that the public, press and politicians have suggested they must, in order to be accepted as part of society, they are then seen as not 'real' Gypsies and Travellers and subsequently threatened with having their racial and cultural identities stripped away (this removal of cultural identity upon settling is enshrined in planning law, but not so in equalities legislation). If Gypsies and Travellers, having been made homeless through being moved on from roadside encampments persistently, move into a house as the only option offered by a council in response to a homeless application, they are seen as not needing a site or roadside accommodation (even if they are included in an accommodation needs assessment, their desire to be on a site rather than in a house may be seen as preference rather than need), fewer sites are built, more Gypsies and Travellers have to go on the roadside, they are moved on and on, and on, perhaps they eventually move into housing – but they are still seen as 'other' even when they conform, or are coerced to conform. This seems to embody the articulation (and re-articulation) within antagonistic practices. There is always conflict involved, sometimes overt, but sometimes implied, but there is no fixed boundary to the antagonistic practices or the groups party to this process of power and control. In other words, if rules and group identities are fixed then it is possible to learn the rules and engage in resisting the dominant power; but if the rules and identities are constantly changing and being rearticulated then resistance is much more difficult.

Figure 7.1: Articulation of Gypsies and Travellers within antagonistic practices

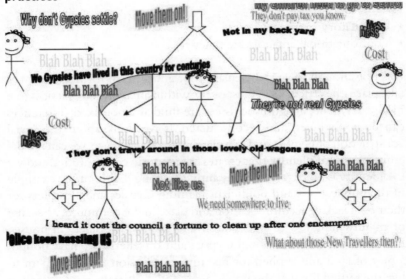

Source: Richardson (2011b)

Gypsies and Travellers resisting through representation

Through continued marginalisation and discrimination, it is possible for dominated groups to develop a heightened sense of awareness of this process of the social construction of identity, re-articulation of 'otherness' and antagonistic practices of power and control. As a result they may forge alliances between micro groups to form a coalition (whether informal or formal) to resist against the power and control. They may, as part of this process, seek to distance themselves from the society that discriminates against them. High levels of discrimination and notions of injustice form part of the cycle of conflict and antagonism that has impeded Gypsy and Traveller participation in a range of institutions and civic forums (CRE, 2006). Such trends have been accentuated by cultural and moral fears that Gypsies and Travellers have of 'outsiders' grounded in fear and mistrust of the wider community (Derrington and Kendall, 2004). At the margins, bonding social capital (intense social networks) has acted as a form of self-help and defence against exclusion and discrimination (Ryder, 2011). Through the maintenance of what Barth (1975) described as 'cultural boundaries', Gypsies and Travellers at times have kept their distance from mainstream society, which in turn has limited the development of formal organisation. Such boundary maintenance can be counter to empowerment, given that it is dependent on greater interaction and participation in a range of decision-making forums. In response to discrimination and hostility, besieged minority groups like Gypsies and Travellers have developed forms of reactive ethnicity, where they construct ethnicity as a defence against racism and discrimination, forming a defensive wall that can offer protection through distancing (Ballard and Ballard, 1977).

While ethnogenesis, or recognition of ethnic difference from wider society, is a process that can represent the power of alliance between groups with similar claims and demands in an area – for instance, Gypsies and Travellers as an umbrella identity for a range of different ethnicities – it can also dilute claims and meanings. Laclau and Mouffe (2001) discuss the notion of 'empty' or 'floating' signifiers in discourse and the lack of fixity in social identities. They suggest (2001, p 113) that:

> The practice of articulation, therefore, consists in the construction of the nodal points which partially fix meaning; and the partial character of this fixation proceeds from the openness of the social, a result, in its turn, of the constant overflowing of every discourse by the infinitude of the field of discursivity.

What Laclau and Mouffe are telling us is that signifiers (and any solid meaning of things) can only ever be partially fixed because the field of discursivity (the context for the debate) is constantly changing and overwhelming any momentary understanding of what a particular node (thing, person, group) is. So, a newspaper columnist may claim to know exactly what a Gypsy or Traveller is, but their attempt to fix meaning is overwhelmed by new information and by wider reactions to their attempt to fix meaning. This changing discourse, which overflows partially fixed meanings of social identity, can be seen to occur not just in the external debate that socially constructs and reconstructs identities (for example the debate about Gypsies and Travellers by the public, press and politicians) but also in the internal debate within and between Gypsy and Traveller groups themselves. This links to a debate on the specific definition of Gypsy and Traveller groups, both by themselves and by others. The very label 'Gypsies and Travellers' is an externally imposed exonym to bring together a range of diverse cultures, races and identities for the sake of convenience and expediency. It is necessary (and is a label that is used throughout this volume) so that the discussion can look at issues, claims and demands that relate to common experiences across a range of groups (for example lack of accommodation, lack of access to healthcare and schooling, and treatment by the public, press and politicians as 'other' in discourse – language and practice). However, there is concern that Gypsies and Travellers should define themselves, their own distinct community, through an internally devised ethnonym. Yet, there are competing claims between groups for labels and a concern over authenticity of claims. For example, some groups would like a general definition to be used for all Gypsies and Travellers and for it to be the same across housing, planning and race law. However, other groups may challenge that and prefer to retain separate and distinct definitions of identity that refer to specific histories, cultures and claims.

While it is important that groups self-define rather than have external labels imposed on them, there is a challenge over 'ownership' of a label and also fixity within a wider discourse. The discourse by the public, press and politicians is out of the control of the groups under discussion, and is a constantly changing identity, as stated earlier. Laclau and Mouffe (2001, p 119) talk about this in terms of control and fiction in representation of identities: '[a representative] can be subjected to such conditions of control that what becomes a fiction is the very fictitiousness of the representation; and on the contrary, a total absence of control can make the representation literally fictitious'.

Lobbying for justice and empowerment

> Gypsies have no conception of democracy or representation.
> It is absurd for anyone to claim in a meaningful and

technically democratic sense to 'represent' the Gypsies on anything. (Smith, 1975, p 6)

This statement by Smith in a Young Fabian pamphlet does not resonate with the democratic landscape we see in the current context, nearly 40 years on. The development of a heightened awareness of identity and marginalisation created a greater sense of unity and political mobilisation to secure equality.

> Large and diverse Romani communities are experiencing a process of ethnogenesis as they discover their cultural and political potential and move from a status of a despised, ignored, and marginal community of 'Gypsies' to that of a 'Romani/Sinti' minority demanding respect and rights. (Gheorghe and Mirga, 2001, p 9)

There are examples of Gypsies and Travellers representing interests in society through professional membership – for example Gypsy lawyers, journalists and police. They are also involved in traditional types of political office: Gypsies and Roma are district councillors and Members of the European Parliament. Such professional leaders although growing in numbers are relatively small in number and are still competing against 'charismatic' leadership, in the shape of strong leaders whose authority is based on status and kin networks rather than organisational and democratic structures. However, in Europe (see Chapter Eleven, this volume) there has been significant progress in community development with the emergence of policy and voice organisations and community leaders well versed in the arts of lobbying, processes that have been mirrored in the last 50 years in the United Kingdom (UK). The importance of this is emphasised by McCarthy (1994, p 28):

> Policy decisions that fundamentally affect Traveller lives are constantly being developed without any input from the Traveller community. Policy decisions reflect the cultural norms of the settled community. How these decisions will affect Travellers is never considered. Without knowledge of this distinct lifestyle, policy decisions cannot be sensitive to their needs.

Hence, it is imperative that Gypsy and Traveller community groups continue to grow and flourish if the foundations of ethnogenesis are to be built upon. An important aspect of this process is capacity building, that is, organisational development and staff training that enables community groups to grow and secure stable financial foundations and offer high-quality services. By virtue of further capacity building, Gypsies and Travellers can build on their present foundations and further mobilise from within the community, enabling them to shape and influence social policy.

The formation of the Gypsy Council in 1966 was a landmark in Gypsy and Traveller ethnogenesis as it was the first national and formalised campaign structure for this community in the UK. However, after initial successes in helping secure government reforms on site provision in the form of the Caravan Sites Act 1968, a series of splits and divisions fractured this organisation (Acton, 1974). It was not to be until the late 1990s that more unified campaigns were to materialise in the shape of what was termed 'Traveller Law Reform' (Ryder, 2011). In 2002, the Traveller Law Reform Bill was drafted by Cardiff Law School and, once it had been brought to his attention by the Irish Traveller Movement in Britain, the Conservative MP David Atkinson announced that he would be introducing the Traveller Law Reform Bill as a Private Member's Bill. This took many by surprise for the Bill proposed to reintroduce a statutory duty on councils to provide and facilitate sites and Atkinson represented a constituency where a number of contentious unauthorised encampments had ignited large public protests. However, rather than proposing draconian enforcement measures, increasingly favoured by others in his party, he contended that the shortage of sites was a principal cause of the growing tensions between Gypsies and Travellers and the settled community (Ryder, 2011). The Bill ran out of parliamentary time, but the foundations for concerted lobbying and representation were laid.

The Traveller Law Reform Bill 2002 was a key moment in lobbying for empowerment and justice for Gypsies and Travellers. It was resolved to lay the foundations of a broad and coordinated campaign by creating some type of forum, including the various lead activists and groups, to mount a campaign in support of the Bill. The coordinating forum that was established in 2002 was named the Traveller Law Reform Coalition.[1] It sought to involve not just constituted and member-based Traveller groups such as the Gypsy Council and Friends, Families and Travellers but also traditional activists. Furthermore, there were no elected officers, a majority of the committee were Gypsies and Travellers and decisions were taken collectively (Ryder, 2011).

The coalition also secured greater access to the parliamentary process through the establishment of the All Party Parliamentary Group (APPG) for Gypsies, Roma and Travellers (prior to 2010, APPG Traveller Law Reform). While the Traveller Law Reform Coalition is no longer a part of the representative landscape, the APPG still listens to Gypsy and Traveller issues and tries to have their voices heard in Parliament where regular discussions are held. Lord Avebury has been a key politician for decades in the struggle for Gypsy and Traveller rights; he is secretary of the group. There are other key moments connected to the APPG, for example the Westminster Panel Review of evidence on the impact of the Localism Bill (since enacted) on Gypsies and Travellers (funded by the Joseph Rowntree Charitable Trust and undertaken by the Travellers Aid Trust). The panel included both authors of this chapter and a number of other contributors to this volume, as well as key figures from the APPG. The panel review attempted to establish the key areas of impact on travelling communities. Expert witnesses from Gypsy and Traveller communities, local government, planning and legal professions, representative voluntary organisations and the police all gave evidence on a range of questions examining the Localism Bill and Big Society (see Ryder et al, 2011).

A major fear raised at the panel review by those working in the Gypsy and Traveller third sector is that opportunities for the employment of community members, the delivery of devolved and effective services and involvement in the design and shaping of services and policy as touted in the Big Society package will be missed by the dearth of Gypsy and Traveller community groups. In recent years the Gypsy and Traveller third sector has grown greatly in terms of resources and staff employed but this growth comes from an incredibly low base, and in comparison to other minority groups the Gypsy and Traveller third sector remains fragile. A profound fear was raised by community groups at the panel review that a loss of funding in the wake of the financial crisis and governmental policies of deficit reduction could stall and even reverse the development of the Gypsy and Traveller third sector at a key point, leading to a loss of confidence, expertise and body of skilled staff from the Gypsy and Traveller community itself (Ryder et al, 2011). Given that it is likely that groups that are the most organised, confident and well resourced will be the best placed to seize opportunities presented by the Big Society, Gypsies and Travellers are likely to be at a disadvantage (Bartlett, 2009). Aside from a lack of funding reducing Gypsies and Travellers' input into the Big Society agenda, there is the issue of trust and community relations. Coalition policy, particularly in the sphere of accommodation (see Chapter Two, this volume), combined with existing notions of injustice (see below) will impede meaningful interactions and partnerships because wider tensions will be pulling actors in opposite directions, presenting an obstacle to inclusive service provision, civic engagement and community cohesion.

Ideas on justice in a policing context

Donzelot (1979), in his work *The policing of families* discusses government through family. He also proposes three 'philanthropic poles' of power held over the family: moralisation, normalisation, and contract and tutelage. These three forms of power have commonalities with the three different types of power (discipline, training and surveillance) identified by Foucault (1979).

Gypsies and Travellers are under the surveillant control by the majority of society in overt and covert ways. It is interesting to outline the more covert type of control and surveillance in wider society, in the context of a framework of control and power. Dandeker (1990) helps to clarify a typology of surveillance, with five main types:

- petty tyranny;
- direct democracy;
- patronage;
- bureaucratic dictatorship;
- rational–legal (see Figure 7.2).

Direct democracy (in Figure 7.2) seems to be the most appropriate model for the current political context in the UK, and it is interesting to note the 'tyranny' of the majority in this categorisation. While Figure 7.1, presented earlier in this chapter, showed articulation of identity in contested space, and there was some element of resistance to control within that – there is evidence from observing the debate about Gypsies and Travellers, and the translation of the debate into public practices and action, a tyranny of the majority over the travelling communities, which puts up barriers to community cohesion, access to public space, accommodation and good health and education outcomes. This tyranny is dispersed throughout society due to the plurality of power and control, but one area that Gypsies and Travellers see tyranny in its most concrete form is through eviction; and the police are seen as the face of that eviction process.

> Almost 40 years ago I watched police officers deliberately kick burning sticks onto children to force the Travellers to move on quickly. Ways to move them have become less

Figure 7.2: Typology of surveillance

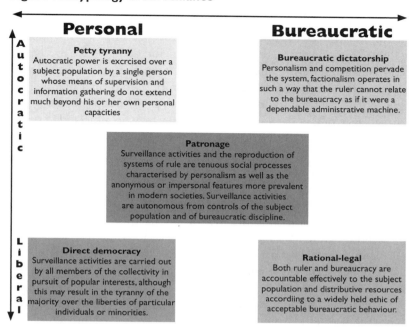

Source: Adapted from Dandeker (1990: 45-51)

crude but equally effective. They depend, it seems to me, on utter and total prejudice and ignorance in almost the whole of our society. (Dawson, 2000, p 4)

Dawson (2000) outlines his views of the treatment of Gypsies and Travellers, by the police and others, and he suggests that there should be more understanding and toleration in our diverse community, particularly following the Macpherson Report (1999). The Macpherson Report (1999), which followed the police handling of the murder of Stephen Lawrence in 1997, found that the police force was institutionally racist. Since then, there have been steps to improve the way that the police operate; particularly looking at their relationships with black and minority ethnic communities.

James and Richardson (2006) noted that proactive, intelligence-led policing approaches resolve problems most efficiently and effectively. However, until more recently, such policies have failed to come to fruition, with police tending to engage with Gypsies and Travellers through enforcement rather than partnership and communication.

A small group of professionals in the police force have recognised the need for understanding and engaging with Gypsies and Travellers, partly to follow the need to combat institutionalised racism, after Macpherson (1999). Traditionally there has been a suspicion of the police by Gypsies and Travellers. This is often because they see the police on eviction days, or are stopped and searched more often than members of the settled community. Bowers (undated, p 13) discussed the police surveillance of Gypsies and Travellers: 'They may be subjected to police surveillance on a regular basis (I witnessed a lot of helicopter and car based police surveillance whilst in Cambridgeshire).' Bowers also analysed his survey of young Gypsy/Traveller attitudes to the police:

> When asked the question: 'what do you think of the police?' 44% said something negative, 40% said they thought the police were OK and 16% said something positive.... Some young travellers definitely had a more positive view of the police than their parents.... Perhaps the most dramatic responses came on the issue of race hate ... not a single person said they had reported an experience of racism to the police: 'It would be worthless reporting a crime'. One 13-year-old Romani boy told me: 'They would just side with the gorgias'. (Bowers, undated, p 13)

One tragic moment epitomised the absence of justice for Gypsies and Travellers, and that was the killing of a 15-year-old boy, Johnny Delaney, by a group of boys in Cheshire in 2003. Witnesses said that Johnny was called names and kicked about the head. In this case the police recognised the racial motivation of the killing, but the court did not. Finding the accused boys guilty of manslaughter, the court did not find that the killing was a racially motivated crime. The police, after the hearing, voiced their disappointment at this lack of justice:

> Detective Chief Inspector Jed Manley, of Cheshire Police, said: 'It was recorded as a racially-motivated incident on the first day of the inquiry under the definition given by the Lawrence Inquiry because of certain comments made at the scene of the incident. I believe that the incident still falls within the definition we would use for a racially-motivated incident, and we believe that is appropriate.' (BBC News, 2003)

Since Bowers' survey of Gypsies and Travellers, and the shocking murder of Johnny Delaney in 2003, work has been done to try to improve the relationship between the police and the travelling community. Notably, Cheshire police force were a lead authority in this attempt to improve relations with the community. In Cambridgeshire police force there was also development work on policies to improve community cohesion, and this culminated in the release in 2005 by the Gypsy Media Company of a CD entitled 'Del gavvers pukker-cheerus' ('Give the police a chance'), although this was heavily criticised in the tabloid press (Sapstead, 2005).

There has been an explicit move, within the police, to train themselves in dealing better with Gypsies and Travellers. John Coxhead, of the Derbyshire Constabulary, published his report *Moving forward* (Coxhead, 2005), and the accompanying annual police and Gypsy conferences, Pride not Prejudice, started in 2004. And yet, there are still lessons to be learned in policing practice. This volume has been completed in the wake of the Dale Farm eviction where the practice of police as practitioners and enforcers of the eviction process (rather than the eviction being carried out by bailiffs) has been called into question. Images of police using tasers were shown across the news channels (see Figure 7.3).

A review of whether the police action was proportionate during the eviction was called for at the Irish Travellers Movement in Britain conference in November 2011. It will be interesting to see whether new policy emerges from the Association of Chief Police Officers as a result of any review.

Justice from local political and community representatives?

This brief section of the chapter will draw on two examples where justice has been lacking – one following a public parade and another following outrageous comments from a local councillor. There is no tragic loss of life in these cases, as in the Johnny Delaney killing, but they are shocking examples in their own spheres.

The first example is from 2003. Residents in the village of Firle in East Sussex had a public bonfire party where they had a caravan with the number plate P1KEY and effigies of Gypsies and Travellers inside, which they set fire to and paraded down the street in a procession. Instead of standing up for Gypsies and Travellers following complaints about the event, the local MP, Norman Baker, compounded the sense of discrimination and injustice:

Figure 7.3: Image of the police evicting Travellers at Dale Farm

Source: Peter Macdiarmid, kindly supplied by Getty Images

> Local MP Norman Baker said residents were upset after 'itinerant criminals' caused damage to land and property, and a degree of anger was understandable. He backed the organisers of Firle Bonfire Society, who denied any racism....
>
> The CRE [Commission for Racial Equality] chairman, Trevor Phillips, said the burning was a clear example of incitement to racial hatred, a crime which carries a maximum sentence of seven years. 'You couldn't get more provocative than this,' he said. (Ellinor, 2003)

The situation in Firle demonstrated an extreme form of prejudice against Gypsies and Travellers. Trevor Phillips, chair of the former CRE, noted in the article above just how provocative the actions of the Firle bonfire party were.

At a local level, some councillors, both at public meetings and in local newspapers, have made highly inflammatory remarks, which can only serve to stoke local conflict, and there is little done to stop or reprimand them. One example of this, in 2007, was a local councillor who suggested that if she had cancer she would strap a bomb to herself and blow up a local unauthorised site, an issue that received national press coverage. The government agency, the Standards Board for England, found that no disciplinary action (other than that indicated in the quote below) was needed to discipline the councillor, which demonstrates acquiescence to this racism and makes Gypsies and Travellers feel further vilified, and even more on the margins of the community. Here is how the item was reported in the tabloid press:

> It was a flippant suggestion born of frustration. But councillor ... has paid dearly for joking that suicide bombing might be the only way to deal with an illegal travellers' site making residents' lives a misery. She and her colleagues were promptly dispatched on 'cultural awareness training' in which they were forced to tour travellers' sites and learn about their history. At the same time, council watchdogs carried out an 11-month investigation into the remark at taxpayers' expense. Mrs X had told fellow councillors that [the] District Council would 'never get rid of the b★★★★★★★' who had created an infamous illegal settlement....The independent councillor ... declared: 'If I had cancer, I'd strap a big bomb around myself and go in tomorrow'. (*Daily Mail*, 2007, p 35)

This district councillor made outrageous and offensive comments about local residents who were Travellers living on an unauthorised site. Some may have construed the comments as incitement to racial hatred and violence, but the Standards Board clearly did not think so. The *Daily Mail* further compounded the lack of justice in its reporting of this so-called 'jibe'.

In both of these two case studies, the initial offensive act or comment was enough to cause feelings of discrimination in the Gypsy and Traveller communities, but the defence of the Firle procession by the local MP, and the lack of disciplinary action from the Standards Board and the reporting in the newspaper in the councillor episode, significantly heighten the sense of injustice.

Conclusion

This chapter has attempted to provide theoretical frameworks for thinking about the notions of empowerment and justice. It has given examples where empowerment through representation has clearly improved in the last decade, but roots this in historical but ongoing challenges of articulating and constructing identities in confrontational, antagonistic practices. Many of the examples of control and power, through discursive and physical actions, represent Lukes' (1974) third dimension of power where it is exercised covertly and where interests are institutionalised and internalised, sometimes without question or recognition.

An examination of notions of justice in this chapter has also used examples of discourse as not just talk, but action – as in the tragic case of Johnny Delaney. Yet, examples of hate-filled talk from people in power, and defence of provocative public displays, are still evident since Johnny's death when we can see from both theory and tragic previous experience that talk and practice/action are part of the same antagonistic discourse. Antagonistic discourse can limit Gypsies' and Travellers' ability to feel confident and secure enough to enter into new forums, developing bridging forms of social capital by forming new relationships and interactions with actors outside of the group and to trust, all of which are central components of empowerment.

In the next chapter, the examples of Gypsy and Traveller identity focus on much more positive representations of culture. Aspects of the impact of public discourse are analysed in detail in Chapter Ten.

Note
[1] Retitled the Gypsy and Traveller Law Reform Coalition in 2004.

EIGHT

Recognising Gypsy, Roma and Traveller history and culture

Thomas Acton and Andrew Ryder

> This House notes June is Gypsy Roma Traveller history month and that it is the first such celebration to be fully supported and endorsed by the Government and provides a tremendous opportunity for children in our schools to hear of the traditions of Gypsies, Roma and Travellers; and congratulates the large number of Gypsies, Roma and Travellers, libraries, schools, teachers and others who have worked hard to organise events around the country. (*Hansard*, Early Day Motion 1858, 23 June 2008)

In 2008, an Early Day Motion was tabled by Julie Morgan MP and 70 other Members of Parliament to encourage recognition of the importance of Gypsy, Roma and Traveller history and culture. This chapter examines the changes that brought history to the fore as a subject within Traveller education and the tensions over the 'ownership' of history (from above, below, state, school or community), but argues that in the partnerships between Gypsies, Roma and Travellers (GRT), schools, libraries and other service providers, the Gypsy Roma Traveller History Month (GRTHM) provides a safe place within which critical narratives of the history of GRT groups can help in the reconstruction of more equal relationships.

The belief that history is an essential part of the curriculum in the improvement of the education of GRT communities is relatively recent. In the 1960s, Travellers and teachers alike believed that what was necessary to bring Traveller children, then widely and deliberately excluded from school altogether, into mainstream society was basic literacy and numeracy, and history was simply irrelevant to them. Across Europe at that time, the great majority of literate non-nomadic GRT still simply disguised, or at least downplayed, their identity in order to avoid racism, whether in the white-collar occupations of the capitalist world or the intelligentsias of state socialism, unless they were also part of culture or folklore industries, where just occasionally Romani ethnicity could be a plus. Kalinin (2000, 2010) and Lemon (2001) show how a private ethnic solidarity could help Roma succeed on an individual basis within the communist bureaucracy. Those still nomadic in the West often disguised their occasional literacy to avoid being held to account by an increasingly regulated world. The fragmented Romani societies were still struggling to come to terms with the fundamental lesson that the Nazi Holocaust had given them: that the steam had run out of the survival strategies of accepting marginalisation or ghetto-isation, which had emerged from the great social catastrophes of defeat, dispersal and genocide that befell them in the 16th century (Acton, 2010). The historical stance of that passive strategy was: 'Let's forget the past, and make what we can of the future without losing ourselves utterly.'

From the end of the 19th century, however, we find lone Romani voices, the Kaslovs, Kwieks and Smiths, and small associations emerging into history to challenge the facelessness hitherto accepted by their people (Acton, 1974). But still in the 1960s, it was possible for a PhD researcher to know of pretty well all the politically active GRT in Europe, and with a little travelling meet most in person. But since then, Romani politics of all kinds have snowballed, and with that the growth of an internationalising class of Romani intellectuals, retaining or rediscovering their ethnic identity because of the growth of educational policies directed specifically at GRT. This has brought about not just a rediscovery of Romani history, but also a radical challenge to European historiography in the area, not only from Europeans themselves seeking to deconstruct the racialisation of Gypsies, but also from GRT intellectuals insisting that the historical narrative of the last millennium has to make sense in terms of GRT being people like them; in other words, the creation of historical narratives cannot be discounted as mere mythmaking, or as irrelevant to current policy, but must be both archivally and sociologically plausible (Marsh and Strand, 2006). Neither 'it's in the blood' nor 'it's a mystery' is an adequate answer to questions about the historical roots of GRT in Europe.

GRTHM in the UK, from its origins, exemplifies both the thirst that has arisen for real history in GRT communities, and the recognition of that thirst by the state education system and by some other state policy makers, and its importance for rebuilding the whole knowledge base of community relations. But it also manifests some of the historiographical problems in reshaping the Gypsy history narrative, which are mirrored by – and arguably hidden at the root of – some of the arguments and divisions that have arisen in the running of GRTHM.

Over the past 50 years, Gypsy politics have fitted uneasily into the British model of 'race' relations, with campaigners taking a long time to have Gypsies and Travellers treated legally as ethnic or 'racial' groups, and struggling and often failing to establish that instances of anti-Gypsyism count as racism (Acton, 2004). Nevertheless, it is anti-racist and anti-colonial organisations that have served as the models for campaigners, and so it is perhaps unsurprising that the precursor to the national GRTHM was organised locally in the London Borough of Brent by the Traveller Education Service coordinator, Rocky Deans, who had been a local stalwart of the UK Black History Month. His awareness of the importance of the struggle of his Maroon ancestors against slavery in Jamaica made him an advocate of the need for being aware of similar struggles in GRT communities. The establishment of GRTHM was the culmination of a long and difficult process of trying to resolve the question of what role GRT culture should play in the curriculum.

The contesting of culture in Traveller education

Since the 1960s and the development of the first caravan schools, the pioneering work of volunteer teachers and educationalists in the early Traveller education network had sought to argue that bringing GRT culture into the curriculum could play a key role in harnessing pupil motivation and nurturing greater participation and achievement (Acton, 1985). These pioneers contrasted their approach with what they called the 'open door' approach of mainstream schools, which simply stated that the schools were there and Travellers could just go to them, ignoring the fact that often (like an Irish Traveller girl on an illegal encampment, Mary Delaney, who was refused admission to school by the London Borough of Croydon in 1977) they would just be turned away as 'not belonging to the area'. When Tory Education Minister Rhodes Boyson, after meeting a delegation led by NGEC secretary Thomas Acton, blocked this loophole in the 1980 Education Act (as his Labour predecessor till 1979, Shirley Williams, signally failed to do) it was because he still believed in the 'open door.' But when Traveller children were enrolled, the deal was that they left their culture at the door.

Nonetheless, the critique that 'a flattening process of assimilation' actually hindered integration was becoming part of the adoption of multiculturalism and interculturalism within mainstream education, and this provided an opening for the materials culturally sensitive to GRT culture, occasionally using Romani and Gammon/Cant language, developed by the voluntary movement. Since those early days of trying to establish an educational framework that could promote inclusion and equality, the role and importance of culture have played a prominent part in the debates and at times there have been struggles between a range of actors as to how Traveller education should be shaped and where it should be located.

In the early days, mainstream integration in the schools system was often very partial; for some pupils it meant separate and unequal treatment, being taught in segregated units or special classes. For some, school meant merciless bullying and the denigration of their culture by racist and assimilationist school authorities. There were others who counselled against mainstream educational participation, arguing that within the nexus of Traveller socialisation practices centred on cultural and economic activities, the rudiments of education could be delivered through onsite educational provision. Yet critics argued that a few hours of education a week in the back of a van was not equality either. A further overarching consideration to these polarised positions was: to what degree could Gypsies and Travellers access and utilise formal education, without the danger of assimilation and cultural compromise?

At times these debates proved to be bitter and divisive (Acton and Kenrick, 1991). Fundamental divisions within the National Gypsy Education Council (NGEC) emerged on this issue when Grattan Puxon, the founder of the NGEC, clashed with the educationalist Lady Plowden over conceptions of the role that formal education was to play, which led to the formation of two factions (Acton, 1974). It was a strong desire to maintain the separate identity and traditions of Gypsies and Travellers by one faction that led to a split in 1973 within the NGEC. The integrationists, composed largely of professional educationalists and headed by Lady Plowden, broke away from the NGEC and established the Advisory Council for the Education of Romany and other Travellers (ACERT).

The debate has moved on considerably since then, with former NGEC and ACERT members sitting together on many different committees in a plethora of new organisations. Acton and Kenrick (1991) show how mainstream education has taken over from the voluntary sector, but the statistics for non-participation and low achievement rates have continued and reveal that some of the tensions and arguments of earlier days are still being played out before us (Derrington and Kendall, 2004; Ryder et al, 2011). Inevitably, they were to surface in the inception and development of GRTHM, with bitter argument as to who was to be the arbiter of this group's identity and what role could be expected of schools and the community itself.

In recent years, the educational authorities have sought to move away from the assimilationist approach of earlier years and have sanctioned and encouraged the promotion of Gypsy and Traveller culture in the curriculum. Ofsted (1996, p 19; 2003b p 5) has recommended the promotion of Gypsy and Traveller culture in the curriculum and staff training and the Department for Education helped fund a website on the Romani language at Manchester University, embodying the insights of Professor Yaron Matras and his team. In part, such promotion is regarded as a tool that will raise staff and pupils' general awareness of Gypsy and Traveller culture and hence reduce friction and in turn improve achievement and participation. The motor for such pronouncements was the important and largely localised work of a number of Traveller Education Services and Gypsies and Travellers engaged in the cultural sector who have used Gypsy and Traveller culture as an effective educational tool.

The establishment of GRTHM as a national event was rather inauspicious in the sense that the germ for its inception was an underspend in the Department for Children, Schools and Families' (DCSF) budget. With only a short amount of time to make a claim for available funds, a number of educationalists and civil servants sympathetic to GRT communities conceived a plan for the national GRTHM. Once the money was formally confirmed there were in fact only about four months to organise the first GRTHM in 2008. This led to a flurry of activity, which included the establishment of a steering group largely composed of Traveller Education Services.[1] As Ryder noted in a speech at the National Association of Teachers of Travellers and Other Professionals' (NATT+) conference in 2009, the context in which the month was conceived was far from ideal, in particular the short amount of time for planning and consultation. However, a number of educationalists had seen an important opportunity to consolidate the various cultural works being undertaken in the educational system and raise the profile and financial support for such ventures. Ryder noted that this had caused tensions but that with hindsight they had acted with honourable intentions and acted decisively when the alternative would have meant losing a brief window of opportunity.

Yet it has to be acknowledged that tensions were caused. There were complaints about a lack of GRT representation on the steering group. This was addressed by co-options and the appointment as first national coordinator of Patricia Knight.[2] Another cause of dispute was the timing of the month: a strong section within the Gypsy Council (formerly the NGEC) asserted that the month of June had been decided by the schools lobby to suit them and that the community had not been consulted. They argued for the month to take place in April, because of the celebration of the anniversary of the first World Romani Congress on 8 April (organised by the NGEC in 1971), which had been adopted by the International Romani Union as Roma Nation Day. Against this position was the simple practicality of June given the greater time that teachers had for innovative activities, especially in secondary schools when exams had been completed, and the possibility of tying the month up with Appleby Fair. Critics responded that such arguments reflected a romanticised and stereotypical view obsessed with 'bowtops' and horses, failing to recognise that Gypsy and Traveller culture is changing and taking new and innovative directions. They argued that GRTHM was centred on schools and the community agenda and the GRT community was being marginalised in the process. This dispute had a largely positive outcome. When the struggle to change the month to June was lost, the unreconciled groups began to organise their own events in competition, partly around 8 April, and partly as alternatives to the official GRTHM in June. Competition, in fact, spurred everyone on to greater efforts, which absorbed most of the energy that people might have spent in quarrelling. As GRTHM anyway became a mosaic of independent as well as 'official' events, the distinction became blurred, especially as Jake Bowers of the Romani Media Company assumed greater importance in preparing the information magazines of the month.

Despite the tensions and divisions, an impressive list of events was organised in the first year. Lord Adonis, the-then Parliamentary Under Secretary of State for Schools stated:

> I have endorsed a national Gypsy Roma and Traveller History Month in June – the first will be in 2008. This will offer us all the chance to raise awareness and explore the history, culture and language of these communities, which is not usually included in the curriculum for all pupils. We can challenge myths, tackle prejudice and be in a position to offer a balanced debate about the issues. We will all be able to celebrate the richness that Gypsy, Roma and Travellers communities bring to our everyday lives through their many and varied academic and artistic achievements. (DCSF, 2009c, p 6)

Indeed, events were held across the country not only in schools but also at fairs, community centres and in libraries. The celebration of the month ensured that there was enough evidence to convince the DCSF that the month should continue to be supported and the department decided to put out to tender the right to coordinate the event and a larger budget over a two-year period. The winning tender involved a consortium consisting of NATT+, the Gypsy Media Company and the Irish Traveller Movement in Britain, with Patricia Knight continuing as national coordinator. The logic behind the consortium was that the month needed to reflect not just school but also GRT interests beyond that. It was resolved as part of a bid that a steering group should be formed with regional representation consisting of one Traveller Education Service and one GRT representative per region. The Irish Traveller Movement in Britain, which led on the community strand of the project, divided the great part of its share of the budget among GRT regional representatives to organise regional events for the month. The regional dimension of the project was further developed through regional heats of a competition entitled 'Travellers Got Talent' in which the regional finalists competed in a national competition. This new strategy did not address all of the previous disputes and some new ones were to emerge centred on whether funding was being equitably distributed and to what degree profit-making ventures should feature in GRTHM. However, this new organisational framework did enable a degree of greater stability and better partnership between schools and the wider GRT communities in the coordination of the month. Patricia Knight comments on the regional structure that was set up:

> GRTHM's reach and impact at a grass roots level was made possible by the voluntary involvement of the regional coordinators, who were all Gypsy Roma or Traveller and esteemed educators, activists and campaigners in their own right. In their regions they held multi-agency planning meetings, mobilised Gypsy Roma and Traveller individuals, and oversaw the applications for funds from community members and Education.... The enthusiasm, experience and dedication of these coordinators made the huge variety of initiatives in GRTHM possible, and resulted in a cacophony of community voices – many heard for the first time speaking about our own history. The regional coordinators were: Siobhan Spencer – National Federation of Gypsy Liaison Groups; Candy Sheridan – the Gypsy Council; Jane and Jo Hearn – Cheshire Voice; Ann Wilson

– Surrey Travellers Action Group; Sally Woodbury – South
West Romany Gypsy Advisory Group; and Sylvester Huzka
– Roma Support Group.... GRTHM was an exercise in
evidencing the slogan of the decade of Roma inclusion –
'Nothing about us without us'. Newly formed alliances
of Gypsy Roma Travellers and our new partners brought
forward the 'Gypsy Voice' in all areas of the planning
and presentation of events for the month. (unpublished
submission to chapter authors, reproduced with permission)

It is evident that during the progress of the development of the month
there were disputes between educationalists and community groups
about where and how the activities should be centred and organised.
Yet despite these creative and cultural tensions, the month has achieved
much by mobilising many community members to organise events
and go into schools to present on their culture, and many young GRT
have been able to feel a sense of pride in their culture in a school
environment, a novel experience for some. Schools and Traveller
Education Services have forged new and meaningful relationships with
young and old GRT. Furthermore, through activities such as 'Travellers
Got Talent', young GRT have demonstrated the new and exciting
directions they are taking GRT culture through popular mediums
such as television competition formats, rap, country and western and
contemporary dance alongside mainstay cultural activities such as
painting, poetry and storytelling.

Putting the history back into history month

An occasional criticism of GRTHM literature was that although it was
using history to raise the consciousness particularly of school children,
teachers would take any old version of GRTHM history they could
download from a convenient website, without looking at the latest
critical insights.

Three main currents in contemporary Romani historiography – the
deconstructionist, the positivist and the revisionist – have developed
since the 1980s as Romani communities have become more interested
in history, leaving behind the earlier lack of concern that the Scottish
poet, Alastair Reid (1963, p170) documented in his memories of
English Gypsies: "'A gennelman come 'ere one day and said as we
is all from India,' one old Gypsy woman told me. 'So I says to 'im,
"Well, maybe we is, Surr, but it don't make a mighty difference, now,
do it, Surr?"'." Over the past 30 years it has become evident what a

difference it does make to disembed the racism entrenched in older narratives of origin.

In the 1990s, the expulsion of racism from the accepted narrative of Romani history seemed to have been accomplished by Fraser's (1992) magisterial *Gypsies*, which seemed to settle all the debates of a century of the *Journal of the Gypsy Lore Society*. But the treatise that settled the battles of Gypsy history proved to be just the starting gun for the wars of Romani studies. Radical deconstructionist Dutch historians, of whom the most systematic is Willems (1997), claimed that although Fraser had clearly repudiated racism as an ideology, his lack of theory prevented him from seeing how the processes of racialisation had shaped the social construction of Romani/Gypsy identity. In this he drew on earlier work by Okely (1983), who had challenged the notion that a 'myth' of Indian origin could explain the current realities of Gypsy culture.

Willems (1997) suggested that 'Gypsy' was a name foisted on a diverse strata of vagrants and marginalised groups by the armchair synthesist Grellmann (1787 [1783]). Grellmann, a German historian, popularised the discovery of the Indian origin of Roma, and brought European understandings of Gypsies within the new 'scientific racism'. After Grellmann, the primary European intellectual explanation of the cultural difference of Traveller groups was not their deviance (although this continued at a popular level) but their racial origin. They were the primitive people who had remained primitive despite 500 years sojourn in civilised Europe, an exceptional case that proved the overriding importance of race.

Willems, however, attracted critics, especially positivist linguists, who sympathised with Fraser's historical positivism, and claimed that Willems and his friends were almost arguing that Gypsies had been invented by Grellmann in 1783, and whatever the truth about the social processes of racialisation, we cannot ignore the indisputable Indian origin of the Romani language (Matras, 2002). Merely to assert, however, that 'Gypsies come from India' is insufficient when clearly the range of GRT groups have complex and intertwined identities and origins. A sociologically and historically plausible account was required of how the Romani language might have arisen in Anatolia in the 11th or 12th century and how this Indian heritage might have been variously embedded in a range of marginal groups that were established during the catastrophic fragmentation of Europe into capitalist nation states and statelets in the 16th and 17th centuries. It is perhaps not surprising that it has been intellectuals themselves of GRT heritage who have demanded that if this history was their ancestors, it should make sense as if it were about people like them, rather than the 'primitives' of Gypsylorist history, although this may cause some pain, perhaps most vividly expressed in Kwiek's (1998) poem I am the Common Rom, a cry of anguish at the moment when reading Romani history persuaded him that his ancestors had been slaves. GRT intellectuals may have to repudiate not only racist images, but also some of the positive, defensive stereotypes embedded in GRT self-images during centuries of persecution, as Hancock (2006) does in a brave, and trenchant self-criticism that is perhaps the founding manifesto of contemporary Romani historical revisionism.

These debates were also part of the 2008 GRTHM in an academic conference at the University of Greenwich where, perhaps for the first time, all those who gave papers were themselves of GRT heritage. This does not mean, however, that they all adopted a common position. In fact, in the collected papers edited by Le Bas and Acton (2010) we find that each of the three positions that are current in Romani historiography can be found. Unsurprisingly, the papers of Hancock, Marsh and Kwiek were revisionist in tone, but those of Belton and Le Bas were broadly deconstructionist, while those of Kalinin, Keet–Black and Jones were still within a classical, Fraserian positivistic framework. It is the last three of these papers, however, that most emphasised the importance of history to individuals living their own life, whether in Russia or Britain. Keet–Black and Jones particularly demonstrated the importance of the work of the Romany & Traveller Family History Society, which, with more than 600 subscribers, has by far the largest formal dues-paying GRT membership of any GRT organisation ever in the UK. Many Society members suggest that family historians ought to be as important as teachers in the running of GRTHM.

In 2010, history became more central in GRTHM as an explanation of the past, rather than just a colourful prop to identity. A key theme was the Porrajmos, or holocaust of Roma under the Nazis. The definitive exhibition of this created by the Verband Deutscher Sinti und Roma was brought to the Mile End Arts Pavilion in London, and GRTHM 2010 was launched there at a reception hosted by the German embassy in London. The event was coordinated by exhibition curator, Eva Sajovac, and GRTHM national coordinator, Patricia Knight. In a powerful and emotive speech, English Gypsy and member of the Derbyshire Gypsy Liaison Group Tom McCready said (Knight, 2010):

> I didn't come here today to bring you a horror story; I came to bring you a story of hope, a story of optimism, and a story of triumph. It's a story of hope, because even during

the darkest chapters of man's existence, be they those past, or those yet to be written. When everything is ripped away from you, remember this. They can't take your hope; they can't take it until you let it go…. It's a story of triumph because the Gypsy people, persecuted for generations, are still here.

GRT voices and contemporary culture

In 2011, a key feature of GRTHM was the regional contest 'Travellers Got Talent', which culminated in a national final at the Royal Festival Hall in London. The competition is to feature in a Sky Television series. Organiser and Gypsy Jake Bowers of the Gypsy Media Company, said:

> Gypsy, Roma and Traveller communities are perceived to be guilty of many things, but capable of nothing, but the final and the regional finals that led up to it quash that myth. They have all demonstrated that Gypsy, Roma and Traveller young people, in particular, have talents, skills and abilities that are largely unrecognised by the world beyond their communities. (Reported in the *Daily Star*, 19 June 2011)

Another key event in 2011 was the Southwark Travellers' Action Group launch of a DVD about Irish Travellers at the Tate Modern gallery in London. Anne Marie O'Brien, an Irish Traveller, outlines why coming to the Tate was important: 'The screening at Tate Modern was excellent as it shows that Travellers are part of the wider community and are welcome into places like the Tate Modern. It brings people from all different areas together and … empowers Travellers to go to different places.' Another Traveller, Vanessa O'Driscoll, who attended the launch reveals why GRTHM is important:

> 'GRTHM is something that many non-Travellers probably haven't even heard of, but it is significant to Travellers themselves. It's a time to stand up and say "we are Travellers and proud!". At present, as the public image of Travellers has been distorted and racism continues just as strongly as ever, we need events like those that take place during GRTHM to really celebrate the positives of being Travellers and support one another. In the future, GRTHM needs to soldier on, and empower Travellers to celebrate and not hide who they are. I think the events that are held need to be wider spread

than just Travellers and those that work with/support them;
it needs go further and reach out to the wider public, to
work on changing perceptions of this culture.'

Isaac Blake is a Romany Gypsy, a dancer and a dance choreographer
and an active force in establishing GRTHM in Wales. With his brother,
Jimmy Blake, and the Black Voluntary Sector Network Wales, he has
established the Romani Cultural and Arts Company to take forward
arts-based community and anti-racist work including coordination
of the all-Wales celebrations of GRTHM. Isaac outlines GRTHM in
Wales in 2011:

'GRTHM in Wales is unashamedly about challenging both
the racism that the Gypsy, Roma and Traveller communities
experience and their own, internalised, racism. It's about
raising aspirations, promoting culture and dispelling the
myth that Gypsy, Roma and Traveller communities are
"hard to reach". We work on a community development
model, but it is a challenging community development
model and we are not afraid to make people feel a little
uncomfortable sometimes.

The community element is maintained, and has been
developed to extend several months ahead of the History
Month, by taking community development and youth
work projects onto local sites across South Wales. In this
way communities, particularly children and young people,
benefit from activities that provide them with constructive
activity, a strong message about the validity of their way of
life, a voice and a stage on which to perform. The 2011 Welsh
History Month event in Newport featured an animated film
made by young people from the Shirenewton site (Cardiff),
a dance performance by young people from the Roverway
site (Cardiff), a drama performance made by a mixed
group of Gypsy, Roma, Traveller and gorger/country folk
working together and artwork from community members
in Bridgend and Torfaen. Importantly, each of the residences
that created these pieces of work took professional art,
community development and youth organisations onto sites
and gave them the skills and experience to stop thinking
of the Gypsy, Roma and Traveller communities as "hard
to reach".'

These voices of Gypsies and Travellers reveal the energy and vibrancy of GRTHM. It is a means by which Gypsies and Travellers can celebrate their survival and cherish what they value and prize in their culture both past and present yet also remember darker stories and episodes of persecution. The month is also a means by which wider strategic alliances can be formed with service providers and sections of local and national government, leading to greater understanding and meaningful change. What GRTHM has also achieved, where Traveller Law Reform campaigns in the past have failed, is favourable and positive media coverage, as quoted above in the tabloid press, which in the past and still sadly in the present has been the source of much vilification towards the GRT minority.

The future

Looking to the future, GRTHM faces new challenges. One is that in an age of austerity and deficit reduction, it appears that the Department for Education will now no longer bankroll this event. The government position has been summarised thus:

> Whilst the Department has no plans to provide further funding for the GRT History Month, schools and Local Authorities can continue to take an active part in GRTHM events if they wish to do so, in the same way as they take part in Black History Month, which has never received funding from central Government. (Ryder et al, 2011, p 50)

As is evident, the Coalition Government will not be as active in its support of GRTHM as the previous administration. It is perhaps a little unfair to use the argument that Black History Month did not enjoy central government support since over the years it received a great deal of support from local authorities where black communities represent a significant section of the population and where they yield political influence and have a growing presence in schools as teachers and governors. GRT communities are not in an equally advantageous position and in the present climate of deficit reduction and drop in charity donations the government is severing the financial lifeline at a difficult time. Nonetheless, the National Federation of Gypsy Liaison Groups and others are preparing funding applications for future years, and it is to be hoped that the event is so embedded within the community and schools network that it will continue in some shape or form regardless of what funding is received.

Failure to support GRTHM could also give out the wrong signals as the Coalition Government has established a cross-governmental ministerial-level group on Gypsies and Travellers. One of the remits of the ministerial-level group is to consider a 'community-led proposal to encourage greater parental engagement and support for children to remain in the education system' (Hanham, 2011). The ministerial-level group needs to consider the value of GRTHM, which has forged new partnerships and understanding between parents, schools and other agencies, partnerships that can lead to broader analyses of means to increase educational participation. The national and local partnerships between GRT and service providers established through GRTHM could provide a proven foundation on which to build a community-led response to educational exclusion. Indeed, many of the advocates and activists involved in GRTHM have continuously stressed that it was important for the month to not focus on superficial representations of the culture, 'bowtop wagons and campfires', and instead explore throughout the year wider structural factors that lead to exclusion and misrepresentation, with GRTHM being the annual culmination of this long-term work.

The principles of GRTHM may also be under threat from the 'traditionalist' history curriculum that Education Secretary Michael Gove is said to want to promote (Penny, 2010). In this curriculum, an emphasis is placed on 'facts', the long narrative thread of history and 'British achievements', which invariably is coded language for the history of elites. The historian Professor Niall Ferguson (cited in Higgins, 2011), who is to advise on the new school curriculum for history, has called for a vision of the curriculum in which children are taught that the 'big story' of the last 500 years 'is the rise of western domination of the world'. Such a curriculum may not give much attention to social history, the story of the oppressed and encouragement of learners to assess and question history critically, in particular their own. This is precisely why GRTHM should continue to develop in the UK in schools, libraries and other community events. And the focus for the month should provide an opportunity not only for a marginalised minority to come forward and publicly take pride in their culture and history but also for the wider community to understand the shameful historical narrative of persecution against GRT communities in the UK.

Hence, it is important that the month is promoted not only on Traveller sites but in schools, libraries and by a range of service providers, including the police, and that GRT communities form partnerships with schools and other agencies. The benefit for GRT communities through such mainstreaming is that acceptance of their lifestyles and identity will prevent the danger of cultural genocide. Such partnerships reflect the fact that although GRT communities are establishing a prime voice in telling their own history, the lessons of history are universal and open to all.

Notes

[1] A key driving force was Peter Saunders of Leeds Traveller Education Service.

[2] A heroine of Romani resistance to the burning of Travellers in effigy during Bonfire night in the village of Firle in Sussex.

NINE

Research with and for Gypsies, Roma and Travellers: combining policy, practice and community in action research

Margaret Greenfields and Andrew Ryder

Introduction

This chapter engages with both the ethical and practical aspects of undertaking partnership research with members of Gypsy and Traveller communities. It is underpinned by an exposition on the philosophy and methodologies utilised in two key research projects, both of which explicitly sought to utilise participatory methods as a way of increasing the skills base of Gypsy and Traveller research partners as well as ideologically rejecting methodological practices that seek to impose mainstream categories and assumptions on marginalised or excluded peoples (Pollner and Rosenfeld, 2000). In other words, these were projects that sought to ethically research 'with' and 'for' Gypsies and Travellers rather than carrying out research 'on' members of these communities.

The earlier of these two studies (perhaps surprisingly, the first in the UK to have employed trained Gypsy and Traveller interviewers to work with their own communities) was the Cambridge Gypsy Traveller Accommodation Assessment[1] (GTAA) undertaken between 2005 and 2006 (Greenfields and Home, 2006). The lessons learnt in that project in relation to supporting community interviewers, and the methodology and training devised to support participants, which has been commended as best practice by the Commission for Racial Equality and the Fundamental Rights Agency (among others), has since been developed and used in other GTAAs across Britain. It has also been developed to an expanded form within the key economic inclusion research undertaken by the Irish Traveller Movement in Britain (ITMB) – the Traveller Economic Inclusion Project (TEIP), the second research project that this chapter focuses on (Ryder and Greenfields, 2010). This latter research, which was financially supported by the Big Lottery Fund with the explicit intention of influencing policy and practice mechanisms for enhancing the economic inclusion of Gypsies and Travellers, was guided, perhaps even more clearly than the Cambridge GTAA, by refined principles of participatory action research (PAR), a mode of action that actively addresses issues of power (and empowerment) and politics (Reason and Bradbury, 2008). Within the remainder of this chapter, the authors set out the case for why PAR is an ethical model that can be applied appropriately to research with Gypsy, Roma and Traveller communities, and argue that utilisation of such a process, despite the challenges that can sometimes occur in operationalising this methodology, offers the best means of undertaking politicised and inclusive intercultural research that gives 'voice' to those who are frequently unheard.

Research with excluded minority ethnic communities: the ethical basis for PAR and intercultural approaches

Before discussing the details of the research projects, it is apposite to define and explore the concepts of both intercultural and participatory action research.

PAR

Participatory action research is research that works explicitly with and for people rather than undertaking research on subjects, a mode of inquiry that has roots in the work of the educationalist Freire (1970) and also that of Gramsci (1971), who famously declared that all people are intellectuals and philosophers or 'organic intellectuals'. In particular, Gramsci was preoccupied with foregrounding the conceptualisation that non-academic (predominantly) working-class people are more than able to take their local knowledge from life experiences, and use that knowledge to effectively address changes and problems in society (Gramsci, 1971, p 258). Freire, in his work on critical pedagogy, argued that a model that places the 'teacher' at the front of the class, 'imparting' information to the passive recipient 'students', disempowers one half of the dyad and silences them. In contrast, by locating this pedagogic model within a research paradigm, it becomes possible to devise translational research where the actors create research models as part of a dynamic process (Freire, 1982) and devise and negotiate the meaning of their findings with the intent of bringing about social change.

While in 'classical' PAR theory – which defines an ideal situation where time and funding are not problematic – the PAR proceeds through repeated cycles, wherein the experienced researchers (typically academic) and members of the partnership community work together to identify major issues and problems that lead into a research project, triggering re-active responses, which in turn are researched in an attempt to evaluate the change that has occurred, the reality, in times of fiscal retrenchment, is somewhat different. In practice, the PAR process is rarely likely to move through more than one cycle. The principle, however, that participants in action research projects practise critical reflexivity, seek to improve democratic research practice and are focused on generating knowledge and improving their skills and learning rather than merely concentrating on outcomes, remains critical to this mode of research (McNiff and Whitehead, 2009).

Participatory action research is thus an explicitly sociopolitical mode of research and the way in which it is undertaken is an active statement of political and policy ideals. While the model can be used to generate knowledge through co-production, and building on pre-existing community networks offers a tool that permits access to individuals who might otherwise be 'unreachable' (as occurred in the Cambridge GTAA), in other circumstances (predominantly where a project is exclusively qualitative in nature), use of PAR methods enables silenced voices to be heard and 'untold truths' to be brought into the public domain (Lundy and McGovern, 2006). Where the voices of community researchers are foregrounded within a narrative, the 'hidden transcripts' (Scott, 1990) that guide (and are embedded within) verbal and practical transactions between people who are marginalised, and those individuals and structures who (potentially) oppress or exclude them, are granted the opportunity to be considered openly. Accordingly, the use of PAR enables the experiences, interpretations, values and discourse of those groups more usually regarded as 'subordinate' in terms of knowledge production to be accorded the respect traditionally paid to data gathered and presented by a group of professional peers engaged in a research undertaking.

The extent of community input into projects and ultimately the degree to which 'professional' researchers/academics control the process of generating knowledge define which mode of participatory research is followed. In essence there are three core models:

- research that involves consultation with community members;
- participatory research, where community members are actively involved in design and knowledge development;
- partnership research, where all aspects of the project are developed and undertaken within a team consisting of 'academics/professional researchers' and 'community researchers'.

Arnstein (1969) discusses this in her classic 'ladder of participation' comprising a set of steps ranging from 'manipulation' (of the public/research subjects) to 'citizen control' (of a project). In her model, the ladder is further subdivided into a triad, consisting of 'citizen power', 'tokenism' and 'non-participation'. At its worst, 'consultation' can merely be 'tokenism' although Arnstein locates the step of 'partnership' within the domain of 'citizen control', a placement that the authors of this chapter feel does not always adequately reflect the power dynamics inherent in participatory research.

For practitioners engaged in PAR in the 21st century, projects that locate community engagement at the highest level of the hierarchy, and that practise partnership research (co-production of research) in its most developed form should (at least in theory) involve analysis, writing of the report, editing, delivery of findings and sharing of accrued assets equally between community and professional researchers with all partners' involvement in the process being equally valued. Where this occurs, Arnstein would probably locate such practice on the rung of 'delegated power' or 'citizen control'.

While the research teams engaged in both the Cambridge GTAA and the TEIP sought to carry out full partnership research, in practice (constrained largely by funders' deliverables and the necessity for the production of technical reports, relatively rigid timetables and the requirements of some aspects of the research, such as use of software and computerised analytical packages) it is probably more realistic to acknowledge that the academic–voluntary sector partners held a greater degree of control (and ultimately responsibility to the funders) in both projects. Hence, both studies can be seen as occupying the extreme end of participatory research (embedded PAR) rather than full-blown partnership/co-production research.[1]

However, our studies do go beyond the level of community member involvement in many action research type studies in this field that have traditionally limited the involvement of Gypsies and Travellers on the terms of the academics or funders of the research. Robinson and Tansey (2006) suggest that this traditional type of involvement is 'dialogic'. However, in more integrated approaches to involving communities there is a 'transformative' element and those involved go beyond being 'users': 'In this [transformative] forum the purpose is to both engage the researched at the problem definition stage and to actively alter the social conditions in which they find themselves' (Robinson and Tansey, 2006, p 152).

Use of PAR is not merely embedded in political activism (a point that the authors of this chapter have had to stress on occasion to funders), there are also sound practical reasons for adopting such a research approach. Meyer (2004, p 454) notes: 'Its strength lies in its focus on generating solutions to practical problems and its ability to empower practitioners – getting them to engage with research and subsequent development'. Thus a 'virtuous circle' is created by '... striv[ing] to include the participants' perspective on the data by feeding back findings ... and incorporating their responses as new data in the final report' (Meyer, 2004, p 454). PAR benefits from enhanced quality of data, validation of findings and approval of the way in which the content has been presented and obtained from community participants, which in turn add credibility to the overall study.

A further strength in PAR methodologies is the embrace of 'interculturalism' as a model for encouraging greater integration and understanding between diverse communities. Theories on race, multiculturalism and assimilation were discussed briefly in Chapter One, this volume. We argue therefore that the use of intercultural research tools can be a powerful weapon in increasing comprehension and breaking down stereotypes between communities. It is this political and philosophical drive to increase community dialogue and support distinct communities in 'giving voice' that has underpinned the adoption of intercultural and participatory action research models within our work.

Challenges in and benefits to using PAR approaches

While philosophically and ethically committed to undertaking PAR, we are aware as experienced researchers that some colleagues have raised concerns pertaining to the difficulties inherent in the use of such methodologies. Accordingly, we feel it appropriate to mention that the use of PAR techniques can lead to potential clashes between the funder, researcher and community groups with whom the research team work, as inevitably there will be vested interests among various participants in the process (Orr and Bennett, 2010). However, if an ethically engaged and mutually agreed inclusive research framework is negotiated between all parties prior to commencing the study, then PAR/co-production approaches hold the potential not only to empower those previously disenfranchised by traditional research processes but also to produce research that captures honestly the predicament of marginalised minority groups such as Gypsies and Travellers.

One major source of tension can be evident in lines of accountability and 'ownership' of data and results, particularly where a 'client' – for example a local authority acting as lead partner or a voluntary organisation – is commissioning the work. While accountability will tend to follow contractual obligations, it is incumbent on the practitioner to withstand pressures that may on occasion be brought to bear, for example if the commissioner body is unhappy with findings that may have significant political impacts (for example in relation to pitch numbers) or which suggest criticism of services offered to clients. We would note, however, in the projects showcased within this chapter, the changes in process and method suggested by the Gypsy and Traveller participants in the research were taken account of and embraced by all parties, demonstrating both a real desire for change on behalf of the commissioning bodies and a genuine commitment to both process and ethical practice. In this way, agreement on the common goals and outcomes for these research projects as well as pre-identifying processes that enabled dissent on occasion, facilitated unity and cooperation between different interest groups (Greenfields and Home, 2006).

As indicated above, traditional research has entailed the academic 'professional' interpreting the actions of the researched through a epistemological lens, which, it can be argued, has actually marginalised and distorted the voice and aspirations of relatively voiceless groups. This disempowering tendency can be avoided (as far as possible) by enabling the 'researched' to act as a co-producer of the research, entrusting them to engage as a partner in the task of analysis and production of findings. However, this may cause genuine tensions, particularly where tradition (including gendered approaches to engagement and status or 'morality' and presentation of 'facts') or notions of inclusion are at odds. In such a setting, the researcher may find themselves called on to protect and defend the interests of minorities within minorities who may be unfairly excluded or diminished by 'the group', who reject their lifestyle, personal characteristics or activities. Where this occurs, the researcher can find themselves confronted with a new and difficult dilemma in terms of how a subject matter should be presented, or whether the academic should 'pull rank' and demand that evidence of variation is incorporated into the outputs of the study. In relation to this factor it should also be noted that when working with PAR or co-production approaches, the academic researcher can become more personally and emotionally involved with the research field than is common, with strong feelings arising through their interactions with Gypsy and Traveller communities. In such circumstances, there is a potential for 'loyalty stressors' and a real risk that a lack of objectivity may come into existence (a state of affairs referred to below when indicating the need to practise reflexive research). Yet despite the difficulties outlined above, we argue that PAR still offers the greatest potential to build trust and produce valid and meaningful research that delivers 'transformative' outcomes (Robinson and Tansey, 2006); an attraction that we propose outweighs the problematic elements and pitfalls, which (as we seek to demonstrate) can be avoided through rigorous training, open negotiation and honest dialogue with all parties to the research.

The research projects

The Cambridge GTAA was one of the earliest GTAAs undertaken in the UK and, perhaps surprisingly, the first project that the authors of this chapter were able to identify in the UK that employed Gypsies and Travellers to undertake research into their own communities' needs. Prior to submitting a tender for the GTAA, the academic team members decided to utilise a PAR model and made this clear from the outset. That the funding authorities were willing to utilise what was – at that point – perceived of as a 'high-risk' strategy with the likelihood of attracting negative media comment (and certainly an approach with greater cost implications than a typical 'quick and dirty' use of professional consultants and pre-trained interviewers) was commendable.

The project benefited hugely from a pre-existing, enlightened local authority approach to engagement with the local Gypsy and Traveller community, which meant that a multi-agency 'Travellers' Forum' (albeit – as was common at that time – operating without the participation of any community members) was already in existence in the locality. In addition, a plethora of pre-existing research and statistics, regularly updated by the local authority research unit team, was readily available. The commissioning of a large multi-district GTAA to map the needs of Gypsies and Travellers at a subregional level permitted a consortium of public authorities (including primary care trusts and the Traveller Education Service/local education authorities, which used the exercise to consult on aspects of their work) to engage in partnership work with the academic members of the team and a specially convened Gypsy and Traveller Advisory Group.

The advisory group, consisting solely of respected community activists, many of whom were 'elders', was conceived of as offering a counterbalance to a typical policy core group, which overwhelmingly consists of 'professional' members. The advisory group worked closely with academic and local authority partners to devise a blueprint for consultation, research and questionnaire design. At the time the advisory group was convened (2005), the decision to have 'closed' advisory group sessions, where Gypsies and Travellers could discuss their opinions on methodologies and research questions unfettered by the presence of academics and local authority staff, was regarded by many commentators as a radical and challenging move (Blackburn et al, 2010), rather than one that inverted the power dynamics historically inherent in relations between local authorities and communities that were more likely to be researched 'on' than researched 'with'.

All interviewers – and advisory group members – were supported in a crash course in interviewing skills, with training, ethics and professional standards identical to that considered appropriate to a postgraduate student. The only variation in the expectation of trainees was that methods were adapted to ensure that training and participation was available to community members who did not have literacy skills or felt uncomfortable in writing. Thus, 'research literacy' was tailored to take account of structural barriers that had impacted on formal education for some community members. Accordingly, 'interview pairs' were developed so that, where required, one partner could scribe for the other, while someone who was potentially more verbally skilled and astute at 'probing' could administer the questionnaire or provide information to participants. Interviewers were paid at the same rate as other (non-community) survey staff working on projects, as at the point of tendering for the project it was decided as a matter of principle that community interviewers would be treated as professionals and partners in all ways. Quality control on data gathered was undertaken by academic team members and it was found that the standard of completed questionnaires was as high, and in some cases higher, than those typically collected by postgraduate students (Greenfields and Home, 2006).

Although data input and analysis were undertaken by academic team members, advisory group members and interviewers were consulted with regard to the findings and provided clarification and interpretations of assumptions. In addition, a focus group was conducted out with interviewers to explore their experiences of participation in the study and their opinions of the overall research process as well as the draft report that had been produced by the academic authors. The review and validation data were then fed back into the report, which was presented to the commissioners jointly by the interviewers, advisory group and academic team. The final report was launched at a public event – attended by local authority staff and officers, members of the media and service providers. After a technical summary and presentation of findings by academics, formal acceptance of the report by the commissioning body and the presentation of university certification to the community team, which identified them as accredited community interviewers, a panel of advisory members and interviewers then hosted the latter half of the event, taking questions from the floor, entering into debate with local authority and public sector staff and raising issues that they wished to discuss with the delegates and funders.

The Cambridge methodology delivered highly successful results and the level of training delivered to participant community members enabled the overwhelming majority of these team members to move on to further employment as interviewers and consultants (for example working with health authorities to identify need), working in both their own localities and other areas of the country. As a model it was highly acclaimed by Gypsy and Traveller communities as providing a conduit for consultation and participation in planning for site delivery at an early stage and despite the many difficulties involved in undertaking a complex large-scale study of this kind (Greenfields and Home, 2006), the methodology was recognised as best practice by a number of agencies, including the Equalities and Human Rights Commission and the Fundamental Rights Agency in Europe, and particular elements of the methodology were subsequently incorporated into the Communities and Local Government guidance on undertaking GTAAs (CLG, 2007). Subsequently, the methodology was replicated in a number of other localities (for example in East Kent, Devon and Cornwall).

The second study to be considered – the TEIP (Ryder and Greenfields, 2010) – came to fruition in response to the ITMB's identification of the fact that no UK policy considerations or discourse had thus far taken account of the changing economic circumstances and increasing levels of financial exclusion of Gypsy and Traveller communities identified both in GTAAs and through anecdotal evidence gathered from frontline and policy agencies such as ITMB and the national charity Friends, Families and Travellers. Overwhelmingly, in terms of policy debate the primary focus since the 1960s has been on accommodation issues, in part because the national shortage of Traveller sites has increased tensions between Gypsies and Travellers and the wider community as long-term site shortages have led to an increase in unauthorised developments and encampments (Richardson and Ryder, 2009a). The highly publicised pressures on land and disputes between sedentary and nomadic people, coupled with lobbying by the Gypsy and Traveller Law Reform Coalition, prompted the Labour government to embark on a large-scale policy review in the early 2000s, culminating in a detailed policy framework for the delivery of sites (see Greenfields, 2007), yet within this review, little notice was taken of broader issues pertaining to economic inclusion.

Emerging evidence from GTAAs during these years of continual policy review indicated that the lack of adequate site provision was continuing to have a detrimental impact on the educational outcomes for Gypsies and Travellers; and alarming education figures released by government departments indicated a decline in attainment for certain travelling communities, linked anecdotally to rising rates of racism in school and greater levels of detachment from education for some community members. Low achievement and participation rates in formal education have thus become a serious cause for concern over a number of years, especially as improved educational achievement has been identified as a central factor that can improve the overall social and economic situation of Gypsy and Traveller communities (DCSF, 2009a) in a post-modern society that increasingly demands that job applicants have qualifications for even fairly low-skilled work opportunities.

A further element that has been posited as leading to increasing rates of unemployment and benefit dependency among Gypsy and Traveller communities (Greenfields, 2006; Cemlyn et al, 2009) has been the relatively rapid rate of change in 'traditional' employment opportunities for Gypsies and Travellers, with steep declines in farm and fieldwork opportunities associated with the increase in mechanisation and in recent decades the greater use of migrant labour organised around the 'gang' system, minimising the opportunities for individual families to obtain harvesting work, coupled with emerging demand for a sedentary labour force.

In contemplating the causes of declining social inclusion experienced by many Gypsies and Travellers, it was clear that a central feature of this debate would need to be the changing nature of the 'Traveller Economy' as employment activities are a clear determiner of material wellbeing and life chances afforded to diverse populations. Such a discussion has a clear intercultural dimension as socioeconomic relations and interaction between the state, mainstream society and minority ethnic communities engaged in both 'ethnic economies' (Light and Gold, 2000) and mainstream employment are fundamental to issues of social justice and community cohesion. Thus, the situation of Gypsies and Travellers needs to be scrutinised within the nexus of access to employment, education and training and life chances, and in turn such examination of employment-related opportunities and outcomes raises issues around cultural and gender norms, expectations and values (Greenfields, 2008) and the changing nature of group identity and 'boundary maintenance' (Barth, 1969).

In recognition of the absence of policy discourse on employment support needs for Gypsies and Travellers, ITMB first began to lobby on this in 2007, jointly organising a seminar with the Department for Work and Pensions (DWP) on the topic of Gypsy and Traveller economic inclusion. At that event, calls were made for the DWP to establish a forum (ITMB, 2007); however, it was subsequently argued that having a special interest group focused on one minority would contravene the DWP policy of 'mainstreaming' minority ethnic employment issues. From that time, ITMB sought funding to identify the challenges facing Gypsies and Travellers, on the grounds that greater information was needed to support government departments in tailoring service delivery for highly excluded 'hard-to-reach' Gypsies and Travellers as well as acting to increase the knowledge and awareness of community representatives working in the policy arena.

In 2009, the Big Lottery Foundation (through its 'community research arm', the Big Lottery Research Fund, designed explicitly to fund third sector based projects) agreed to finance a major 15-month study, hosted by ITMB, which would work in partnership with key community and research activists to explore barriers to economic inclusion, and (seeking to celebrate success) identify the mechanisms used by (some) Gypsies and Travellers to secure economic inclusion. The TEIP was explicitly designed to utilise PAR techniques with the intended outcomes of training community members to aid them in influencing local and national policy and practice in relation to financial inclusion planning for marginalised minority communities while enabling ITMB to develop an evidence-based knowledge resource that could be disseminated through various mechanisms to assist in enhancing Gypsy and Traveller economic inclusion.

For many participants (both interviewees and interviewers) involved in the TEIP, action research and an expectation of strong Gypsy and Traveller involvement in the research process were a natural continuation of previous projects (such as the Cambridgeshire GTAA and others identified below) that utilised such methods. In the case of the TEIP, which unlike earlier projects was located across a very wide area of England, it was necessary to identify and recruit community interviewers via a series of national activist networks and then to train these community researchers in a range of qualitative research methods – in this case, including the use of more 'open-ended' interviewing techniques than are used when a relative simple questionnaire is administered. In common with a number of practitioners who have worked with diverse communities (Gunaratnam, 2003), it is our experience that community interviewers can, in some circumstances, be far more effective in gaining access to interviewees than 'external' researchers and indeed appreciate the nuances of what they are hearing more than even an experienced 'outsider', a rationale that used to justify the involvement of GTAA interviewers in earlier projects when PAR was considered unusual in working with Gypsy and Traveller communities.

Not only did the funders and advisory panel members of the TEIP note that community involvement adds value to the overall programme and moreover that such team members can provide important cultural advice and guidance to the academic team, it was also acknowledged throughout that the employment of community interviewers is a clear declaration that a research project is striving to be inclusive and respectful of participants' worldview while enhancing community cohesion and trust between parties to the research (in other words – adhering to principles of intercultural research practice).

The interview team – consisting of both male and female Gypsies and Travellers (as well as a lead researcher, Andrew Ryder, who is not from a Gypsy/Traveller background) – came from a relatively narrow age range; however, during the life of the project they conducted semi-structured interviews with 95 respondents of diverse ages and both genders, distributed across the English regions living in a variety of accommodation types. The sample reflected a broad cross-section of ages and employment types, with activities ranging from traditional self-employed traders engaged in typical 'Traveller trades' such as scrap metal dealing, to professional and degree-educated Gypsies and Travellers in managerial positions. In addition, a number of community group members with campaign and advocacy experience, and individual service providers, were interviewed to identify good practice in terms of training and employment as well as to highlight the benefits of affirmative action to community enhancement and the development of role models.

One key theme that emerged from discussions with research team members was an awareness that the recruitment of community members meant that there was no question that such a study would be perceived of as a 'quick and dirty' research – so-called when a researcher extracts information and uses it in a way that has no intrinsic value for the community being researched. In contrast (and following the best PAR practice), Gypsy and Travellers would not be constructed as passive 'research subjects' (an approach critiqued by Greenfields and Home, 2006), a technique that is both unethical and that over time decreases the willingness of Gypsies and Travellers to participate in projects that appear to have little benefit for them (Brown and Scullion, 2009). Accordingly, from inception to dissemination, the TEIP team sought to develop active partnership and enhanced participation from the community being researched that both maximises community 'buy-in' as well as remaining true to the political and philosophical roots of community development and action research.

The dissemination phase of the project was planned carefully to ensure that research participants (interviewees as well as researchers) were invited to participate in regional seminars and contribute to the identification of broad policy goals. Participants were also given access to the final version of the report, which incorporated findings from the regional seminars, and were invited to the launch event, which took place in the House of Commons in November 2010. Ongoing activities emerging since the launch of the report include liaising with third sector groups who work to promote the economic interests of other excluded groups (for example the Black Training and Enterprise Group [BTEG]), an activity which at a time of national fiscal retrenchment is likely to prove crucial to ensuring that Gypsy and Traveller issues remain on the broader black and minority ethnic sector agenda. Not only are agencies such as BTEG active in organising campaigns such as 'Need not Greed' (lobbying for greater understanding and sympathy for workers trapped in the 'informal economy' and/or low-wage exploitation), but also by forming broader alliances with a range of excluded groups the TEIP is able to promote an intercultural campaign agenda while developing an 'empowerment network' (Gilchrist, 2004).

Forging alliances with marginalised groups thus averts the negativism of 'dual closure' (Parkin, 1979), where the most excluded demonise or 'buy in' to negative media representations of other groups at the margins, and instead offers the possibility of broad coalitions of the excluded, which might form effective networks of empowerment (Gilchrist, 2004). Such intercultural exchanges with other minority and interest groups (including the state) can thus facilitate a process of reflection on the part of both community members and the broader research team. As Greenwood and Levin (1998, p 99) note:

> Having analysed political economics, social structures and
> ideological systems from around the world and over long

periods of time, professional researchers develop a sense of where the local systems fit into a larger range of variation. This broader contextualization is useful in action research because many groups suffering from acute problems feel stuck in a particular view of the situation and have a difficult time developing a sense of alternative courses of action. By setting the local situation in the context of these broader comparisons, the professional action researcher can assist the local group in opening up its sense of the situation and some options for the future.

Justifying the use of PAR techniques

As has been argued above, the involvement of Gypsy and Traveller community members in research can be justified not only on the grounds of social justice, but also by enhanced delivery of high-quality research findings that are enhanced by accessing individuals who might otherwise be 'hard to reach' for academic researchers. Several authors have identified that the impact of the misuse of research has been acute for Gypsies and Travellers both in the UK and internationally (for example during the Second World War when racial stereotyping was used as a justification for genocide; see Kenrick, 2004) and the legacy of such unethical practice has retained immediacy among community members to this day. Okely (1983) reported that in her early experiences of contact with Gypsy communities she found that highly structured interview questionnaires designed solely by external professionals were counterproductive to a research project, forcing her to rethink her approach, and more recently, anecdotal evidence suggests that other academics continue to experience similar difficulties, noting that consultations that involve interrogative interviews have aroused Gypsies and Travellers' suspicions that inquisitive 'outsiders' will bring harm towards the community or their family.

By using PAR techniques, research partners are able to ensure that interview topics and approaches are culturally apposite (in the case of TEIP, using a 'conversational' style of interview was identified as being conducive to Gypsy and Traveller engagement – particularly across gender and age boundaries – as empowering the interviewed and enabling them to set out their concerns, interests and aspirations without undue restriction). Thus, PAR embeds internal validity into a report by capturing the mood of those being interviewed, especially where the authors adopt a 'call to context' (Delgado, 1995) and, in the case of TEIP through making significant use of direct quotations, to ensure that Gypsy, Roma and Traveller voices are able to speak directly to the reader.

We do not make any attempt to claim that the above examples (Cambridgeshire GTAA and the TEIP) are the only successful use of PAR with Gypsies and Travellers and are delighted to note that increasing numbers of publications reflect on this technique. Indeed, Gypsy Council members used PAR methods to survey the inhabitants of a Kent village (Horsemonden) whose parish council had banned a Gypsy horse fair held there for generations (Acton, 2007) and the resulting report found that most villagers actually favoured the fair's continuation. The publication of those community-driven findings went a significant way to leading to the fair's reinstatement the following year. Similarly, the Ormiston Trust consultation on behalf of the East of England Regional Spatial Strategy (which gathered community views and aspirations on accommodation as part of a process to map a strategy for site delivery) explicitly reported:

> Participatory research has developed somewhat in the last few years as a means to empower individuals and to collect 'better' more 'real' data. Hence inclusion of 'non professionals' has tended to place them as instruments of data collection. Many projects are criticised for this type of inclusion, where participants remain divorced from the wider research process and have little influence over what is being asked. This project, unusually, offered Gypsies and Travellers that opportunity since they were asked to be involved in the design of the questions, the sequencing and structure of the questionnaire as well as developing skills in collecting and recording of the data. (Ormiston Trust, 2007, p 6)

Thus, involvement and awareness of research methods by community members increase a desire to become research active, and in turn successful outcomes justify popular involvement in a range of future projects – which may range from education or health needs assessments to recruitment to community fora.

We argue therefore that the use of PAR and associated techniques avoids the risk of imposition of burdensome and damaging initiatives on those individuals and communities less likely to be able to 'speak to power' when standardised (particularly quantifiable) research methods are used. We are aware, however, that in taking this stance we may well be accused of engaging in politicised action, over-claiming the benefits of PAR and failing to explore the criticisms of action research that have been made by a number of commentators:

> Given the truly pitiful conditions in which the majority of Roma live, those who study them can easily lose their objectivity and become de facto Gypsy activists.... I do find purportedly unbiased studies that overlook the fundamental principles of scholarly research and presentation quite disturbing, however those 'activist authors' may be motivated by a twisted sense of political correctness in so far as they over-emphasise the injuries the Roma have indisputably suffered at the hands of the prejudiced majorities while simultaneously ignoring the Gypsies' responsibility for their predicament and belittling the efforts of states and organisations to assist them. My approach is that of a social scientist and not of a Romanologist or a Gypsy activist. (Barany, 2002, p 18)

One response to the argument that non-participatory modes of research are more reliable than the methods for which we argue is to challenge the concept of scientific neutrality. We propose that the notion that one can be neutral is a fallacy while acknowledging that the qualitative researcher cannot assume they can observe with detachment and certainty in the same manner as a scientist working in a laboratory (Robson, 1993, p 65). Good-quality research and sound outcomes are more likely to be forged by the researcher explicitly acknowledging the impact and influence of their personal views and the life history that they bring to the research field while remaining scrupulously critical of their own practice, engaging with trusted – yet critical – colleagues who will challenge their findings, and remaining impassively incorruptible in the face of potentially conflicting pressures from research funders, commissioners and participants.

Such is the isolation and exclusion experienced by some Gypsies, Roma and Travellers that the action researcher (and indeed community research partners involved in the interview process) will in all likelihood feel at times overwhelmed with appeals for help and assistance for a broad range of problems. Here caution needs to prevail: if the researcher is relied on too greatly as a source of primary support rather than directing those in need to agencies better equipped and resourced to give help, then research outcomes and funding could potentially be compromised or the researcher may find themselves in conflict with their primary aim. The action researcher therefore has to be both selective and focused in forwarding a 'change agenda' as well as coldly self-critical. The value of clear reflexive practice is at its most important in such circumstances to ensure that the academic researcher does not became so engaged that their practice falls below the standard of professionalism owed to the community, themselves and their professional discipline.

Conclusion

In this chapter, the (academic) researchers involved in the Cambridgeshire GTAA and the Traveller Economic Inclusion Project have set out the case for undertaking research with Gypsies and Travellers that is participatory, partnership based, action orientated and seeks to give something back to the community being researched. To do otherwise, and *en passant* to treat Gypsies and Travellers who are one of the most excluded minorities in society as nothing more than a passive research subject on which to model and demonstrate some distant abstract argument, is perverse and alien to our political philosophy. Not all research projects can emulate the scope of Gypsy and Traveller participation as set out by the above examples and in this we acknowledge that we were fortunate in that these projects were well funded and resourced. However, most forms of research provide scope and opportunity to give something back to the 'researched' in terms of participation and honest dialogue between the parties to a study and, in so doing, such research embellishes both ethical social science practice and reputation and aids intercultural dialogue.

Notes
[1] See Chapter Two for a discussion on accommodation and planning issues.

[2] At the time when the Cambridge GTAA was undertaken, this was regarded as a radical-enough departure from research undertaken with Gypsies and Travellers in the UK up until that point (Blackburn et al, 2010).

TEN

'Stamp on the Camps': the social construction of Gypsies and Travellers in media and political debate

Joanna Richardson and Richard O'Neill

> Language is legislation, speech is its code. We do not see the
> power which is in speech because we forget that all speech
> is a classification, and that all classifications are oppressive....
> (Barthes, 1977, p 460)

Introduction

This chapter examines the circular nature of anti-Gypsy discourse –
that it allegedly reflects popular opinion, but also creates folk devils
and moral panics (Cohen, 1972) that feed the negative discourse even
further. A framework for analysing media representation of Gypsies
and Travellers will be discussed, in order to understand the impact that
discourse in newspapers, on television and in Westminster can have,
and also to attempt to understand why the media reports in such a
way. The chapter will focus on two case studies: (a) the 'Stamp on the
Camps' media campaign in 2005 and (b) the television series Big Fat
Gypsy Weddings in 2011. These moments in media and public discourse
provide useful case studies to illustrate conceptual theories on discourse,
racism and control; but also offer insights into the responses of key
institutions such as political parties, media regulatory bodies, equality
bodies and community groups.

The current context for analysis of media debate is shifting following
the News International 'hacking scandal' of 2011 and the subsequent
Leveson Inquiry into the scandal and the regulatory framework. The
analysis in this chapter is mindful of the shifting context for media
regulation, but concentrates on newspaper and television media
representation of Gypsy and Traveller issues between 2004 and 2011.

Discourse in the news: a framework for 'othering'

> Thus news is a practice: a discourse which, far from neutrally reflecting social reality and empirical facts, intervenes in what Berger and Luckman [1966] call 'the social construction of reality'. (Fowler, 1991, p 2)

This linguistic construction of social reality is a powerful tool in creating categories and sorting them into 'conflictual opposites' (Fowler, 1991, p 6). With the example of Gypsies and Travellers, the news constructs Gypsies/Travellers and the settled community as conflictual opposites. After a while, this construction of reality sees Gypsies and Travellers as embodying the enemy of the 'normal' settled community.

Fowler (1991) examined values in the news and referred to 12 contextual factors formulated by Galtung and Ruge (1973). The concept for Galtung and Ruge was that the more values there are in an event, the more newsworthy it is. Many of the 12 factors apply to news stories about Gypsies and Travellers, but two in particular strike a chord:

- 'Reference to persons' or 'personalisation' (promoting feelings of identification, empathy and disapproval). What do Gypsies and Travellers 'stand for'? Media analysis research on Gypsies and Travellers (Richardson, 2006b) sees them as 'standing for' a cost to the taxpayer, causing a mess and being 'other' to the settled community.
- 'Meaningfulness' (including 'cultural proximity' and 'relevance', this relates to consensus and conforming to norms). The ramifications of stereotyping in the press are clear: when an event is reported in the news it reinforces the stereotype; and the fact that a stereotype is part of the event makes it more newsworthy.

The media is not merely a reporting mechanism that reflects events and feelings, it also helps to create and shape events and feelings. Dean (2011) demonstrates that the media does not just report on government, it also shapes policy and political decisions. This shaping can perhaps be seen in the 'U-turns' taken by the Coalition Government during 2011 on justice reform (particularly sentencing). Health reforms were also subject to media shaping; this was discussed by Van Cleemput in Chapter Three, this volume. Clearly, it is not just the media impacting on government policy, but government policy does also drive media priorities. Dean (2011) refers to the 'disappearance of the housing correspondent' as a good example of how government dictates the media agenda – so when housing becomes a lower policy priority for government, this is reflected in the perceived news value in the media.

The media is now more pervasive than ever thanks to the improvement of information and communications technology (ICT). Social media, for example Facebook and Twitter, have seen positive campaigns (such as in support of the Green Revolution in Iran in 2010) and this sort of online collective action – 'clicktivity' – can be a democratic force for positive change, but it can also have negative connotations. Online comments about programmes and television series like Big Fat Gypsy Weddings compound the effect of media stereotyping. This accessibility of the media (and the accessibility of the population for the media to broadcast to) is a reasonably new phenomenon. It is for this reason, and in the current context of highly capable ICT, that the media influence over public perceptions and actions should not be underestimated.

The negative images used to portray Gypsies, Roma and Travellers in some sections of the media serve as a tool to highlight their 'otherness' and their so-called deviancy from societal norms. By labelling Gypsies, Roma and Travellers as 'other', society is actually making them 'other'; they are constructing their identity as different (Richardson, 2006a). The role of Gypsies, Roma and Travellers as folk devils is played out in government policy decisions and reinforced by the media, feeding back again into government, which then reacts to media representation with the introduction of populist policies (as was seen in the *Daily Express* 'campaign' against East European Roma, January 2004, discussed later in this chapter).

Case study on newspaper representation of Gypsies and Travellers: 'Stamp on the Camps' media campaign

There has been little let-up in the anti-Gypsy discursive debate in the popular press, the town hall and Whitehall over the past decade; but helpful and positive voices have also added to the debate (such as speeches from Trevor Phillips of the Equalities and Human Rights Commission and Alvaro Gil-Robles, former Commissioner for Human Rights in Europe). There has also been some examination of press representation. For example, Richardson's (2006a) book *The Gypsy debate: Can discourse control?* examined media debate on Gypsies and Travellers and drew parallels with reporting on asylum seekers. Dean's (2011) more recent work also included examination of media representation of asylum seekers, which resonates with those monitoring the Gypsy and Traveller stories in the press. Richardson and Ryder (2009b) presented a detailed analysis of the 'Stamp on the Camps' media campaign, and this was discussed further in Richardson (2010b). Other works have also looked at Gypsies and Travellers in the media: Ní Shuinéar's (1997) work attempted to understand 'why Gaujos hate Gypsies so much' through examination of a range of media, including newspapers, poems and books. Other work from academics in the area of representation in the media includes Bhopal and Myers (2010). However, the positive and evaluative voices do not appear to have dinted the appetite for writing and reading anti-Gypsy articles in the press.

One of the key flashpoints in the past decade was *The Sun's* 'Stamp on the Camps' campaign in the run-up to the 2005 General Election. It ran two headlines and numerous pages over a three-day period. *The Sun* editorial on 9 March 2005 declared:

> The rule of law is flouted daily by people who don't pay taxes, give nothing to society and yet expect to be treated as untouchables. These people are far removed from the traditional Romany people with their admirable moral code. The villain of the piece is the Human Rights Act, which our judges have limply interpreted to mean that these wandering tribes have a right to family life and respect for their homes which outweighs any harm they might do to the environment or rural communities.

Greenslade (2005) suggests that this was a personal agenda for the-then editor Rebekah Wade (now Brooks). He states that *The Sun* story was:

> ... a heavily spun version of what his department really did – or 'rubbish' as one of his [Prescott's] spokesmen said – but it was just the kind of hook the *Sun's* editor, Rebekah Wade, had been looking for. By coincidence she had been moved to tackle the topic after being shown an encampment in Lancashire and being told by a member of her staff about a similar example in Essex. So her Wednesday front page, picturing a traveller camp with the headline 'Meet your neighbours ... thanks to John Prescott' [see Figure 10.1] eclipsed the *Mail's* efforts. Then, on Thursday, both papers attempted to outdo each other with lurid tales and also redoubled their attacks on Prescott.

Figure 10.1: 'Meet your neighbours' – *The Sun* headline during the 'Stamp on the Camps' campaign

Source: *The Sun*, 9 March 2005

The *Daily Mail* and the *Daily Express* joined in the campaign with their own headlines and an extensive number of pages given over to stories on Gypsies and Travellers. The media discourse resonated with many and was used unashamedly in 'dog-whistle'[1] tactics for the electorate by the leader of the Conservatives – Michael Howard backed *The Sun*'s campaign as part of his pre-election strategy. Howard suggested that Gypsies and Travellers were a 'special interest' group hiding behind human rights legislation and said that the Conservatives would tackle 'illegal' sites through a Gypsy trespass law (Grice and Brown, 2005; Richardson and Ryder, 2009b).

While some politicians used the campaign to what they thought would be political advantage, other key figures condemned the debate. The former Commissioner for Human Rights, Alvaro Gil-Robles, was 'truly amazed' at the headlines:

> [T]o judge by the levels of invective that can regularly be read in the national press, Gypsies would appear to be the last ethnic minority in respect of which openly racist views can still be acceptably expressed. I was truly amazed by some of the headlines, articles and editorials that were shown to me ... it is clear that much more serious efforts are required

to accommodate their needs and promote greater tolerance towards them than are currently in evidence. (Gil-Robles, 2005, p 43)

The Sun's 'Stamp on the Camps' campaign was also only one year on from the *Daily Express* newspaper's 'campaign' to stop Roma 'flooding' into Britain post accession to the European Union (see Figure 10.2); some of the journalists working at the newspaper voiced disquiet at the editorial pressure they were under to write such articles during this 2004 series of articles (Kundnani, 2004).

Figure 10.2: 'The Great Invasion 2004' – the *Daily Express* illustration on its front page, 20 January 2004

Source: The Daily Express, 20 January 2004

Both the *Daily Express*'s and *The Sun*'s campaigns were extreme points of anti-Gypsy discourse, but they were also part of a longer-entrenched, ongoing, negative, political and media discourse at local, national and European levels.

'Stamp out the Prejudice'

Gypsies, Roma and Travellers were deeply affected by the negative reporting and campaigning that revolved around *The Sun* newspaper and the Conservative Party's election campaign. There was reported fear among Gypsy and Traveller people (Spear, 2005).

The Gypsy and Traveller community were not passive victims, however, and advocacy groups such as the Gypsy and Traveller Law Reform Coalition organised a counter campaign entitled 'Stamp out the Prejudice', which was launched in April 2005 by the All Party Parliamentary Group for Traveller Law Reform. The Gypsy and Traveller Law Reform Coalition also submitted complaints to the Press Complaints Commission about *The Sun* reports and to the police for inciting racial hatred.

As a result of *The Sun* newspaper articles and Conservative campaigning, media interest in the issue was intense. The broadsheet newspapers helped to redress the negativism of the tabloids, and *The Guardian* and *The Independent* were prominent in challenging the prevailing negative and racist discourse. In some cases the tabloids also stood up for Gypsies and Travellers – the *Daily Mirror* (editorial, 22 March 2005) proclaimed:

> The British people face serious problems.... But what do the Conservatives think the Big Issue is? Gypsies. Yes, a small number of Travellers. This is not only nonsense but dangerous, vile nonsense.... By the standards of morality and decency, it is the worst sort of gutter politics.... What is going on in this country is no longer just about how we will be ruled for the next few years. It is a war for the soul of Britain....

Parliamentary allies also leapt to the defence of Gypsies and Travellers. Labour MP Kevin McNamara said of Mr Howard's remarks on Travellers:

> There is, I feel, a whiff of persecution about the way the Roma have been treated throughout Europe. They are easily discernible, they are an easy target to attack, to blame all sorts of difficulties on – to appeal to people's basest motives and I really do feel there is the whiff of the gas chambers about this. (Sturcke, 2005)

Church leaders and equality leaders joined in the condemnation. For example, the Commission for Racial Equality (CRE) coordinated the monitoring of the resulting increase in harassment against Gypsies, Roma and Travellers, which prompted the intervention of Trevor Phillips, the chair of the CRE. In an article that he wrote for *The Observer*, which received widespread coverage, he noted the increase in racial abuse and stated:

> Jews, Muslims and Gypsies tell the CRE that they are under siege in Britain. They have good reason to feel threatened.... Our language and tone may unintentionally create the climate for a moment of rage to turn into tragedy. The political and media bandwagon will roll on untouched after the election; but in its wake it will leave thousands of broken lives, scarred by racial abuse and intimidation. (Phillips, 2005)

Monitoring the press in 2005 – the Gypsy Media Advisory Group

Richard O'Neill, the co-author of this chapter and founding member of the Gypsy Media Advisory Group, recounts the decision for communities to come together and try to monitor the press representation of Gypsies and Travellers:

'In 2005 so concerned were we as a group of Gypsies and Travellers about the negative press and media coverage we as communities were receiving on a daily basis, that we decided to set up a group to monitor and to try and counteract it. This was fairly early days for many of the new and younger Gypsy/Traveller campaigners and before the popularity of Facebook, Twitter and other social networking sites. It's also true to say that not all Gypsies and Travellers who were in the group were even online at that point as this was also prior to good and reasonably priced mobile internet connections.

Starting the group we had no idea just how much negative press and media was being produced nationally by the hundreds of regional and local newspapers. After only 10 days of collecting negative stories it soon became clear that as volunteers it wouldn't be possible to even start to deal with the sheer volume that was being produced. Having worked on a number of campaigns, especially around combating the negative press and media towards fatherhood and men's health in the settled community, I assessed that we would need at least one full-time, paid person to simply catalogue the negative stories produced by press and media, let alone try and tackle and counteract them.

This really was a sobering realisation that this thing called the media was stronger than anyone or any group; even the Prime Minister couldn't stop them from reporting negatively about his private life. I think there was a sense of despair about this too, in that whatever you did they always had the last word. We went to a number of meetings with the Press Complaints Commission, which also showed the futility of trying to get the press to admit they were wrong or even to print apologies regarding Gypsy/Traveller stories.

So we as a group decided individually to focus our time and effort on a number of different initiatives and mine was to promote the positive aspects of Traveller culture through the arts, particularly the Gypsy Expressions website (www.journeyfolki.org.uk), which was created to showcase Gypsy and Traveller poetry and short stories and storytelling.'

While there is no longer a Gypsy Media Advisory Group, as noted by O'Neill above, there is still a great interest and motivation in monitoring press stories on Gypsies and Travellers. *Travellers' Times* is a publication that was developed by the Rural Media Company in 2009, it has a website and twitter-feed, which is updated regularly with the latest news, and on its website it has a 'Media Watch' area where articles discussing Gypsies and Travellers are archived. Richardson (2006a) coded and categorised media representation of Gypsies and Travellers, and this work needs to be continued through a systematic monitoring of the media and lobbying, through the Leveson Inquiry, through the Independent Press Complaints Commission and through political representatives to try to improve how Gypsies and Travellers are represented in political and media discourse.

Complaints against *The Sun*

In 2005, the media played a central role in stoking the furore that revolved around the 'Stamp on the Camps'. Complaints were made about *The Sun*'s reporting to the police and Press Complaints Commission (PCC). In late 2005, the Crown Prosecution Service (CPS) ruled that after reviewing the evidence it felt that *The Sun* had not incited racial hatred: this was because no direct link could be found between the reported acts of racial abuse following the reporting and the reports themselves. A number of campaigners argued that this showed the weakness of hate crime legislation. Only after the conclusion of the CPS investigation did the PCC proceed to evaluate whether *The Sun* had infringed the PCC's code of practice. The complainants argued that the code of practice had been broken, particularly clauses on accuracy, harassment and discrimination.

Richard O'Neill remembers the meetings with the PCC to discuss the complaint:

> 'In the case of the meetings with the PCC, it was clear that getting anything resolved was futile. Our concerns were politely acknowledged and then dismissed and it was clear that there was nowhere else to go. There were other people at the meeting from organisations not connected to Gypsies or Travellers who were much more experienced than I in this field, but despite their best arguments the outcome was the same. They didn't find that the article was as bad as we thought it was. And that was that. I remember leaving the meeting feeling both angry and depressed.
>
> I'm sure that many people who have never experienced a racist attack verbal or physical don't realise how devastating it can be. And whatever people think, the media definitely have an effect on the way that groups like Gypsies and Travellers are viewed.'

However, the PCC found that *The Sun* had not broken its code of practice. The argument from the PCC to support its finding was that as no single individual had been named in the reports and directly attacked, which would have meant that they could legitimately complain of being discriminated against, then the code had not been broken. Thus, it seemed possible for a British newspaper to malign a whole ethnic group in racist terms so long as no individual was named. The Gypsy and Traveller Law Reform Coalition, with the support of the Equality and Diversity Forum (an umbrella group of equality groups in the UK), met the PCC and pressed it to reform its code but this request was refused. The campaign to reform the PCC code of practice continues but a major hurdle is the fact that the PCC is a self-regulating press body appointed and run by the newspapers themselves. The 'hacking scandal' of 2011 at the *News of the World*, however, brought about the Leveson Inquiry and the political and public appetite for a change in the regulation of the press. This seemed to be a tipping point in the political and public conscience that highlighted the weakness of the PCC, in a way that the offensive headlines of 2004 and 2005, and the subsequent lobbying by Gypsy and Traveller activists, were unable to achieve.

A failure to secure more responsible reporting on Gypsies, Roma and Travellers has meant that negative and inflammatory reporting continues unchecked. There continue to be many examples of newspaper articles and speeches in Parliament that are also racist and inflammatory, but are met with very little outrage, apart from in the Gypsy and Traveller communities. In some cases, the resulting actions may not be so visible – instead, more benign racism may result in change of leadership in local elections, high turnout to objectors' meetings in planning cases and so on. There is no less a link between the news–political discourse, it just takes place on a longer basis with a more drip-drip approach so it barely causes a stir.

Case study on television representation – Big Fat Gypsy Weddings

The examples looked at so far have been from newspapers, or the new electronic medium for print media. There is also the need to examine the representation of Gypsies and Travellers in television media. A number of media studies have focused on electronic and television media, for example the work of the Glasgow Media Action Group. The group's first publication was entitled *Bad news* (Glasgow Media Action Group, 1976), which focused on electronic media, in this instance television news. In its theoretical stance it is linked with the work of Fowler (1991) in its use of Galtung and Ruge's (1973) 'news values'. These aforementioned 'news values' are the first of four main filtering processes for television news; the other three being (a) time/resources, (b) 'television values', or what looks good visually, and (c) 'cultural air/ideological atmosphere' (Glasgow Media Action Group, 1976: x).

The television series Big Fat Gypsy Weddings aired in the summer of 2011. According to the programme makers, Channel 4, it was a:

> Revealing documentary series that offers a window into the secretive, extravagant and surprising world of gypsies and travellers in Britain today.... Warm, intelligent, engrossing and funny, Big Fat Gypsy Weddings tells intimate stories on an epic scale, laying bare an exotic unseen Britain that exists right on our doorstep. (www.channel4.com)

There were six episodes:

- 'Born to be wed';
- 'No place like home';
- 'Desperate housewives';
- 'Boys will be boys';
- 'Bride & prejudice';
- 'My big fat Gypsy Christmas'.

The write-up of the series by Channel 4 suggested that the programmes 'laid bare the exotic', and this certainly seemed to be evident in the treatment of the people and issues in the programmes, where 'exoticism' rather than cohesion seemed to be the lens through which Gypsies' lives were depicted.

The impact of the series on the community, and on the perception of the community in popular discourse, cannot be underestimated. The debate in newspapers and in online discussion forums was on the size of the dresses, grave-side etiquette and fist-fighting. Within these articles and subsequent public online comments there were inherent presumptions on whether or not Gypsies, Roma and Irish Travellers pay taxes – either Income Tax or Council Tax – and therefore whether they contribute to the wider community. Some comments reflected one dominant perception: that their lifestyle and culture does not contribute socially to the community, and that if they do not pay taxes, they are not contributing economically either.

Many Gypsies and Travellers were outraged by both the content of the programme and the comments that followed each episode in debates online. An official complaint was made to Ofcom (the independent regulator and competition authority for the UK communications industry) and a number of articles and television appearances were undertaken by members of the travelling communities. The producers suggested that the programme aimed to challenge prejudice but just a glimpse through chat sites shows how divisive the response has been. Many Gypsies suggested that the programme did not represent the norms of their communities and they claimed that the most extreme aspects were chosen in the final edit. It is understandable that the programme makers needed to hook the viewer with sensational images and simple messages; however, there is much more to the travelling communities than big wedding dresses. Members of the Gypsy and Traveller communities appealed to the Advertising Standards Agency (ASA) to investigate the 'Bigger. Fatter. Gypsier' advertising campaign for the programme. The ASA originally cleared the campaign in March

2012, but following an appeal by groups such as the Irish Traveller Movement in Britain (ITMB), the ASA's independent reviewer asked the regulator at the end of May 2012 to undertake a full investigation (Sweney, 2012).

While many Gypsies and Travellers found their portrayal in the series to be negative and stereotypical, Richard O'Neill found that there were mixed views:

> 'Big Fat Gypsy Weddings, although scorned by a number of Gypsies and Travellers, has been watched by a record number of non-Travellers and while it has a negative side it has also encouraged people to look differently at the travelling communities and many people have come up to me since it was aired and said things like "I didn't know that the morals were so strong in the Gypsy community". I think attitudes are changing and I think the arts can do a tremendous amount of work in helping this. However, the makers of programmes like BFGW should have been honest with viewers that their programmes were made primarily to entertain rather than to inform.'

Jane Jackson of *Travellers' Times* encapsulated the concerns of many Gypsies and Travellers about the series in a complaint to Ofcom:

> The series publicity and voice-over (i.e. voice of authority) is badly misrepresenting several distinct Gypsy and Traveller communities by describing certain customs as common to all, by filming extreme cases (because no one else would take part in the programme for fear of exactly what has happened) and by not working with any community leaders to get the facts right. This is cheap, nasty media exploitation of the GRT [Gypsy, Roma and Traveller] communities, who have no access to the media themselves to redress the balance. (Jackson, 2011)

As noted in the complaint, no experts or community members were invited to assist in the research for the series and a number of practices by a handful of Travellers, most notably 'grabbing', in which young Traveller men attempted to grab girls and kiss them to gauge whether they were suitable for marriage, were portrayed as common rituals for this community. Added to this were general sub-themes of hyper masculinity, sexism, domestic violence and the sexualisation of children.

Perhaps some of the behaviour displayed was typical of the Travellers featured in the series but the cardinal sin was to create the impression that these are features that are endemic to this community and are thus highly dangerous. Richards (2011) commented:

> .... My Big Fat Gypsy Wedding ... avoids any accusation of being brave by its craven acquiescence to the lowest forms of prejudice and ignorance, and will lead, sure as eggs is eggs, to an increase in murderous attacks on travellers and bullying of traveller children in schools. It is hard to think of another social group, culture or ethnicity about whom such a programme would be made without a chorus of outrage. It seems there is no-one to speak up for the Gypsies.

However, unlike with the 'Stamp on the Camps' incident there has been a notable lack of condemnation from leaders of civil society such as Trevor Phillips or the press: as Paul Richards noted, the legitimate 'chorus of outrage' did not materialise. No doubt, criticising a programme that appeared on a superficial level to sympathise with female Travellers who were portrayed as victims of sexism and male domination is not something easy to do. Indeed, responses were divided and divisive, with some communities suggesting that it did not represent them, but that it might represent other travelling communities.

Many of the complaints about the series were made about the programmes themselves. However, it was in the discussion forums, on a number of websites, where the debate got really nasty. Across the spectrum of newspaper websites, tabloid or broadsheet, politically Left and Right, one can see readers' comments after any story. Those stories on Gypsies and Travellers seem to attract predictable and uninformed comments, sometimes using extremely offensive language. It is incumbent on internet service providers to take down defamatory material 'swiftly' since the case of *Godfrey v Demon* (2000)[2] and this was reinforced following the settlement out of court in the case of *Gina Ford v Mumsnet* (2007)[3]. Comments online about Gypsies and Travellers tend to refer to whole communities rather than individuals; nevertheless, there is a need for publishers to be mindful of race relations legislation and particularly comments that could incite racial hatred either in their reports or in comments about their reports.

Since Big Fat Gypsy Weddings was shown, to mixed reaction, there has been another television series of eight programmes aired on Sky Biography channel: A Gypsy Life for Me. This series followed the fortunes of Gypsy and Traveller contestants in the Travellers Got Talent competition and was presented by Gypsy journalist Jake Bowers, and included Gypsy author Violet Cannon and Gypsy author, *Travellers Times* editor and artist Damian Le Bas. It is impossible not to be impressed by the intellect and talent of the producers, judges and participants in the programmes; however, it is unlikely that these images will be seen by anywhere near as many viewers as Channel 4's Big Fat Gypsy Weddings because it is on a special-interest Sky channel.

Gypsy and Traveller culture, with its strong sense of community and protective and intense social networks, is in fact something that could be held up as a paragon of moral behaviour in any debate on what is acceptable social behaviour in our society today. While these values were alluded to in some parts of the BFGW programmes, they were hidden among the stereotyping, taffeta frills and bare-knuckle fighting. Furthermore, as with all communities, Gypsies and Travellers are moving with the times and women are slowly being accorded the same rights as men, as is testified by the growing number of female campaigners and activists for Travellers' rights. Of course there are some who go against these progressive trends but it would be wrong, as was the case with Big Fat Gypsy Weddings, to give the impression that a particular youth subculture is the cultural norm for a whole minority.

The series prompted a strong wave of protests from Gypsies and Travellers, complaints were sent to Ofcom and a protest Facebook site was established that has around 2,000 members. However, the problem is that Gypsies and Travellers will not be in a stronger position to challenge such depictions of themselves as shown in the series until their place is more assured in the media and other cultural platforms as reporters, commentators, artists and public faces who can present views and images that challenge these dangerous distortions. There are Gypsies and Travellers working in all facets of British society – the legal profession and indeed the media.

The co-author of this chapter, Richard O'Neill, is a successful writer, broadcaster and artist who specialises in storytelling and working with children in schools. He talks about his work:

'In 2005, I started to work with a number of Traveller Education Services around the country as a professional storyteller, using stories both from my family and personal experience of being a Traveller and the rich culture we have and the lessons that could be learned from storytelling. This seemed to catch the imagination of a number of head teachers who were not only under pressure to prove that their schools took diversity issues seriously but also were in need of boosting the speaking, listening and creativity skills of their pupils.

What has been clear from my work in hundreds of schools and museums is that most people have never been up close and personal with a Gypsy person, never seen anything positive coming from the community. Through storytelling and also through my writing I have been able to show the positive aspects of the Traveller communities as well as tackling some of the negative behaviours of a very small minority; also showing the long and positive history of Traveller and non-Traveller communities working and living together in many areas around the country. Working in schools, libraries, theatres and museums not only allows me to show the 'real Traveller life' as many Travellers perceive it, but also to have interaction with parents and other members of the communities I work in.'

Conclusion: the cycle of news and views

Public debate over proposals for new Gypsy and Traveller sites can provoke extremely adverse and racist reactions from the local community, the media and politicians (Richardson, 2007a). The newspapers report these reactions and often provoke further debate, either in the council chamber or, as has been seen more recently,

Figure 10.3: The churn of news and views

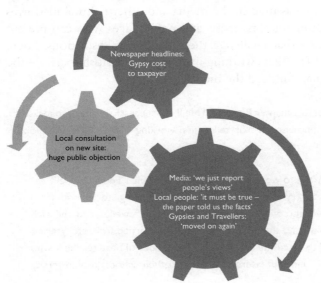

online in the comments sections of newspaper articles or on Twitter. The point here is that the cycle of news and views (see Figure 10.3) is not just an academic debate – there is a manifestation of the words into actions – discriminatory discourse leads to physical disadvantage, or fear of reprisal.

Unless positive action is taken, the cycle of this marginalisation of Gypsies and Travellers means that there is continued hostility towards the travelling community, there is a reluctance to back the provision of more sites, and Gypsies and Travellers continue to be moved on from place to place and are seen as outside the mainstream depictions of community and are 'other'. The events of 2011 leading to the Leveson Inquiry on press regulation showed that there was a line of taste and decency that could be crossed in the method of investigative journalism and lurid headlines. It is notable that the offensive coverage of Gypsies and Travellers in the press was not a strong enough test of the public and politicians on the acceptable levels of taste and decency; but as Trevor Phillips pointed out in 2003, there is a long way yet to go before Gypsies and Travellers are treated with the same courtesy as the rest of the UK population.

The process of rebutting the dominant media stereotype is under way in developments such the television series A Gypsy Life for Me and through Gypsy Roma Traveller History Month, but this needs to step up another gear, for as the series Big Fat Gypsy Weddings demonstrates, stereotypes and negative depictions that were common in the tabloid press have crossed over into mainstream and prime-time television. The series has garnered some of the highest ratings in Channel 4's history and the perception is that the public have now got a taste for such viewing and media focus. Europe's history of 'othering' and marginalising of this minority has, as many Gypsies, Roma and Travellers are painfully aware, all too often generally been played out in genocide, ethnic cleansing and violent attack.

The media does have a challenging role, particularly in the context of 24-hour news and social media use. We hope that both the media and political debate will be led by those who wish to set an agenda for creating ingenuity, honest deliberation and celebration of differences. There are very positive steps being taken by Gypsies and Travellers to attempt to influence the media debate, for example the capacity-building and media training and the web-based media monitor, both of which are run by *Travellers' Times*, and the Sky Biography television series A Gypsy Life for Me. What is needed next is for politicians and leaders in the press industry to respond to the excellent work being produced by Gypsies and Travellers, often in the face of continued hostility and negativity in mainstream political and media discourse.

A failure to secure more responsible reporting of Gypsy, Roma and Traveller issues means that negative and inflammatory reporting continues unchecked, and a major hurdle to improving the situation rests with the Press Complaints Commission as self-regulator. However, the 'hacking scandal' of 2011, following revelations of the activities of the *News of the World*, resulted in the Leveson Inquiry and the accompanying political and public appetite for a change in the way the press is held to account. This scandal and the Leveson Inquiry seemed to be a tipping point in the social conscience that had not previously been pricked by the offensive reporting of Gypsy and Traveller issues.

Notes

[1] The independent strategist for the Conservatives used this term to refer to certain issues to which voters would respond.

[2] In this case the plaintiff asked his internet service provider [ISP] to remove a comment posted on a forum purporting to be from him, but which was in fact forged. The ISP did not remove the comment and the case was settled out of court, but the judge ruled at the pre-trial motion that a transmission by an ISP of a defamatory comment constituted publication under defamation law; and this resulted in a set of rules known as 'notice and take down'.

[3] Following the precedent set by *Godfrey v Demon*, the Gina Ford case tested the 'notice and take down' rules following postings on the chat site mumsnet. This case was also settled out of court, but during the dispute the debate on 'free speech' and the responsibilities of 'online' content providers continued.

ELEVEN

EU Framework for National Roma Integration Strategies: insights into empowerment and inclusive policy development

Iulius Rostas and Andrew Ryder

Introduction

The origins of Roma communities and their arrival in Europe were discussed in Chapter One. It has been estimated that Europe has a Gypsy, Roma and Traveller population of between 10 and 12 million people (Fundamental Rights Agency, 2010). They are Europe's largest minority ethnic group but their predicament presents one of the greatest challenges to the achievement of European ideals on equality and justice. According to a recent European Parliament report:

> The Roma EU [European Union] citizens are one of the most marginalised groups in the EU, facing deep and intractable social problems related to low levels of education, high unemployment, inadequate housing, poor health, and wide-ranging discrimination, all of which are interrelated and create a vicious circle of social exclusion from which it is difficult to extract themselves on their own. In some areas of Central and Eastern Europe the Roma unemployment rate reaches 80–90%. Mortality rates and life expectancy are significantly below the EU average. In addition they often suffer segregation in education and housing, a significant factor in their social exclusion. (European Parliament, 2011b, p 7)

Another disturbing indicator of the level of marginalisation endured by Roma is the degree of xenophobia directed at this group in both the East and West of Europe, ranging from the mass fingerprinting of

Roma including minors in Italy (ERRC, 2008) to blanket deportations in France without individual consideration and in defiance of EU free movement conventions (ERRC, 2010) and including modern-day pogroms in countries such as Bulgaria (ERRC, 2011c). A number of countries such as Hungary have witnessed the rise of far-right groups that are reviving the hate speech and even symbols of fascism, leading to the scapegoating of Roma (ERRC, 2009). Violent attacks targeting Roma communities have intensified. In Hungary, nine lives, including two children, were lost in a campaign of racist and orchestrated terror (ERRC, 2011d).

A number of programmes have been adopted on Roma issues by the Council of Europe and the EU since the 1980s; an early focus was on improving educational outcomes for this minority (Liégeois, 2007). Following the Copenhagen European Council in 1993, the EU increasingly emphasised the importance of protecting ethnic and national minorities as a norm and as a political precondition for the accession of Central and Eastern European candidate member states. EU accession states in Central and Eastern Europe were, prior to EU admission, expected to address Roma exclusion and adopt coherent and inclusive policy and legal frameworks (Taba and Ryder, 2012). Another important dynamic was the elaboration of the Council of the European Union Directive 2000/43/EC, implementing the principle of equal treatment between people irrespective of racial or ethnic origin, a binding instrument for member states of the EU. It prohibits 'direct or indirect discrimination based on the grounds of racial or ethnic origin' (Article 1), including in the field of education (Article 3(g)). The directive requires states to implement effective remedies for people persecuted by discrimination, and to give standing to organisations to seek enforcement of the directive.

Despite these initiatives and commitments, profound exclusion and persecution towards Roma continue to this day and are not only to be found in Central and Eastern Europe – they are also evident in the West, as is reflected by a range of periodic reports by the European Commission against Racism and Intolerance (ECRI, 2010) Thus, Gypsy, Roma and Traveller communities across Europe are highly marginalised and vulnerable, often as a result of political inertia and a lack of resources, but also accentuated by economic problems and ingrained racism. Their plight thus constitutes a major challenge for EU member state and European social policy.

Since 2000, the EU has provided, through the Open Method of Coordination (OMC), a framework for national strategy development as well as for policy coordination between EU countries on issues relating to poverty and social exclusion. This coordinated action at European level is reflected in national action plans. It is claimed that it encourages EU countries to examine their policies critically, and highlights how some perform well in certain areas, spurring on others to perform better (Meyer et al, 2010). The financial crisis has created huge challenges to attempts to increase social inclusion in Europe and the EU has responded with the formation of the European Platform against Poverty and Social Exclusion. The European Commission is claiming to place the fight against poverty at the heart of its economic, employment and social agenda – the Europe 2020 strategy. A common target for this EU OMC framework is to lift at least 20 million people out of poverty and social exclusion in the next decade (European Commission, 2010). An offshoot of this broad economic and social strategy is the EU Framework for National Roma Integration Strategies (hereafter referred to as the 'Roma Framework'), an initiative that was introduced as part of Hungary's presidency of the Council of the EU.

The Roma Framework is based on the OMC and could be described as a roadmap for introducing binding minimum standards at EU level for identified priorities. The focus is on member states to be guided by the framework to devise national strategies to address Gypsy, Roma and Traveller exclusion, focusing on access to education, employment, healthcare and housing. In addition, it is envisaged that a national strategy will identify disadvantaged micro-regions or segregated neighbourhoods, where communities are most deprived. Member states are called on to allocate sufficient funding from national budgets, which will be complemented, where appropriate, by international and EU funding (European Commission, 2011). The Roma Framework is to be coordinated and monitored by the European Commission, which will establish a specific task group to carry out this function.

In a number of statements, the European Commission has stressed the importance of Roma participation in the Roma Framework (OSRI, 2011). A communication from the European Commission to the Parliament and the Council declared:

> Determined action, in active dialogue with the Roma, is needed both at national and EU level. While primary responsibility for that action rests with public authorities, it remains a challenge given that the social and economic integration of Roma is a two-way process which requires a change of mindsets of the majority of the people as well as of members of the Roma communities. (European Commission, 2011, p 1)

Key outcomes of the EU Framework for National Roma Integration Strategies

National Action Plans by EU member states based on and seeking to achieve:

- minimum standards for Roma in housing, education, healthcare and employment;
- micro policy to address acute poverty and segregation;
- monitoring, synergy and deliberation;
- empowerment, partnership and dialogue with Roma and civil society;
- resources from national and EU funding streams.

The Framework is a 'soft form' of governance where policies are formed through deliberation within an EU Framework.

This chapter gives a brief historical overview of policy in Europe towards Roma communities. It also seeks to identify whether the Roma Framework is conducive to ethnogenesis, that is, the political and cultural mobilisation of this minority, and provides opportunities for community engagement and inclusive policy development in the design and monitoring of the framework's national integration strategies and other outputs. Analysis of these processes also provides, in a European context, insights into relations and forms of dialogue between the Roma and centres of power but also internal channels of communication within Roma communities. In analysing community engagement in the Roma Framework, the authors argue that Roma participation is critical to the success of any policy and suggest a number of approaches to address this issue.

Europe-wide Roma strategies

The EU Roma Framework is not the first attempt at framing a Europe-wide approach on Roma issues. The Hapsburgs in the 18th century initiated a Roma policy across the Empire, which, inspired by enlightenment principles, sought to 'civilise' the Roma by proscribing nomadism and forcing them to settle and assimilate by placing Roma children into the care of non-Roma families (Fraser, 1995). A more sinister manifestation of a Europe-wide policy was the Nazi Final Solution in which Roma and Jewish communities were exterminated as part of a policy of genocide across large swathes of Europe (Kenrick and Puxon, 2009). In the post-war period, although not directed through a central policy for the whole Soviet Bloc, Soviet Bloc countries took their cue from policies influenced by Soviet ideology and set about the proletarianisation of Roma, compelling them to take largely industrialised labour positions and to attend school. Thus, the Roma were to be absorbed into the proletariat, 'civilised' and reformed through socialisation, work and education (Bíró, 2011).

The legacy of this policy was the emergence of a small Roma middle class; however, the majority were consigned to low-skilled labour and were highly vulnerable when in the immediate post-Communist period heavy industry was privatised and streamlined, leading to large-scale Roma unemployment and poverty (Gheorghe and Mirga, 2001). Thus, the present challenge facing Europe is a large Roma minority experiencing acute economic, social and racial exclusion. However, this problem cannot be pinned solely to a failed socialist experiment. In the West, many countries, be it Italy, Spain, Sweden or the UK, among numerous other states, often following their own national programme, set about trying to reform, regulate and repress Gypsy, Roma and Traveller traditions (Ryder and Greenfields, 2010). The result, as with socialist experiments and transitions to capitalist systems, has been greater marginalisation and cultural dislocation. The central thread in this narrative of failure has been that states have sought to impose without dialogue their own template for change upon the Roma, who have been expected to passively conform.

The Roma voice in Europe

Recent European policy on Roma has been more benign than the policies that came hitherto: since the 1980s a series of directives from the Council of Europe and the EU have sought to promote measures to increase educational inclusion and outlaw racism and promote the application of Structural Funds to address exclusion (Liégeois, 2007). However, the democratic deficit has continued and consultation with Roma communities has been minimal but in recent years there has been some limited progress with the emergence of civil society organisations, such as the European Roma Rights Centre (ERRC) and the Open Society Institute (OSI). These organisations combined in a network of other transnational organisational structures, the European Roma Policy Coalition (ERPC) alongside the European Roma Information Office (ERIO) have sought to develop an EU monitoring brief, information service and lobbying strategy on behalf of Roma (McGarry, 2010). Furthermore, there have been a small number of Roma Members of the European Parliament (MEPs), although never more than a small number (apart from Hungarian MEP Livia Járóka in the present Parliament, there has been Juan Ramirez de Dios from Spain and Viktoria Mohacsi from Hungary). Estimates calculate that proportionally there should be 24 Roma MEPs (McGarry, 2010).

Attempts have been made to bridge the gaps that exist and create a European platform and voice for Roma communities through the European Roma Traveller Forum (ERTF) founded in 2004, which is composed of Gypsy, Roma and Traveller delegates from the member states of the Council of Europe and which is represented by a General Secretary and Secretariat (Liégeois, 2007). However, there has been criticism of the ERTF in the sense that it has failed, according to some critics, to forge meaningful communication with and legitimacy among Roma communities in Europe (Nirenberg, 2009). Furthermore, there has been criticism that some transnational Roma political action, especially in some forms of Roma nationalism, is over-focused on concepts which have little resonance with grassroots communities. This Roma nationalist agenda has its modern roots in the first-world congress of the International Romani Union in London in 1971 where a flag and nationalist aspirations were formally adopted (Acton, 1974). It has been claimed that this nation-building agenda has led to some activists directing their energies towards European institutions and a small clique of fellow Roma activists, rather than the more challenging task of forging meaningful relationships with centres of power at local and national levels as well as empowerment networks with Roma at the grassroots and other disadvantaged groups (Kovats, 2003).

Another pan-European initiative is the 'Decade of Roma Inclusion 2005–2015' where a number of Central and Eastern European countries, at the initiative of the Open Society Institute and the World Bank, have sought to develop a framework programme to address Roma social and economic exclusion by setting goals for improvements in four priority areas: education, employment, health and housing. Roma involvement in the design and delivery of the programme has been an important dynamic in this initiative. The decade sought to bring forward a new generation of Roma leadership by restricting involvement in some key forums to a younger generation of Rom leaders. This caused frustration for some older and more traditional Roma leaders (Roma Press Agency, 2005). However, there have been claims that the decade initiative has also failed to create genuine dialogue with grassroots Roma communities and that non-governmental organisations (NGOs) funded by the philanthropist George Soros have been a dominant voice for Roma communities in this process, yet often lack clear channels of communications and legitimacy from the communities they seek to represent. It should also be noted that progress has been bedevilled by vague targets and limited resources (Taba and Ryder, 2012).

Another important development has been the Roma Platform. The Roma Platform meetings are decided on and chaired by the member state holding the presidency of the European Council. They bring together national governments, the EU, international organisations and Roma civil society representatives. The meetings aim at stimulating cooperation and exchanges of experience on successful Roma inclusion policies and practices. The first Roma Platform in Prague in 2009 established a set of 10 common basic principles to effectively address the inclusion of Roma. These included commitments on the 'involvement of civil society' and the 'active participation of the Roma' (European Commission 2011 website: www.ec.europa.eu). Such statements imply commitments to forging a dynamic partnership with Roma communities, involving them actively in decision making and policy design.

Given this desire to nurture the Roma political voice, it is surprising therefore that the EU Roma Framework has failed to involve Roma more widely in its design. The initial outline was framed by a number of Roma experts and the Roma MEP Livia Járóka who belongs to the Hungarian centre-right Fidesz Party. MEPs had the opportunity to debate and propose amendments to the strategy on the Civil Liberties, Justice and Home Affairs Committee (LIBE) of the European Parliament and then the wider Parliament. The process of policy design is as important as the aim and result for Roma, or to use the slogan adopted by Roma at the launch of the Decade of Roma inclusion: 'Nothing about us without us' (Haupert, 2010). Thus, there is a danger that an EU Roma Framework, as with other recent pan-European Roma initiatives as already outlined, may have little community 'buy-in' or active consultation with Roma communities and will thus have little support or awareness among Roma and therefore more limited chances of success.

At the Roma Platform meeting in Budapest 2011, Roma civil society was strongly critical of the lack of engagement with them in the development of the Roma Framework. Additionally, in February 2011 a group of European and Hungarian Romani and non-Romani organisations sent a letter to the Hungarian government (at the time holding the EU presidency), appealing for open consultation with NGOs on EU Roma policy-related initiatives (ERRC, 2011a). However, this appeal came too late to allow such groups to have much influence on the framework, given that the European Parliament voted as a whole on the Roma Framework in March 2011. The European Commission presented its proposal in April. The European Council (member states) adopted the policy framework at its meeting on 24 June

2011 and member states had to devise a national strategy on this issue in liaison with Roma civil society by the end of 2011 (OSI, 2011).

A key challenge for the future of the Roma Framework will be to ensure that dialogue is meaningful and inclusive. However, while there are high expectations in declared European Roma policy and the framework, at least in theory, for Roma to organise themselves and to participate in the democratic process and policy making, authorities ignore the historical past and lack of such traditions among Roma communities. With few exceptions, in the past Roma had no models of organising and expressing their interest in society in a similar manner to other groups. As a vulnerable group that faced severe exclusion throughout their history, Roma developed specific survival strategies and practices, often based on intense forms of social capital, adapted to the context in which they lived. Thus, expecting Roma to be able quickly to develop representative institutions similar to those of other groups in society is not only unrealistic and ethnocentric but also indicates a lack of knowledge and understanding of the Roma situation.

Ensuring representation through democratic means of a deeply 'undemocratic' and marginalised community represents serious challenges. In a number of Gypsy, Roma and Traveller communities there are practices that are not compatible with democratic values. Equality of women, early marriages, clan formation and representation – these are just a few issues that Roma leaders would have to address in developing inclusive representation. As the campaigner for Roma rights Azbija Memedova has noted on the topic of gender:

> '... respect should first come from inside the community. Romani men have to recognise the multiple factors contributing to Romani women's inequality and address them at all levels as the Romani women activists do. Only in this way can we speak about a real human rights movement. There are some positive steps in this regard, but we have a long way to go. (Memedova, 2004)

Such practices are often indirect products of exclusion, with marginalised Gypsy, Roma and Traveller communities clinging to traditional customs as a compensatory instrument of pride or status. As Cahn, former director at ERRC, notes:

> Some of the refusals to address human rights issues in Romani communities are motivated by defence of traditional community practice; there are many segments

of the community that do not want to give up the practice of child marriage for example, and ground this refusal in a defence of community norms. (Cahn, 2007)

Changing such perceptions warrants contributions from intellectuals and civil society but ultimately change may be dependent on internal community debates and the removal of structural causal factors of exclusion, which may engender more bridging forms of social capital and likewise life strategies that depart from tradition, which include participation in broad human and civil rights agendas. The authors of this chapter would argue that there may be opportunities in the Roma Framework to make some progress on these goals.

Arguments for dialogue on policies towards Roma

A range of arguments can be employed for the inclusion of Roma in policy development, including moral arguments, legitimacy, identity, solidarity, aggregation of interests and trust. As noted, Roma participation was one of the 10 principles on Roma inclusion presented by the Roma Platform and approved by the European Council in June 2008. Thus, the European Commission is under a moral pressure to stick to its principles.

Legitimacy in democratic systems stems from the fact that power is exercised as a result of collective decisions. Thus, not only should all citizens have a theoretical chance to participate but also the state should ensure that, especially in issues concerning specific groups, these groups are practically involved and, in certain conditions, have a veto on issues (as, for example, the denomination of the ethnic group).[1] In addition, the way minorities and the most vulnerable are treated becomes a test for the liberal democratic system – a point the former President of the Czech Republic, Vaclav Havel, raised when he declared that the treatment of Roma was a litmus test for civil society (Kamm, 1993).

One factor that was not properly considered in the adoption of the EU Roma Framework is the relation between state institutions and Gypsies, Roma and Travellers. The relations with the state administration and with others lack trust and reciprocity. As noted earlier, due to a long history of exclusion since their arrival in Europe, Roma profoundly distrust state institutions (Rostas, 2009). The relations between Roma and non-Roma are not based on cooperation and reciprocity, being rather dominated by distrust, limited interaction and ethnic tensions. Ignoring these realities and failing to include Roma in the policy-making process thus constitutes a recipe for failure.

Deliberation on the Roma Framework and the national strategies will allow Roma not only to participate, and facilitate trust formation, but also to communicate their preferences (and ethnicity) to the wider public. Deliberation and public communication influence the perception of Roma at individual and group levels with regard to who they are, what their relations are with wider society and their capabilities. The deliberation on policy options is not only about the aims but also about the means as to how to achieve those aims. If there is imposition and not aggregation of interests in society then designed solutions will not produce sustainable effects. While the intensity of minorities' priorities might balance the strong majoritarian tendencies in a democratic system, the democratic theory on the protection of politically insular minorities is blurred;[2] those minority groups irrespective of their options and their interests will be rarely if ever supported by a majority. Moreover, when such a minority is also deeply unpopular, the problems become more complex and there is a need for special mechanisms for the protection of such minorities (Sartori, 1987). Ackerman (1985, pp 720, 722) defines political insular minorities as those groups that are 'systematically disadvantaged in the ongoing political process' and, as a result, 'they have little bargaining power that makes it especially difficult for them to strike bargains with potential coalition partners'.

Roma in Europe present all the characteristics of a politically insular minority that needs special protection. An analysis of their current situation, the way they are involved in national politics, the way their interests are aggregated at national level, the lack of a home state and the strong racist attitudes towards them, limit the bargaining power of Roma in relation to other groups in society. These arguments support the need for an EU Roma policy. In fact, the expectation of Roma activists from 2005 was that the EU should adopt a Roma Strategy backed by strong financial and political instruments. It can be argued that a framework for policy coordination is not a strong-enough policy instrument to foster Roma Inclusion. Despite these concerns there may be valuable opportunities for Roma empowerment.

The role of NGOs

Someone not very familiar with the situation of Roma in Europe might ask why NGOs should represent Roma and not other institutions. This is a valid question as the representation function of the NGOs is not a primary function. They are not subject to regular public scrutiny and the leaders of NGOs are not elected by those who they claim to speak on behalf of. The representative weakness of Roma civil society is reflected in recent comments by Gheorghe (Gheorghe and Pulay, 2011, p 27), who has stated: 'Most Roma organisations still operate as "sects" and rather than "churches", since they are not yet part of a broader mass movement'. Furthermore, accusations could be made that NGOs too often reflect the views and aspirations of the philanthropists and foundations that bankroll them, which may have a different worldview to the Roma (Trehan, 2001). Thus, NGOs do not have a constituency and in a democratic sense it could be argued that they lack legitimacy. While these points make sense from the point of view of theory of democracy, there are still some aspects to consider before denying any role that Roma NGOs should play in policy making. However, if NGOs are not perfect interfaces of communication between Roma communities and centres of power, how can wider Roma involvement in decision-making processes be achieved?

There is no recipe for ensuring Roma participation. Often officials are asking for a partner to negotiate and work together in improving the situation of Roma; often there is no such solitary partner entrusted by Roma themselves. When working with Roma, one might be challenged and asked to rethink some rules: it requires consultations with numerous groups from which one might get contradictory views. There might be conflicts among Roma leaders, factions and indeed schisms and different interests asserted. As a result, policy makers could feel uncomfortable in making decisions on issues that they feel are not going to satisfy all Roma interests. However, they have to act as issues arise and there is a constant pressure on them from governments, international organisations and internal dynamics. Hence, to varying degrees governments have consulted and negotiated with a range of Roma civil society actors. However, as Acton and Ryder demonstrated in Chapter Eight, these processes can be fraught and destabilising where mistakes are made.

It would appear, according to some commentators, that there has been a constant practice among governments, international organisations and also donors to invite to their table only those Roma representatives who have not challenged them and served their interests rather than Roma communities (Liégeois, 2007). Policy makers have preferred to work with specific groups of Roma for other reasons such as: English proficiency of Roma activists, their knowledge of administrative and bureaucratic procedures and their ability to use modern communications (Nirenberg, 2009). They have not taken into account that too often these Roma activists have no constituency. The involvement of Roma activists has been most often individual in character rather than institutional. Those Roma activists who have not met the criteria for participating in the discussion, although having support in their communities, have been gradually removed from the negotiation table.

In the last 40 years, especially after the fall of communism in Central and Eastern Europe, Roma set up political parties, NGOs or joined mainstream organisations or churches. However, there are often objections among Roma to the work of these organisations, questioning their commitment to improve the situation, as they were seen as the 'Gypsy industry' (Bíró, 2011). The mainstream churches, with the exception of the neo-Protestant ones, paid little attention to Roma and their vulnerability. As these religious groups were themselves in a minority and often marginal, their capacity to put on the public agenda issues faced by Roma was very limited. Roma political parties were also unsuccessful in attracting Roma voters and playing a role in the political arena in most European states (McGarry, 2010).

Thus, the only partner left for policy makers are Roma NGOs. Irrespective of the objections about their representation, NGOs are the institutions developed by Roma that might claim they represent the voice of the Roma or have the potential one day to do so. So far the NGOs have provided the best platforms for Roma activists, which have managed to prepare some for institutional and political power. It should also be noted that the NGO sector has played a significant role in enabling Gypsy, Roma and Traveller women to play a greater role in articulating the aspirations of their communities, a development that has generated positive results but also challenged traditionally male-dominated culture (Bíró, 2011). These are the main reasons why policy makers should take into account these voices and should invite them to the negotiation when designing and deciding policies towards Roma. However, there is a need for a long-term programme to transform these NGOs into representative, grassroots-based and knowledgeable partners for local and national governments and international organisations (OSRI, 2011) – partners who can play an active role not just in policy design but also in delivery and coordination. This might be challenging as it seems that no government, donor or international organisation is directly interested in such a long-term project. Such a course of action should be a central component of the EU Roma Framework and national integration strategies.

Roma involvement in policy processes in Central and Eastern Europe

The capacity of Roma NGOs as negotiating partners with governments on policy making is supported by empirical evidence. Examples from Bulgaria and the Decade of Roma Inclusion might serve as lessons on how to set up such negotiation platforms. In 1998, the Roma and pro-Roma organisations in Bulgaria formed a coalition that negotiated with the government the Framework Programme for Roma Integration. The coalition was led by Rumayn Russinov, the leader of the Human Rights Project, a Sofia-based human rights NGO (Roma Participation Program, 2002). The greatest success of the coalition was in firmly establishing school desegregation on the public agenda, and leading the way in internationalising the issue.

The Decade of Roma Inclusion also presents models of good practice for the involvement of NGOs: with the support of the Open Society Institute and the World Bank, coalitions of Roma and pro-Roma NGOs have been set up in most of the participating countries. These coalitions monitor the progress achieved by each government in implementing its commitments contained in the national action plan. In this way, the Roma hold accountable the governments and provide feedback on the government policies (Decade of Roma Inclusion website: www.romadecade.org).

As noted already, sections of Roma civil society have become aloof and distant from real communities, in some cases no longer understanding the needs, aspirations and dynamic of local communities. This need to think and act at the local level is articulated by Gheorghe (Gheorghe and Pulay, 2011, p 36): 'Local knowledge must be taken into account in detailed negotiations about aims and implementation, leading to a better fit between actual situations and general principles. This means making alliances with local actors for any NGO that claims that they can handle everything by themselves is implausible.' The Roma Framework could provide the impetus for NGOs to take new localised directions, acting as a bridge between Roma communities and the EU and local and national governmental bodies, helping to mediate policy design and delivery.

Proposals to facilitate Roma empowerment

As has been noted, some of the proposals and aspirations related to the Roma Framework are calling on deep cultural change on the part of some Roma communities. The MEP Livia Járóka and others in the

European Parliament have championed for the framework to address the specific needs of Roma women, by involving them in the development of policies and stopping the practice of child marriages (European Parliament, 2011c). Such change cannot be imposed alone by decree for already national laws on marital age have failed to end this practice among very traditional but also marginalised Roma where exclusion has too often led to them withdrawing into cultural enclaves and stubbornly maintaining certain traditions as part of the cultural nexus that binds strong social networks that offer protection and reassurance in a hostile world. Such 'distancing' has for some traditional Roma communities extended to self-exclusion and or limited interaction with mainstream agencies and institutions. The framework also envisages major change in how Roma communities work and organise themselves economically and politically. It talks about micro credit schemes that will promote self-employment and entrepreneurialism (European Commission, 2011). Again, such economic strategies will mark huge shifts in behaviour and present major challenges especially for those families assimilated during Communist times into the industrial workforce, where traditional work practices became obsolete, and who in the transition to capitalism have endured intergenerational unemployment in industrial areas in the former Soviet Bloc. Such families have limited traditions of entrepreneurialism and a great deal of targeted support will be needed to rectify this. Likewise, the development of Roma NGOs, employment as mediators and participation in democratic and policy forums, including national elections, will also mark a major shift in behaviour for some Roma communities. As part of a process of change, communities will need to see the prospects of any Roma Framework and resulting national programme holding real benefits for their communities. This change and innovation needs to be carefully negotiated through a process of intercultural mediation. These arguments serve to further reinforce the need to ensure that there are inclusive mechanisms for service design and delivery in the Roma Framework and national integration strategies.

The Roma Framework does in fact envisage developing targeted services and approaches and the involvement of Roma staff/mediators in projects (European Commission, 2011). However, consideration may need to be given to other inclusive forms of service delivery such as 'personalisation' and 'co-production', which involve consultation and partnerships in the delivery of targeted services (Ryder, 2011). The European Commission (2011) indicates the potential for such alliances by acknowledging that there may be issues at local and national levels where governmental agencies may lack the expertise for a particular project as part of the national strategy. Therefore, member states should consider entrusting the management and implementation of some parts of their programme to intermediary bodies such as international organisations, regional development bodies, churches and religious organisations or communities as well as NGOs with proven experience in Roma integration. Social enterprise and cooperative ventures may also be means by which the bonding social capital of some Roma communities can be used as a resource, as it has been noted that such intense social networks can provide important foundations for such enterprises (see Chapter Six, this volume). Moreover, social enterprise can help to address community problems but also provide opportunities for employment in a manner that can reflect community aspirations.

A significant impediment to inclusive policy proposals (as outlined above) is the dearth of existing Roma community groups that are localised. In the UK, it has been noted that there are only about 20 Gypsy, Roma and Traveller community groups on the national Register of Charities despite having a Gypsy, Roma and Traveller population of 300,000 (Ryder and Greenfields, 2010). Similar observations can be made in other countries in the East and West of Europe. Furthermore, the development of Roma staff into effective community workers and service providers requires long-term support and mentoring, especially where formal education levels are low. If the number of Roma employed in community initiatives or partnerships between Roma community groups and service providers is to be increased then there is a pressing need for extensive resources to be applied to capacity building in the Roma third sector (Ryder, 2011). Thus, the EU and national governments need to ensure that funding is available for the development of such groups and that, where good practice exists, it is disseminated.

A number of community groups are effectively using 'positive action' approaches to train and develop Gypsy, Roma and Traveller staff who although lacking formal qualifications have a number of skills and qualities that can be used to help them develop into highly effective community workers (Ryder and Greenfields, 2010). Another option is to promote networks between local Roma groups where those that are established shadow and support the development of new groups as is the case with the UK National Federation of Gypsy Liaison Groups. Financial support for community group development is especially pressing as in the financial crisis a number of local Gypsy, Roma and Traveller NGOs are under acute financial pressure and some are in danger of ceasing their operations (Ryder et al, 2011). The Roma Framework needs to highlight and actively promote the approaches and partnerships outlined above that make use of active dialogue and partnerships and the 'positive action' employment and development of Roma community groups.

The Roma Framework notes that important monitoring roles will be performed from a range of groups, including the Fundamental Rights Agency, countries' own monitoring mechanisms, peer reviews as well as 'national contact points', which will be government agencies or civil servants (European Parliament, 2011b). The European Commission has stated that 'robust monitoring' processes should be in place. Communication will be facilitated by the Roma Task Group within the European Commission, which is to become a permanent internal body for focused discussion between directors in the relevant Commission Directorates-General (OSI, 2011, p 3). However, for the process of measuring the success of the Roma Framework and ensuring that the Commission is aware of progress made then clear channels of communication need to be developed with Roma communities in this process. The EU Roma Platform will be of use in this respect but something more localised will be needed not only to provide a clear picture of what is or is not happening in each of the 27 member states but also to enable Roma communities to play an active role with national, regional and local institutions in devising strategies to make the Roma Framework applicable to a particular member state. This is also of particular importance as has been noted above, as the Roma Framework envisages focused work in localised spaces (micro regions) of acute economic exclusion and segregation (European Commission, 2011).

Ongoing dialogue and partnerships between Roma groups and external institutions will be an important component in this process; indeed, the European Commission has stated that national strategies within the Roma Framework should 'be designed, implemented and monitored in close cooperation and continuous dialogue with Roma civil society, regional and local authorities' (European Commission, 2011, p 9). One means to involve Roma in the policy-making process is to support the establishment of negotiations with groups of Roma NGOs that will become partners of the authorities in policy formulation. Such structures could be established also at regional and local levels, ensuring that the voice of Roma communities is taken into account at all levels of decision making. Priorities should be set at a local level in the specific context of the community. In support of such localised initiatives we can quote the oft-used adage 'All politics is local'; this should be applied to the Roma Framework to make it relevant and meaningful to local Roma communities.

One means by which localised engagement can be promoted is by NGOs and governmental agencies seeking to consult and mediate through deliberative democracy – a concept centred on the notion of citizens and their representatives deliberating about problems and solutions in an environment that is conducive to reflection and a mutual willingness to understand the values, perspectives and interests of others. This involves the possibility of reframing their interests and perspectives in light of a joint search for common interests and mutually acceptable solutions (Lengyel, 2009). Thus, through local ad-hoc assemblies and focus groups, important insights on the Roma issue could be gained, which could complement those negotiations that will take place between Roma NGOs, representatives and governmental agencies. For some traditional Roma communities, such mechanisms for dialogue might be conducive forums to input into policy development and could build on the Kris – a tribunal instigated to deal with internal disputes and is adjudicated by Roma elders (Cahn, 2000). In the Kris, speeches for and against a course of action or judgement are made and attempts are sought to find consensus. As Acton notes when commenting on the Kalderash Kris, '[t]he ultimate legitimacy of the decision of the Kris is that it re-establishes consensus; it is a remarkably democratic institution' (cited in Cahn, 2000).

Another means to ensure that Roma are included in consultations is to stage panel reviews of national policies and the situation confronting Roma based on the deliberative policy development model of the panel review organised by the Travellers Aid Trust (TAT), which culminated in the report *A big or divided society? Final recommendations and report of the panel review into the impact of the Localism Bill and Coalition Government policy on Gypsies and Travellers* (Ryder et al, 2011). As was the case in the UK, such a panel review can combine and fuse deliberative democracy with more traditional forms of dialogue between NGOs and governmental actors. The panel was composed of a broad range of politicians from the main political parties including those in government and a number of established academics and legal experts who included Gypsies and Travellers. A majority of the participants presenting to the panel were Gypsies and Travellers, not just NGO activists but Gypsies and Travellers with no previous experience of political participation. Through the panel research and report, TAT hoped that a positive and constructive contribution would be made to wider debates, thus a wide range of stakeholders were invited to participate and it was hoped that the process would further dialogue and understanding (Ryder et al, 2011).

The panel review concept could therefore be replicated in EU member states and help in the design and delivery of the Roma Framework in individual member states. An important principle in ensuring that the views of the Roma Task Group/European Commission and 'national contacts points' are balanced with the views of the Roma community themselves is ensuring clear and transparent lines of communication between these entities and Roma society at all levels. The panel review model fulfils such criteria. An important way of ensuring that these deliberative panels reflect accurately the voice of Roma communities and reach and include key Roma voices is through the process being project managed, as in the UK, by NGOs that work for Gypsy, Roma and Traveller communities.

Conclusion

A key message in this chapter is that transparency and clear lines of communication are essential pillars of the EU Roma Framework, which to date have not been adequately mapped out. The EU is accused in many quarters, and not just by Roma interests, of being aloof and out of touch. An inclusive Roma Framework that empowers Roma communities and fosters inclusive policy development and partnerships could effectively address such criticisms but moreover present a model of good practice that the EU can replicate for other minority interests, thus leading to the development of informed and effective EU economic and social policy that adds to the cohesion and validity of the EU. Empowerment, transparency and the design of meaningful policies are key components that will contribute towards the formation of trust between Roma communities, NGOs and centres of power, which to date has all too often been lacking but which is an essential foundation on which social inclusion should be built for the Roma at local, national and European levels. Key to meaningful progress is the development of a democratic, grassroots Roma politics.

A key challenge that could undermine Roma participation and further mobilisation is the economic crisis. The Roma Framework has the potential to become an interventionist and targeted project requiring massive investment at European and national levels to achieve its stated aims. This contradicts the political realities on the ground where governments are limiting social services and cutting social expenditure (Richardson, 2010a). The EU Commissioner, László Andor, at the Sixth Roma Platform in Brussels in November 2011 described such political downgrading and sidelining as creating a 'social time bomb' that could explode at any moment (Andor, 2011). However, it has been noted that the EU has a budget of EUR 50 billion per year in Structural Funds to resolve structural economic and social problems. To date a negligible amount of these funds has targeted Roma; this failure carries wider costs as the cost of non-inclusion of Roma is also high in terms of welfare expenditure and non-productive workers (OSRI, 2011).

Another potential stumbling block is the level of racism among the wider population. It is important to emphasise that without the support of the majority population no significant policy change and implementation can be made as regards Roma. Here Roma participation in a range of forums outlined, and the emergence of new role models and advocates both locally and nationally, will have a fundamental role to play in persuading majority society of the need for the development of inclusive policies towards this minority. However, in addition to persuasion, another instrument that needs to be considered is enforcement. A key challenge will be the determination displayed by the European Commission in intervention against the member states that are reluctant to devise Roma integration strategies or contravene European equality conventions. Making the receipt of European funding conditional on achieving Roma Framework goals could be imperative. Debates as to the need for greater central direction and intervention in the face of EU member state recalcitrance but correspondingly fears of the issue being 'Europeanised' with member states abdicating responsibility, will no doubt be shaped by the success or failure of the Roma Framework. However, in these debates sight should not be lost of the vital importance of involving Roma. This discussion ultimately brings into play concepts of minority rights and the role of governmental agencies in protecting the interests of minorities, issues that are discussed in more depth in the final chapter of this volume.

Notes

[1] In January 2011, a Romanian MP submitted a Bill to the Parliament proposing the use of the denomination 'tigan', a highly pejorative term in the Romanian language, instead of 'Roma' in order to avoid confusions between the Roma and Romanians. This Bill generated a controversy as to who has the right to decide on the denomination of the ethnic group, involving the Parliament, Government, Romanian Academy, research institutes and human rights groups and ended up in the courts of law. From the democratic theory point of view, this issue should be decided by the minority itself, which should have a veto over its own denomination.

[2] The concept of discrete and insular minorities was developed by the United States (US) Supreme Court in the case *United States v Carolene Products*. The case concerned the federal regulation of milk content. The Supreme Court decided that it is the duty of the legislative branch to regulate interstate commerce and even if it chose to set minimal standards for milk quality, the judicial branch should not interfere. However, in footnote 4, it asserted that in non-economic regulation cases, the Court might adopt a higher level of scrutiny when cases concern rights of a non-economic nature such as those under the First 10 Amendments, political rights, or legislation directed at discrete and insular minorities. Based on this provision, the Supreme Court used the strict scrutiny test in subsequent cases, protecting the integrity of the political process or involving 'suspect' classification, such as race, creed or religion, examining statutes that had the potential to abridge individual liberties (*United States v Carolene Products*, 304 U.S. 144 Footnote 4 (1938)).

Part Three

Conclusions

Conclusion and next steps: inclusion, space and empowerment for Gypsies, Roma and Travellers?

Joanna Richardson and Andrew Ryder

This book set out to examine a range of issues affecting Gypsies and Travellers (such as accommodation, health, education, social policy and employment). Throughout the chapters we explored cross-cutting challenges, including social inclusion, discursive control, media power, representation, empowerment, justice and contested spaces. We conducted our analysis in a reflexive way, asking about the place of the researcher (Chapter Nine) and exploring power relationships in the representation of Gypsy and Traveller communities and the issues relating to them (Chapters Seven and Eight). There are a number of ideas weaving in and out of the specific and cross-cutting issues that this book has sought to examine. In this conclusion we select some of the prominent themes identified throughout.

Challenges of policy reform

Policy reform under the Coalition Government saw a coupling of localism with a process of marketisation: services are put through processes of commissioning, potentially undermining strategic decision making and local democracy. Localism appeals to notions of individualism, the free market and laissez-faire social policy and belief that these reforms will be cost cutting: an attractive proposition in an age of deficit reduction (Carswell and Hannan, 2008). The vacuums that are left are to be filled by forms of 19th-century philanthropism, volunteerism and welfare strategies based on business models, which constitute the 'Big Society' or what could equally be termed the 'small state'. The conclusions drawn in this book (particularly in Part One) are that Gypsies, Roma and Travellers could be further marginalised in this policy framework, by virtue of the fact that at present they lack the resources to take advantage of opportunities to deliver services or in light of a lack of popular support and understanding are unlikely to feature prominently or favourably in any localist-driven social policy agenda in a particular community. These issues of localism, public service commissioning agenda, choice, personalisation of services and individual budgets cut across a number of service areas, and the discussion on health, education and social care in Chapters Three, Four and Five demonstrated the impact that these changes in public services may have for Gypsies and Travellers, as well as discussing the opportunities, provided there is good leadership in public services, and partnership with Gypsies and Travellers, for improvements to be made.

Gypsies, Roma and Travellers are systematically disadvantaged and have little bargaining power (Chapter Eleven). As noted in a number of chapters in this book, the Coalition Government reforms offer some opportunities for Gypsies, Roma and Travellers to potentially have a greater say in policies and services that affect them but these opportunities will be limited by the weak state of the Gypsy and Traveller third sector (Chapters Seven and Eight). Overall, the threats and challenges are great; the dismantling of strategic decision-making bodies in planning and health, and the fragmentation of Traveller Education Services, could do much to undermine the interests of Gypsies, Roma and Travellers (Chapters Three and Four). This is most clearly reflected with regard to the question of Traveller sites, where greater powers in the planning system and the ability to initiate referenda could do much to thwart site provision (Chapter Two). In the following section we focus on Gypsies and Travellers but then widen the discussion to include the experiences of Roma communities in the rest of Europe and reflect on a number of global themes.

Let us legislate for 'reality' rather than 'perception' – the problem of 'fairness'

Running through the political reforms, in particular with regard to Gypsies and Travellers, are perceptions of 'fairness'. Fairness in this particular discourse does not seem to rely on fairness of outcome but instead on 'all things being equal' and treating everyone the same, regardless of need and existing disadvantage. Statements by government ministers and departmental press releases have raised the spectre that previous policies on Gypsies and Travellers were somehow unfair and damaged community relations by causing resentment on the part of the settled community to the advantages that the planning system allegedly gave to Gypsies and Travellers. A press release from the Department for

Communities and Local Government (DCLG, 2011) stated: 'the old planning rules created a *perception* of special treatment for some groups, undermining the notion of fair play in the planning system and further harming community cohesion' (emphasis added).

In one parliamentary debate, the following sentiments as to the planning system and Gypsies and Travellers were raised: 'There is anger in the country.... There is a view that there is one law for the settled community and another for Gypsies and Travellers' (Williamson, 2010). In the same debate, another Member of Parliament argued there was a 'two-tier system – a parallel track, with one side for those who play by the rules and another for those who seek to flout them' (Patel, 2010). These arguments seem to reject notions of positive action but also offer a skewed analysis of fairness and equality.

'It's political correctness gone mad!'

The Human Rights Act (HRA) has assumed the role of a villain and has been cast as an instrument that has unfairly privileged Gypsies and Travellers by supporting unauthorised encampments and developments (Richardson and Ryder, 2009a). The Coalition Government is reviewing the Act, but it cannot easily scrap human rights obligations within it, because they are based on the European Convention for Human Rights and thus a core component of British European Union (EU) membership. However, there is talk that a Bill of Rights may downgrade the role of the Act in British domestic law. The lack of popular support for the Act is a cause for concern, given that the Council of Europe has noted that: 'Our common future depends on our ability to safeguard and develop human rights, as enshrined in the European Convention on Human Rights, democracy and the rule of law and to promote mutual understanding' (Council of Europe, 2008, p 4).

The public need to accept that Gypsies and Travellers have been able to invoke human rights arguments where inequality and site under-provision is clearly evident. Under rules of proportionality, the interests of the settled community are also protected and sites have failed in the planning process under proportionality where the inconvenience to wider communities and damage to the environment of a Gypsy Traveller site is considered to be of greater interest. Again, such a process of education and persuasion is not simple given the sustained invective against what is depicted as an EU tyranny of 'political correctness' (Wilson and Bloomfield, 2010). However, such battles do need to be fought and won if more liberal notions of minority rights are to prevail and counteract the hegemony of a neoliberal narrative.

Going local

A fundamental weakness and moral flaw of localism (seen through the lens of Gypsy and Traveller needs) is that the weak and vulnerable in society will be left in some cases to the mercy of local majorities that have little care or regard for unpopular or politically weak minorities or interests (Chapter One). Hence, alongside opposition to Traveller sites, some communities will choose to oppose wind farms, care homes, affordable housing and so forth for a number of self-interested or prejudicial decisions (Chapter Two discussed the challenges to new planning development). This scenario, which reflects the notion that the views of the majority in a local area should always be of ultimate import, can be questioned on the grounds that it can conflict with the interests of the 'greater good' – a principle that is accepted by many when applied to transport, energy and environmental protection (Parvin, 2011) but not so readily when applied to minority interests, in particular the needs of Gypsies and Travellers. Here local majorities can form a tyranny and be driven by prejudices that can deny a minority fundamental rights such as a decent place to live and access to services (Fung, 2002). This is a fear noted by the Communities and Local Government Select Committee inquiry into localism:

> A range of organisations representing the interests of vulnerable, marginalised or minority groups expressed fears that a decentralised system in which 'bureaucratic accountability' mechanisms had been dismantled would leave services for such groups at the mercy of the vagaries of local politics and funding choices made under the pressure of cuts. (DCLG Select Committee, 2011, point 59)

There is therefore the potential for illiberal actions in localism if one accepts that an important part of the liberal tradition is the protection of minority rights. As Parvin (2009, p 354) notes:

> [T]he centralisation of decision making power also fulfils another function of liberal democratic political systems – namely the protection of minority groups from the tyranny of the majority ... liberal democratic principles may not always be best served by devolving decision making power

down to local communities because it is entirely possible that local communities might use this power to enact policies or initiatives that violate liberal principles and make the lives of certain members worse.

However, such notions of liberalism are increasingly being questioned by both the Left and Right where emphasis has been placed on an 'integration' agenda that has rejected multiculturalism and instead placed an emphasis on notions of 'Britishness' and conformity (Chapter One). One criticism of this approach is that it has classified separation (ghettoisation) as a product of personal choice and cultural bonds but has neglected the role of racism, poverty and inequality leading to some communities forming cultural enclaves for protection and security or by having no other choice.

Localists might well respond to criticism of their ideal communities, which are shaped and formed by the majority of inhabitants residing there, that if some are unhappy in such communities then they can just move to a community where they feel happier, as was espoused by the classical liberal thinker Nozick (1974), who with his conceptions of the minimalist state laid the foundation for localism. Aside from such an approach 'ghettoising' minorities where they are forced to huddle together in greater numbers to secure the rights and treatments they aspire, it further puts a brake on fair policies towards minorities as local authorities will be discouraged from being fair by the fear that their area will attract greater numbers of such minorities than say a neighbouring authority that is not driven by an equalities or fairness agenda. This 'honey pot' effect, as it is termed, is well known with regard to Gypsy and Traveller issues, where local authorities claimed that those in the past who did provide sites took on the responsibilities that neighbouring authorities were failing to provide for their local Gypsy and Traveller populations, who thus went to the areas where sites were being built. Such a picture of ghettoised and 'lottery code' communities is thus an aspect of localism that needs to be considered more carefully by its proponents in terms of fairness and social inclusion but also community cohesion. Local communities thwarting or opting out of national projects or ideals based on protection and care for minorities and the vulnerable hold the potential to trigger a great deal of discord and conflict. It was to avoid such conflict and to break the log jam of nimbyist opposition to strategic projects that notions of civic leadership were accepted in the past where councillors, for example, were prepared to face and oppose the views of the majority in the interests of a greater good.

Empowerment and justice: the need for governance and leadership

Firm and strong civic leadership, not afraid to challenge prejudice or take seemingly unpopular decisions for the greater good, has been recognised as a key component in Traveller site delivery (Richardson, 2007a). Chapter Seven of this book sought to examine the extent to which Gypsies and Travellers were empowered in society, and whether there was justice when things went wrong. However, it was found that in many cases, past and present civic leadership has buckled and backtracked in the face of strong local opposition to sites and more generally to Gypsies and Travellers in public, political and media discourse (Chapter Ten). Hence, although strong and central safeguards are needed to deliver equality, it can only be guaranteed if a process of public persuasion and education can also take place in tandem. The regional strategies attempted this by placing a strong emphasis on dialogue and consultation on site delivery and some notable converts were made in particular at councillor level; but this dialogue often failed to percolate and inform communities at a grassroots level (Ryder et al, 2011).

Such a process of percolation may be a long-term proposition involving more positive images in the media and the school curriculum; but it is also for Gypsies and Travellers to be known and to be accepted in communities (Chapters Eight and Ten). However, such persuasion and mind-changing processes cannot take place in the short term or even before a site is built; in some cases civic leadership may have to force through site development measures in the courageous hope and belief that they are doing the right and humane thing and that with time local populations will accept such need (Richardson, 2007a). Part of this process involves accepting elements of positive action but also human rights principles. Where special mechanisms exist on site delivery these should not be viewed as an unfair advantage but instead as a form of 'positive action' that is enabling Gypsies and Travellers to catch up and for the huge inequality of under-provision of sites to be addressed (Richardson, 2011b). Such mechanisms should be viewed as part of a minority rights framework where the state recognises that for minorities to receive protection and equality then special frameworks can be warranted. Positive action measures, awareness raising, community employment, empowerment and targeted measures have featured strongly in the good practice alluded to in this book but will be vulnerable in a localist framework that appears to be harnessed to major cutbacks and the fragmentation of strategic interventions and governance in health, education, accommodation and wider social policy.

Local democracy and central safeguards and interventions are not always or necessarily at odds. Empowered participatory governance (Fung and Wright, 2001) can create public buy-in and support and tailoring of policy to meet local needs and circumstance. It creates space to be informed by expert local knowledge, which can be combined with a form of centralism that ensures that marginalised groups' needs and aspirations are taken account of. It is a form of governance that provides space and scope for local voices and aspirations but within a framework that provides safeguards and protection, and ultimately a role for central power if those guaranteed standards are infringed. This is a model that could be applied successfully to social policy for Gypsy, Roma and Traveller communities (and in a wider context) at both national and European levels, with those who are the focus of policy being given effective involvement in the design and delivery of services.

Such a participatory role for Gypsies, Roma and Travellers will necessitate new forms of representation and interaction (Chapter Eight) with wider communities. Ideas on identity within and between a range of diverse Gypsy and Traveller groups, a process of ethnogenesis (Chapters Seven and Eleven), raise profound questions with regard to identity and what social inclusion means and whether it reflects the aspirations and interests of Gypsy, Roma and Traveller groups.

A new future in Europe?

Many of the arguments presented in the United Kingdom (UK) about the struggle and conflict between localism and laissez-faire social policy can also be projected onto debates in the wider sphere of Europe. Here debates are being waged as to the role of governments and the European Union in reversing Roma exclusion, with some sections of the political elite hesitant or loath to see the state embark on more dynamic and interventionist measures, and in some cases bending to localised and reactionary pressures and embracing and orchestrating populist arguments where the Roma are blamed for their own misfortune as part of a moral underclass discourse that pathologises Roma exclusion. In such a policy discourse, Roma often find themselves cast as passive subjects in paternalist and rigid forms of social policy, which fail to empower and provide new opportunities and directions. A challenge to such approaches could be presented by the European Framework for National Roma Integration Strategies (hereafter referred to as 'the Roma Framework').

The Roma Framework presents a model of where central authority can be a force of good, but although it is interventionist and the prospect has been raised for intervention where states err in their responsibilities for Roma, it is not overtly prescriptive. Much scope is placed on the formulation of localised and regional initiatives under the framework where Roma communities are given a say in the design of measures to alleviate exclusion and the prospect is raised for dynamic partnerships with service providers and local and national centres of power (Chapter Eleven). Again drawing a parallel with social policy in Britain, failure in the past in part stemmed from policies being imposed on Gypsies and Travellers that constituted in effect a form of assimilation, which led to these templates for conformity being despised and/or rejected and the sites where they were placed being labelled as reservations (Chapter Two).

Change may necessitate a paradigm shift from global neoliberalism and what has been described as the 'race to the bottom' in which nation states reduce welfare and intervention to make themselves more competitive and attractive to investors (Chomsky, 2000). Evidence suggests that the adoption of neoliberal economic policies in Central and Eastern Europe has come at a high price for Roma communities now confronted with the legacy of deindustrialisation, namely mass unemployment but also the role of scapegoat. An alternative is presented in 'global responsibility', which is embedded in social justice and human rights. It is a worldview that seeks to promote responsible citizenship worldwide, based on the principles of solidarity, subsidiarity, the dignity of the human person and the common good, and offers a global counter-hegemonic discourse (Richardson, 2011b). In this context the Roma Framework could offer a solution.

At the launch of the Roma Framework the Vice President of the European Commission, Viviane Reding, described the framework as 'beyond all expectations' and declared that '[t]his is a beginning of a new future' (EU Presidency, 2011). There are long-held dreams of a 'new future' for the Roma, but these visions have foundered either being based on assimilationist templates or lacking resources and political commitment (Chapter Eleven). The framework, despite criticism of a lack of consultation and involvement in its design by Roma communities, has been applauded by Roma civil society as an opportunity to reverse the profound levels of exclusion and discrimination endured by this group (ERRC, 2011b).

However, there are forces at play that are moving in the opposite direction and Europe could witness the accentuation of Roma exclusion. The financial crisis is leading to cuts in welfare services

(Richardson, 2010a) and interventionist social strategies across Europe, leaving the prospect that the Roma integration strategies as envisaged by the European Commission may be somewhat shallow and out of sync with desired social policy aims at a European level. Solutions will also be weakened by EU member states working within a flexible framework to meet general but poorly defined goals. A failure of policy will ensure that the cycle of Roma exclusion characterised by the most marginalised living in crippling poverty, in effect third-world conditions, with some living in shanty towns, segregated ghettoised communities or on the side of the road in a caravan, will continue.

The authors of this volume would argue that local dialogue and caring communities need to be balanced and given some direction by national or European governmental agencies willing to offer strong intervention to protect the interests of the vulnerable and excluded and promote equality. Acceptance of this 'Rawlsian' notion or social contract based on justice (Rawls, 1971) is a central feature of finding effective and inclusive social policy responses on the Gypsy, Roma and Traveller issue in the 21st century in both the UK and Europe. A lack of direction and intervention on the Roma issue at a European level could stall Roma inclusion. Likewise, EU members will not make reasonable progress without a degree of unison. European states may resist action if they sense that their neighbours are lagging behind and persecution and continuing exclusion of Roma communities in certain states will prompt migrations on a scale that could destabilise other states' relations and policies towards Roma. Thus, as the authors have demonstrated in discussion of material related to the UK, a localist, or state-by-state, approach where problems are ignored, action is not taken or misconceptions challenged will mean that the consequences will be profound for Gypsy, Roma and Traveller communities but also for the nature and the sense of justice entwined with European society and identity, which has sought to reflect the ideals of the 'social contract'.

Marginalisation and exclusion

It is evident that the financial crisis had led to doubts and insecurities in the political and economic establishment, hence some have been drawn to scapegoating rather than assisting Gypsies, Roma and Travellers. The increased desire for old and new 'folk devils' to act as a focus of anxiety and blame has seen age-old stereotypes against the Roma revived and mobilised for political ends (Chapter Ten; Richardson, 2006). Acute poverty in some cases leads to Roma appearing to conform to these stereotypes of deviancy and criminality but such superficial analysis pathologises poverty and fails to place it in a coherent context of limited life chances and profound anti-Gypsyism in European society. Hate discourse is taking ever-more sinister manifestations as is evidenced by Far Right pogroms and other hate campaigns. However, such invective and attack are not just confined to the Far Right: they are also taking root in what is considered the political centre and popular public opinion. Hence, for Gypsy, Roma and Traveller communities in Europe, the future rather than offering a new and promising future could merely repeat previous narratives of demonisation and exclusion.

If this scenario follows then exclusion is likely to be accentuated by self-exclusion by Gypsy, Roma and Traveller communities where distancing and alternative life strategies will be devised by those living at the margins (Chapter Seven). Individuals also exclude themselves from their own culture and identity because of past trauma in the social care system (Chapter Five). Gypsies, Roma and Travellers are also excluded from accessing services that many people take for granted, either through lack of a place to settle and call home or through discrimination from the wider community. Exclusion from a range of public services can result in poor health (Chapter Three), low educational attainment (Chapter Four) and difficulty finding employment (Chapter Six). Faced with such challenges it is likely that many Gypsies, Roma and Travellers will, as has been the case so often in the past, look to themselves for support and active solutions. However, the opportunities for such manoeuvrability are reduced given the growing crisis within the 'Traveller Economy' and self-employment and entrepreneurial mechanisms, once so strongly evident in Gypsy and Traveller communities in Britain, are steadily being undermined by a shortage of sites, a problem accentuated by an inability to upgrade skills as a consequence of educational exclusion (Chapter Six) – a problem that exists on an even greater scale on the continent where assimilationist policies have broken Roma entrepreneurial traditions. Exclusion for Gypsies, Roma and Travellers, as with other vulnerable minorities, holds the danger of them looking too much to themselves and their own for protection, forming cultural enclaves further cut off from wider society and through a form of reactive identity actually contributing to isolation through self-exclusion.

Spatial exclusion or 'ghettoisation' for Gypsies, Roma and Travellers has been a byproduct of exclusion and policy and has compounded isolation. These communities, be they in isolated rural sites or sites occupying marginal space located in deprived areas and/or adjacent to waste, industrial areas, rivers and railway lines, acquire reputations as dangerous places, and thus may become ghettoes where 'dangerous classes' are formed (Mee and Dowling, 2000). The occupation of marginal space has led to the 'othering' of this minority (Kendall, 1997). In such discourses the 'space' itself rather than structural factors is identified as the culprit for exclusion in a form of spatial 'determinism' that links exclusion to a dysfunctional and deviant localised culture (Gough et al, 2006). The localist agenda, which gives undue influence to local communities to determine how many sites should be developed and where they should be located, is likely to add to this cycle of segregation (Chapter Two).

Hooks (1991) argued that being located at the margins of society can provide some advantage for the excluded as 'spaces of radical openness' can be formed, more removed from the gaze of dominant society. Thus, excluded communities occupying 'marginal space' can more readily form an ideology of resistance. The identification of certain spaces as theirs is a prominent element in the construction of Gypsy and Traveller identity. Gypsies who occupy their own land often argue that such occupancy enables them to escape the interference and loss of autonomy that residency on a local authority site brings; likewise nomadism as practised through the occupancy of unauthorised encampments is also cherished by some as an accommodation and lifestyle choice that can bring freedom and cultural independence.

On the other hand, such lifestyle choices have in recent years increased the chance of conflict with wider society as Gypsies and Travellers have increasingly been compelled to launch retrospective planning applications to live on their own land or occupy prominent public spaces on account of the growing shortage of unused land and greater regulation that land is now subjected to. The use of space by Gypsies and Travellers in such a way can be deemed to present a challenge to 'majoritarian' society, which has led to an increase over the last 30 years in draconian measures to curb these lifestyle choices (Richardson, 2006a). For others, greater control over lifestyle has been imposed through the regulations attendant with local authority sites or the assimilation that has befallen many Gypsies and Travellers who have entered into housing because of the shortage of sites and curbs on nomadism (Shelter, 2007). Spatial exclusion, along with the lack of cultural manoeuvrability this incorporates, is one of the most distressing dimensions of exclusion for Gypsies, Roma and Travellers and one of the greatest challenges for decision makers is matching the rhetoric of 'mixed communities' by developing Traveller sites or inclusive Roma accommodation that facilitates interaction and friendships with the wider community. Eradicating spatial and resulting service segregation is one of the biggest issues that needs to be addressed if social inclusion and acceptance of Gypsy, Roma and Traveller communities in the UK and Europe is to be achieved.

An important issue to consider in terms of social policy is that the programme offered to Gypsies, Roma and Travellers should reflect their aspirations. Thus, a strong case needs to be made for Gypsy, Roma and Traveller involvement in the design and delivery of policy and research (Chapters Six and Nine). In this sense the message of the 'Big Society' is of use but as noted the resources have not been supplied to make such involvement a reality for a broad range of groups but especially the most vulnerable (Chapters Seven and Eleven). As argued in this volume, innovative services and partnerships based on co-production, intercultural mediation, partnerships with third sector groups, mutualism and deliberative policy all hold the potential to create dynamic and inclusive models for progression and participation in services, economic activity and decision making.

Identity

An inclusive and flexible social policy regime would clearly have implications for Gypsy, Roma and Traveller identity and improve on the past trauma experienced by those who have had their identity taken away during their experiences of social care (Chapter Five). If unfettered by external restraint and pressure, then Gypsies, Roma and Travellers will be free to make choices and adaptations that will enable them to retain what they consider to be the best of their culture in a way that maintains and enhances economic, cultural and social capital. Such a process will create a strong and viable form of identity that can effectively challenge and counter discrimination. For some, this ideal policy context would reflect traditional aspirations and bolster cultural practices such as self-employment, entrepreneurialism, nomadism and dwelling in caravans (Chapter Six). At the same time, constructive and beneficial relations with the state and wider society will facilitate intercultural dialogue and partnership, creating an environment that is conducive for new and innovative forms of adaptation (Chapter Nine).

This intercultural and adaptive process might witness an ever-greater number of Gypsies, Roma and Travellers accessing higher education and entering into professional occupations in a form that would enable them to retain their identity. Such processes as evidenced in this volume may also lead to greater equalisation of gender roles among Gypsies, Roma and Travellers, leading to more women taking on new and dynamic roles as economic entrepreneurs, service providers and community advocates. If social policy moves in the opposite direction then the danger of assimilation will increase but also conflict and resistance, leading for some to greater levels of distancing and the formation of rigid and 'reactive' identities, but will also act as a clear indicator of the existence of a divided and unequal society.

Dream for the future

The UK educationalist Arthur Ivatts OBE describes Gypsies, Roma and Travellers:

> ... as the jewel in the European crown.... If the non Roma/ Gypsy peoples of Europe can come to terms with their wilful race hatred, persecution and discrimination of the Roma/Gypsies, then the peoples of Europe together as a mixed, but racially unified society, will be well equipped to face the new and challenging social and racial demands of globalism. (Ivatts, 2005, p 1)

The experiences of Gypsy, Roma and Traveller communities, as outlined in this volume, suggest that British and European public policy and social policy face huge challenges in that test. While we do not suggest that the period under the New Labour government was a 'golden age' for Gypsies and Travellers in Britain, there are challenges presented by the cumulative effect of policy measures brought in by the Conservative-led Coalition Government. There are initiatives within a European framework, but these could be stronger and we must recognise the impact of the economic crisis (Richardson, 2010a) on the ability of national governments to deliver European programmes.

The authors hope that they have made some meaningful contributions to these important debates affecting Gypsies, Roma and Travellers in Britain and Europe. Our dream for the future, as the title of the book suggests, is that Gypsies, Roma and Travellers will be afforded accommodation, empowerment and inclusion in British (and European) society.

References

ACERT (Advisory Committee for the Education of Romany and other Travellers) (2011) Angela Overington's contribution to ACERT AGM, 24 September, online at: http://acert.org.uk/agm-2011-angela-overington.html.

Ackerman, B. (1985) 'Beyond Carolene Products', *Harvard Law Review*, vol. 98, no 4, pp 720-22.

Acton, T. (1974) *Gypsy politics and social change*, London: Routledge and Kegan Paul.

Acton T.A. (1985) 'Gypsy education: at the crossroads', *Special Education: Journal of the National Council for Special Education*, vol 12, no 1.

Acton, T. (ed) (1997) *Gypsy politics and Traveller identity*, Hatfield: University of Hertfordshire Press.

Acton, T.A. (2004) 'Modernity, culture and Gypsies: Is there a meta-scientific method for understanding the representation of Gypsies? And do the Dutch really exist?', in N. Saul and S. Tebbutt (eds) *The role of the Romanies: Images and counter-images of Gypsies/Romanies in European cultures*, Liverpool: Liverpool University Press, pp 98-116.

Acton, T. (2007) 'Human rights as a perspective on entitlements: the debate over gypsy fairs in England', in M. Hayes and T. Acton (eds) *Travellers, Gypsies, Roma: The demonisation of difference*, Newcastle-Upon-Tyne: Cambridge Scholars Press.

Acton T.A. (2010) 'Is tradition the enemy of history?', in L. Orta (ed) *Mapping the invisible: EU-Roma Gypsies*, London: Black Dog Publishing, pp 20-23.

Acton T.A. and Kenrick D.S. (1991) 'From summer voluntary to European Community bureaucracy: the development of special provision for Traveller education in the United Kingdom since 1967', *European Journal of Intercultural Studies*, vol 1, no 3, pp 47-62.

Ahmad, W. (2000) *Ethnicity, disability and chronic illness*, Buckingham: Open University Press.

Andor, L. (2011) *Getting Member States to draw up their Roma Integration Strategies – Opening of Roma Platform*, Sixth meeting of the European Roma Platform Brussels, 17 November (EU Speech/PressRelease), online at: http://europa.eu/rapid/pressReleasesAction.do?reference=SPEECH/11/771&amp&aged=0&language=en&guiLanguage=en.

Andrews, E. (2009) 'Want to see a GP – Gipsies come first as NHS tells doctors travellers must be seen at once' , The *Mail Online*, online at: www.dailymail.co.uk/news/article-1193810/Want-GP-Gipsies-come-NHS-tells-doctors-travellersseen-straight-away.html#ixzz0PlCE0eRj.

Anthias, F. and Yuval Davis, N. (1992) *Racialised boundaries*, London, Routledge.

Arnstberg, K. (1998) 'Gypsies and social work in Sweden', in Williams C., Soydan, H. and Johnson, M. (eds) *Social work and minorities*, London: Routledge.

Arnstein, S. (1969) 'A ladder of citizen participation', *Journal of the American Institute of Planners*, vol 35, no 4, pp 216-24.

Atkin, K. and Chattoo, S. (2006) 'Approaches to conducting research', in J. Nazroo (ed) *Health and social research in multiethnic societies*, Abingdon: Routledge, pp 95-115.

Auswind (Australian Wind Energy Association) (2007) *Wind farms and landscape values: Foundation Report*, online at: www.cleanenergycouncil.org.au.

Avebury, E. (2005) House of Lords Debate, 23 March, *Hansard*, col 299.

Bachrach, P. and Baratz, M.S. (1970) *Power and poverty, theory and practice*, New York: Oxford University Press.

Badman, G. (2009) *Report to the Secretary of State on the Review of Elective Home Education in England*, London: HMSO.

Ballard, R. and Ballard, C. (1977) 'The Sikhs: the development of South Asian settlements in Britain', in J.L Watson (ed) *Between two cultures*, Oxford: Wiley-Blackwell.

Bancroft, A. (2005) *Roma and Gypsy-Travellers in Europe: Modernity, race, space and exclusion*, Avebury: Ashgate Press.

Barany, Z. (2002) *The East European Gypsies: Regime change, marginality and ethnopolitics*, Cambridge: Cambridge University Press.

Barth, F. (ed) (1969) *Ethnic groups and boundaries: The social organization of culture difference*, Oslo: Universitetsforlaget.

Barth, F. (1975) 'The social organisation of a pariah group in Norway', in E.F. Rehfisch (ed) *Gypsies, tinkers and other Travellers*, London: Academic Press.

Barthes, R. (1977) *Selected writings introduced by Susan Sontag*, London: Jonathan Cape Ltd.

Bartlett, J. (2009) 'Getting more for less: efficiency in the public sector', London: Demos, online at: www.demos.co.uk/files/Getting_more_for_less.pdf?1248779976 (11 September).

Battu, H. and Mwale, M. (2004) 'Ethnic enclaves and employment in England and Wales', Centre for European Labour Market Research Discussion Paper.

BBC News (2003) 'Boys guilty of killing "Gypsy"', 23 November, online at: http://news.bbc.co.uk.

Bellamy, R. (1993) 'Liberalism', in R. Eatwell and A. Wright (eds) *Contemporary political ideologies*, London: Allen and Unwin.

Belton, B. (2010) 'Knowing Gypsies', in D. Le Bas and T. Acton (eds) *All change: Romani studies through Romani eyes*, Hatfield: University of Hertfordshire Press.

Belton, B. (2005) *Gypsy and Traveller ethnicity: The social generation of an ethnic phenomenon*, London: Routledge..

Bennett, M. (1998) *Basic concepts of intercultural communication*, Boston: Intercultural Press.

Bentham, J. S. (1987) *Utilitarianism and other essays*, London: Penguin Classics.

Bentley, T. and Gurumurthy, R. (1999) *Destination unknown: Engaging with the problems of marginalised youth,* London: DEMOS.

Berger, P. and Luckmann, T. (1966) *The social construction of reality: A treatise in the sociology of knowledge*, Harmondsworth: Penguin.

Bhopal, K. (2000) *Working towards inclusive education: Aspects of good practice for Gypsy Traveller children*, International Centre for Intercultural Studies Institute of Education, University of London.

Bhopal, K. and Myers, M. (2010) *Insiders, outsiders and others: Gypsies and identity*, Hatfield: University of Hertfordshire Press.

Bíró, A. (2011) 'The price of Roma integration', unpublished text presented at the conference 'The Price of Roma Integration', Snagov, Romania, 22 September.

Blackburn, H., Hanley, B. and Staley, K. (2010) *Turning the pyramid upside down: Examples of public involvement in social care research*, Eastleigh: INVOLVE/NIHR.

Blair, T. (1996) Speech to Labour Party Conference.

Blakemore, K. and Giggs, E. (2007) *Social policy: An introduction*, New York, NY: Open University Press.

Blaxter, M. (1990) *Health and lifestyles*, London: Routledge.

Blunkett, D. (1999) 'Excellence for the many, not just the few: raising standards and extending opportunities in our schools', Speech to the Confederation of British Industry, 19 July.

Bourdieu, P. (1986) 'The forms of capital', in J.G. Richardson (ed) *Handbook of theory and research for the sociology of education,* New York: Greenwood Press.

Bourdieu, P. and Wacquant, L.J.D. (1992) *An invitation to reflexive sociology*, Chicago: University of Chicago Press.

Bourne, J. (2006) *In defense of multiculturalism*, Institute for Race Relations Briefing, Paper No 2.

Bowers, J (no date) *Prejudice and pride: The experiences of young Travellers in Cambridgeshire*, Cambridgeshire: Ormiston Children and Families Trust.

Briscoe, B. (2007) *The road ahead: Final report of the Independent Task Group on Site Provision and Enforcement for Gypsies and Travellers*, London: Communities and Local Government.

Brown, P. and Scullion, L. (2009) 'Doing research with Gypsies and Travellers: reflections on experience and practice', *Community Development Journal*, vol 45, no 2, pp 169-85.

Brown, P. and Niner, P. (2009) *Assessing local housing authorities: Progress in meeting the accommodation needs of Gypsy and Traveller Communities in England*, Equality and Human Rights Commission.

Brunner, E. (1997) 'Socioeconomic determinants of health: stress and the biology of inequality', *BMJ*, vol 314, p 1472.

Brunner, E. and Marmot, M. (1999) 'Social organization, stress and health', in M. Marmot and R.G. Wilkinson (eds) *Social determinants of health*, Oxford: Oxford University Press.

Buck, S. (1998) *The global commons: An introduction*, Washington: Island Press.

Burchardt, T., Le Grand, J. and Piachaud, D. (1999) 'Social exclusion in Britain 1991–1995', *Social Policy and Administration*, vol 33, no 3, pp 227-44.

Cabinet Office (2010) *Inclusion health: Evidence pack*, London.

Cahn, C. (2000) *Nexus: Domestic violence, Romani courts and recognition*, ERRC, online at: www.errc.org/cikk.php?cikk=644.

Cahn, C. (2007) 'The unseen powers: perception, stigma and Roma rights', ERRC, 20 November.

Cameron, D. (2011) 'PM's speech on Big Society', 15 February, online at: www.number10.gov.uk.

Carswell, D. (2007) 'Open Democracy', *The Localist Papers*, no 6, London: Centre for Policy Studies, online at: www.douglascarswell.com/upload/upload8.pdf.

Carswell, D. and Hannan, D. (2008) *The plan: Twelve months to renew Britain*, London: Carswell.

Cemlyn, S. (2000a) 'Assimilation, control, mediation or advocacy? Social work dilemmas in providing anti-oppressive services for Traveller children and families', *Child and Family Social Work*, vol 5, no 4, pp 327-41.

Cemlyn, S. (2000b) 'From neglect to partnership? Challenges for social services in promoting the welfare of Traveller children' *Child Abuse Review*, vol 9, no 5, pp 349-63..

Cemlyn, S. and Briskman, L. (2002) 'Social welfare within a hostile state', *Social Work Education*, vol 21, no 1, pp 49-69.

Cemlyn, S., Greenfields, M., Burnett, S., Matthews, Z. and Whitwell, C. (2009) *Inequalities experienced by Gypsy and Traveller communities: a review*, Research Report No 12, London: Equality and Human Rights Commission.

Children, Schools and Families Committee (2009) *Looked after children*, London: HMSO.

Chomsky, N. (2000) 'Globalization and its discontents: Noam Chomsky debates with *Washington Post* readers', *Washington Post*, 16 May, online at: www.chomsky.info/debates/200000516.htm.

Clark, K. and Drinkwater, S. (2002) 'Enclaves, neighbourhood effects and employment outcomes: ethnic minorities in England and Wales', *Journal of Population Economics*, vol 15, no 1, pp 5-29.

Clark, C. and Greenfields, M. (2006) *Here to stay: The Gypsies and Travellers of Britain*, Hatfield: University of Hertfordshire Press.

Clark, C. and Ó'hAodha, M. (2000) 'We were the First Greens: Irish Travellers, recycling and the State', *Radstats*, vol 73, no 1, online at: www.radstats.org.uk/no073/article1.htm (accessed 19 July 2011).

CLG (Communities and Local Government) (2012a) *National Planning Policy Framework*, March, online at www.communities.gov.uk.

CLG (2012b) *Planning policy for traveller sites*, March, online at www.communities.gov.uk.

CLG (2012c) *Progress report by the ministerial working group on tackling inequalities experienced by Gypsies and Travellers*, London: CLG.

Cohen, S. (1972) *Folk devils and moral panic: The creation of Mods and Rockers*, London: Mac Gibbon and Kee.

Collingwood, R.G. (1989) *R.G. Collingwood: Essays in Political Philosophy*, ed. D. Boucher, Oxford: Oxford University Press.

CONSCISE (2003) *The contribution of social capital in the social economy to local economic development in Western Europe, Final Report 3*, online at: www.conscise.mdx.ac.uk.

Cossée, C. (2005) *Travellers' economy in Europe: What Recognition?*, Study for the ETAP Transnational Project EQUAL European Programme.

Council of Europe (2008) 'Living together as equals in dignity', White Paper on Intercultural Dialogue.

Coxhead, J. (2005) *Moving forward: How the Gypsy and Traveller communities can be more engaged to improve policing performance*, London: The Home Office.

Craig, G. (2007) 'Cunning, unprincipled, loathsome: The racist tail wags the welfare dog', *Journal of Social Policy*, vol 36, no 4, pp 605–23.

Crawley, H. (2004) *Moving forward: The provision of accommodation for Travellers and Gypsies*, London: Institute for Public Policy Research.

CRE (Commission for Racial Equality) (2004) *Gypsies and Travellers: A strategy for the CRE, 2004–2007*, London: CRE.

CRE (2006) *Common ground: Equality, good relations and sites for Gypsies and Irish Travellers*. London: CRE.

Cripps, J. (1977) *Accommodation for Gypsies: A report on the working of the Caravan Sites Act 1968*, Department of Environment and Welsh Office.

Dahl, R. (1961) *Who governs? Democracy and power in the American city*, New Haven: Yale University Press.

Daily Express (2004) Headline, 20 January, p 1.

Daily Mail (2007) 'An explosive remark', 24 January, p 35.

Daily Mirror (2005) Editorial, 22 March.

Dandeker, C. (1990) *Surveillance, power and modernity*, London: Polity Press.

Dawson, R. (2000) *Crime and prejudice: Traditional Travellers*, Derbyshire: Robert Dawson.

DCLG (2010) Bi-annual caravan count online, July.

DCLG (2011) 'Eric Pickles: time for fair play for all on planning', Press release, 13 April, London: DCLG.

DCLG Select Committee (2011) *Third report – Localism*, London: DCLG.

DCSF (Department for Children, Schools and Families) (2006) *Ethnicity and education: The evidence on minority ethnic pupils aged 5–16*, London: DCSF.

DCSF (2008a) 'Improving the outcomes for Gypsy, Roma and Traveller pupils: literature review', online at www.education.gov.uk/publications/eOrderingDownload/DCSF-RR077.pdf.

DCSF (2008b) *The inclusion of Gypsy, Roma and Traveller children and young people*, London: DCSF.

DCSF (2009a) *Improving the outcomes for Gypsy, Roma and Traveller Pupils – what works? Contextual influences and constructive conditions that may influence pupil achievement*, London: DCSF.

DCSF (2009b) *Guidance for Local Authorities and Schools on setting education performance targets for 2011, LA statutory targets for Key Stages 2, 4, Early Years' outcomes, children in care, underperforming groups and attendance.*

DCSF (2009c) *The Inclusion of Gypsy, Roma and Traveller Children and Young People*, www.education.gov.uk/publications.

DCSF (2010) *Working together to safegaurd children: A guide to interagency working to safegaurd and promote the welfare of children,* Nottingham: DCSF Publications..

Dean, M. (2011) *Democracy under attack: How the media distorts policy and politics,* Bristol: The Policy Press.

Dearling, A., Newburn, T. and Somerville, P. (eds) (2006) *Supporting safer communities: Housing, crime and neighbourhoods,* Coventry: Chartered Institute of Housing and Housing Studies Association.

Delgado, R. (ed) (1995) *Critical race theory: The cutting edge,* Philadelphia, Temple University Press.

Derrington, C. (2007) 'Fight, flight and playing white: an examination of coping strategies adopted by Gypsy Traveller adolescents in English secondary schools', *International Journal of Educational Research,* vol 46, no 6, pp 357-67.

Derrington, C. and Kendall, S. (2004) *Gypsy Traveller students in secondary schools: Culture, identity and achievement,* Stoke on Trent: Trentham Books.

DfE (2010a) *The importance of teaching: the Schools White Paper,* online at: https://www.education.gov.uk/publications/standard/publicationdetail/page1/CM%207980.

DfE (2010b) 'New endowment fund to turn around weakest schools and raise standards for disadvantaged pupils', Press notice, 3 November.

DfE (2010c) 'Permanent and fixed period exclusions from schools in England 2008/09', online at www.education.gov.uk/rsgateway/DB/SFR/s000942/index.shtml.

DfEE (Department for Education and Employment) (1998) 'A step change in Traveller education', Charles Clarke's speech to the biennial conference of the National Association of Teachers of Travellers (NATT), Leicester, 12 November 1998, unpublished.

DfES (Department for Education and Skills) (2003) *Aiming high: Raising the achievement of Gypsy Traveller pupils,* London: DfES.

DfES (2005a) 'A new relationship with schools: improving performance through school self-evaluation', online at www.education.gov.uk/publications/standard/publicationDetail/Page1/DFES-1290-2005.

DfES (2006) *Care matters: Transforming the lives of children and young people in care,* London: HMSO.

DfES (2007) *Care matters: Time for change,* London: HMSO..

DH (Department of Health) (1998) *Caring for children away from home: Messages from research,* Chichester: Wiley.

DH (2009) *About the Pacesetters programme,* online at http://webarchive. nationalarchives.gov.uk/+/www.dh.gove.uk/en/managing yourorganisationn/equalityandhumanrights/pacesettersprogramme/ dh_078778.

DH (2010) *Inclusion health: Improving primary care for socially excluded people,* London: DH.

DoE (Department of the Environment) (1994) *Circular 01/94: Gypsy sites and planning,* London: DoE.

Donzelot, J. (1979) *The policing of families, welfare versus the state,* London: Hutchinson & Co.

Donzelot, J. and Hurley, R. (1997) *The policing of families,* Baltimore: Johns Hopkins University Press.

Doyal, L., Cameron, A. and Cemlyn, S. (2002) *The health of Travellers in the South West region,* Bristol: South West Public Health Observatory.

Duncan, T. (1996) *Neighbours' views of official sites for Travelling people,* York: Joseph Rowntree Foundation.

Earle, F., Dearling, A., Whittle, H., Glasse, R. and Gubby (1994) *A time to travel? An introduction to Britain's newer Travellers,* Lyme Regis: Enabler Publications.

Economic and Social Data Service (1997) SN 3685 – Fourth National Survey of Ethnic Minorities, 1993–1994, online at: www.esds.ac.uk/ findingData/snDescription.asp?sn=3685.

ECRI (European Commission against Racism and Intolerance) (2010) *Fourth periodic report on the UK,* online at: www.coe.int/t/ dghl/monitoring/ecri/Country-by-county/United_Kingdom/ UnitedKingdom_CBC_en.asp.

EHRC (Equality and Human Rights Commission) (2009) 'Gypsies and Travellers: simple solutions for living together', online at: http://www. equalityhumanrights.com/key-projects/good-relations/gypsies-and-travellers-simple-solutions-for-living-together/.

Ellinor, R. (2003) 'Caravan Burned in Village Bonfire', The *Guardian,* 30 October, p 7.

ERRC (European Roma Rights Centre) (2008a) 'Persistent segregation of Roma in the Czech education system', online at www. romaeducationfund.hu/publications/studies-and-researches.

ERRC (2008b) 'Rights groups demand european commission clarify its position on fingerprinting Roma in Italy', online at: www.errc. org/cikk.php?cikk=2980.

ERRC (2009) 'Hard times for Roma: economics, politics and violence', online at: www.errc.org/cikk.php?cikk=3046.

ERRC (2010) 'ERRC provides European Commission evidence of French violations of EU law', online at: www.errc.org/cikk. php?cikk=3715.

ERRC (2011a) 'Civil society appeal for consultation on EU Roma Strategy development', Press release, 15 February.

ERRC (2011b) 'ERPC: Coalition applauds EU leaders' endorsement of Roma Framework', Press release.

ERRC (2011c) 'Bulgaria must ensure the safety of its Romani citizens', online at: www.errc.org/cikk.php?cikk=3934.

ERRC (2011d) 'Attacks against Roma in Hungary: January 2008 – July 2011', online at: www.errc.org/cms/upload/file/attacks-list-in-hungary.pdf.

EU Presidency (2011) 'Roma integration: the Presidency takes Aaction', 8 April.

European Commission (2010) 'Stepping up the fight against poverty and social exclusion'.

European Commission (2011) 'Communication from the Commission to the European Parliament, The Council, the European Economic and Social Committee and the Committee of the Regions – An EU Framework for National Roma Integration Strategies up to 2020'.

European Dialogue (2009) 'EU member states: A mapping survey of A2 and A8 Roma in England: patterns of settlement and current situation of new Roma communities in England', Report prepared for DCSF, online at: equality.uk.com/Resources_files/movement_of_roma.pdf (accessed: 14 November 2011).

European Parliament (2011a) 'The European Commission will consistently execute the Roma Strategy – Praise to the hard work of the Hungarian EU Presidency and the Rapporteur', Press release by MEP Lívia Járóka, Brussels, 25 May.

European Parliament (2011b) 'Measures to promote the situation of Roma EU citizens in the European Union'.

European Parliament (2011c) 'EU Strategy on Roma Inclusion: MEPs set out priorities', Press release, 14 February.

Feder, G. (1989) 'Traveller Gypsies and primary care', *The Journal of the Royal College of General Practitioners*, vol 39, pp 425-9.

Finch, J. and Mason, J. (2000) 'Family relationships and responsibilities', in N. Abercrombie and A. Warde (eds) *The Contemporary British Society Reader*, Cambridge: Polity Press, p 170.

Fisher, I. (2003) *Deprivation and discrimination faced by Traveller children: implications for social policy and social work*. Social Work Monographs, Norwich: University of East Anglia Press.

Fordham Research (2008) *London Gypsy and Traveller accommodation assessment*, London: Fordham Research.

Forester, J. (1999) *The deliberative practitioner: Encouraging participatory planning processes*, Boston: MIT Press.

Forester, J. (2009) *Dealing with differences: Dramas of mediating public disputes*, Oxford: Oxford University Press.

Foster, B. and Walker, A. (2010) *Traveller education in the mainstream: The litmus test,* London: Mark Allen.

Foucault, M. (1969) *The birth of the clinic: An archaeology of medical perception*, trans. A.M. Sheridan, London: Tavistock Publications.

Foucault, M. (1979) *Discipline and punish: The birth of the prison*, Harmondsworth: Penguin.

Foucault, M. (1980) *Power/knowledge*, ed. C. Gordon, Harlow: Pearson Education Ltd.

Fowler, R. (1991) *Language in the news: Discourse and ideology in the press*, London: Routledge.

Fraser, A. (1992) *The Gypsies*, London: Blackwell.

Fraser, A. (1995) *The Gypsies: The peoples of Europe* (2nd edn), London: Blackwell.

Freire, P. (1970) *Pedagogy of the oppressed*, New York: Continuum Publishing Company.

Freire, P. (1982) 'Creating alternative research methods: learning to do it by doing it', in B. Hall, A. Gillette and R. Tandon (eds) *Creating knowledge: A monopoly*, Toronto: International Council for Adult Education, pp 29-37.

Fundamental Rights Agency (2010) 'The fundamental rights position of Roma and Travellers in the European Union – factsheet'.

Fung, A. (2002) 'Creating deliberative publics: Governance after devolution and democratic centralism', *The Good Society*, vol 11, no 1.

Fung, A. and Wright, E.O. (2001) 'Deepening democracy: Innovations in empowered participatory governance', *Politics and Society*, vol 29.

Galtung, J. and Ruge, M. (1973) 'Structuring and selecting news', in S. Cohen and J. Young (eds) *The manufacture of news, social problems, deviance and the mass media*, London: Constable.

Garrett, P.M. (2004) *Social work and Irish people in Britain*, Bristol: The Policy Press.

Garrett, P.M. (2005) 'Irish social workers in Britain and the politics of (mis)recognition', *British Journal of Social Work*, vol 9, no 2, pp 1-18.

Gheorghe, N. and Mirga, A. (2001) *The Roma in the twenty-first century: A policy paper*, Princeton: Project on Ethnic Relations.

Gheorghe, N. and Pulay, G. (2011) 'Choices to be made and prices to be paid: potential roles and consequences in Roma activism and policy.

Gilchrist, A. (2004) *The well-connected community: A networking approach to community development*, Bristol: The Policy Press.

Gillborn, D. and Gipps, C. (1996) 'Recent research on the achievements of ethnic minority pupils', Ofsted report. London: HMSO.

Gil-Robles, A. (2005) 'Report by Mr Alvaro Gil-Robles, Commissioner for Human Rights, on his visit to the United Kingdom, 4-12 November 2004', Strasbourg, Council of Europe.

Glasgow Media Action Group (1976) (Members of the group: Beharrell, P. Davis, H. Eldridge, J. Hewitt, J. Oddie, J. Philo, G. Walton, P. and Winston, B.) *Bad news*, London: Routledge.

Goffman, E. (1968) *Stigma*, Harmondsworth: Penguin.

Gough, J., Eisenenschitz, A. and McCulloch, A. (2006) *Spaces of social exclusion*, Oxon: Routledge.

Gove, M. (2010) 'It's not simply an academic question – why we need radical reform of vocational education', Speech to the Edge Foundation, online at www.education.gov.uk/inthenews/speeches/a0064364/michael-gove-to-the-edge-foundation.

Gove, M. (2011) Speech to The Policy Exchange on Free Schools, 20 June, online at: www.education.gov.uk/inthenews/speeches/a0077948/michael-goves-speech-to-the-policy-exchange-on-free-schools.

Gramsci, A. (1971) *Selections from the prison notebooks*, London: Lawrence and Wishart.

Granovetter, M. and Swedberg, R. (1992) *The sociology of economic life,* Westview.

Greatrex, J. (2011) 'Revealed: the 24-hour a day vigil at Meriden Gypsy site', The *Sunday Mercury*, 17 April, www.sundaymercury.net.

Greenfields, M. (2002) 'The impact of Section 8 Children Act applications on Travelling families', PhD (unpublished), Bath: University of Bath.

Greenfields, M. (2006) 'Family, Communities and Identity', in C. Clark and M. Greenfields (eds) *Here to stay: The Gypsies and Travellers of Britain*, Hatfield, University of Hertfordshire Press, Chapter 2.

Greenfields, M. (2007) 'Accommodation needs of Gypsies/Travellers: new approaches to policy in England', *Social Policy & Society*, vol 7, no 1, pp 73-89.

Greenfields, M. (2008) *A good job for a Traveller?*, High Wycombe: Buckinghamshire New University Press.

Greenfields, M. (2011) *An SROI evaluation of Irish Traveller movement: Britain's Community Development Programme for Traveller women*, High Wycombe: IDRICS/BNU.

Greenfields, M. and Home, R. (2006) 'Assessing Gypsies and Travellers' needs: partnership working and "The Cambridge Project"', *Romani Studies*, vol 16, no 2, pp 105-13.

Greenfields, M. and Smith, D. (2010a) 'A question of identity: the social exclusion of housed Gypsies and Travellers', *Research, Policy and Planning* (2010/1), vol 28, no 3.

Greenfields, M. and Smith, D. (2010b) 'Housed Gypsy Travellers, social segregation and the reconstruction of communities', *Housing Studies*, vol 25, no 3, pp 397-412.

Greenslade, R. (2005b) 'Stirring up tensions', The *Guardian*, 14 March, online at: www.guardian.co.uk/media.

Greenwood, J. and Levin, M. (1998) *Introduction to action research: Social research for social change*, Thousand Oaks: Sage Publications.

Grellmann, H. (1787 [1783]) *Die Zigeuner: Ein historicher Versuch* über *die Lebensart und Verfassung, Sitten und Schicksale dieses Volks in Europa, nebst ihrem Urspringe*, 2nd edn, Göttingen: Johann Christian Dieterich [1st edn 1783, Leipzig].

Grice, A. and Brown, C. (2005) 'Labour labels Howard "a serial opportunist"', *The Independent*, 22 March, online at: www.independent.co.uk/news/uk/politics/labour-labels-howard-a-serial-opportunist.

Gropper, R. and Miller, C. (2001) 'Exploring new worlds in American Romani Studies: social and cultural attitudes among the American Macvaia, *Romani Studies*, vol 11, no 2, pp 81-110.

Gudeman, S. (2001) *The anthropology of economy*, London: Blackwell.

Gunaratnam, Y. (2003) *Researching 'race' and ethnicity: Methods, knowledge and power*, London: Sage.

Hajioff, S. and McKee, M. (2000) 'The health of the Roma people: a review of the published literature', *Journal of Epidemiology & Community Health*, vol 54, pp 864-69.

Halpern, D. (2005) *Social capital*, Cambridge, MA: Polity Press.

Hancock, I.F. (2006) 'On Romani origins and identity: questions for discussion', in A. Marsh and E. Strand (eds) *Gypsies and the problem of identities*, London: IB Tauris/Istanbul: Swedish Institute in Istanbul.

Hancock, I.F. (2010) 'Mind the doors! The contribution of linguistics', in D. Le Bas and T. Acton (eds) *All change – Romani studies through Romani eyes*, Hatfield: University of Hertfordshire Press.

Hanham, Baroness (2011) 'Answer to written question by Lord Avebury', *Hansard*, 7 May, online at: http://services.parliament.uk/hansard/Lords/bydate/20110627/writtenanswers/part023.html.

Haupert, A. (2010) 'Roma communities need results, not promises', 17 June (Blog).

Hawes, D. and Perez, B. (1996) *The Gypsy and the state: The Ethnic cleansing of british society*, Bristol: The Policy Press.

Hayes, J. (2010) 'Foreword to the Wolf report', in A. Wolf, *Review of vocational education: The Wolf Report,* online at: https://www.education.gov.uk/publications/standard/publicationDetail/Page1/DFE-00031-2011.

Healey, P. (2005) *Collaborative planning: Shaping places in fragmented societies*, Basingstoke: Palgrave Macmillan.

Hennessy, M. (2011) 'UK pub chain which barred Travellers faces investigation', The *Irish Times*, online at: www.irishtimes.com/newspaper/frontpage/2011/1124/1124308057833.html.

Higgins, C. (2010) 'Right-wing historian Niall Ferguson given school curriculum role', *The Guardian*, 31 May, p 10.

Holloway, S. (2002) 'Outsiders in rural society? Constructions of rurality and nature-social relations in the racialisation of English Gypsy-Travellers, 1869–1934', *Environment and Planning D: Society and Space*, vol 21, pp 695–715.

Home Office (2002) *Secure borders, safe haven: Integration with diversity in modern Britain,* White Paper, London: HMSO.

Hooks, b. (1991) *Yearning: Race, gender and cultural politics*, London, Turnaround.

ITMB (Irish Traveller Movement Britain) (2007) *Paper on economic inclusion for Travellers*, London: ITMB.

ITMB (2010) *Roads to success: Economic and social inclusion for Gypsies and Travellers*, London: ITMB.

Ivatts, A. (2005) *The education of Gypsy/Roma Traveller and Travelling children*, Position paper for the National Strategy Group, Department for Education and Skills.

Ivatts, A. (2006) *The situation regarding the current policy, provision and practice in elective home education (EHE) for Gypsy, Roma and Traveller children*, London: DfES.

Jackson, J. (2011) 'One big fat Gypsy protest: how to complain to OFCOM', *Travellers Times*, January, online at: www.travellerstimes.org.uk.

Jackson, S. (2006) 'Looking after children away from home: past and present', in S. Jackson (ed) *In care and after: A positive perspective*, London: Routledge.

James, Z. and Richardson, J. (2006) 'Controlling accommodation: policing Gypsies and Travellers', in A. Dearling, T. Newburn and P. Somerville (eds) *Supporting safer communities: Housing, crime and neighbourhoods*, Coventry: Chartered Institute of Housing and Housing Studies Association.

Jenkins, R. (1996) *Social identity*, London: Routledge.

Jones, M.W. (2010) 'The RTFHS: a special family history society', in D. Le Bas and T. Acton (eds) *All change: Romani studies through Romani eyes*, Hatfield: University of Hertfordshire Press,.

Kalinin, V. (2000) 'Oh, this Russian spirit abides everywhere: a dialogue of the imagination with Dr Donald Kenrick', in T. Acton (ed) *Scholarship and the Gypsy struggle*, Hatfield, University of Hertfordshire Press.

Kalinin, V. (2010) 'The construction of the history of the Roma in the "Great Land" (Russia): notions of Roma history and identity in Imperial, Soviet and Post-Soviet Russia' in D. Le Bas and T. Acton (eds) *All change: Romani studies through Romani eyes*, Hatfield: University of Hertfordshire Press.

Kamm, H. (1993) 'Havel calls the Gypsies "litmus test"', *New York Times*, 10 December.

Karlsen S. and Nazroo, J. (2000) 'Identity and structure: rethinking ethnic inequalities in health', in H. Graham (ed) *Understanding health inequalities*, Milton Keynes: Open University Press, pp 38-57.

Keet-Black, J. (2010) 'The importance of the Romany Traveller Family History Society', in D. LeBas and T. Acton (eds) *All change: Romani studies through Romani eyes*, Hatfield: University of Hertfordshire Press.

Kelly, G. (2009) 'So you love us, Mr Brown. but do you trust us?', The *Times Educational Supplement*, 30 October, available at: www.tes.co.uk/article.aspx?storycode=6026515.

Kendall, S. (1997) 'Sites of resistance: places on the margin – the Traveller home place', in T. Acton, *Gypsy politics and Traveller identity*, St Albans: University of Hertfordshire Press.

Kenrick, D. (1999) *The Gypsies during the Second World War: In the shadow of the swastika*, Hatfield: University of Hertfordshire Press.

Kenrick, D. (2004) *Gypsies: From the Ganges to the Thames*, Hatfield: University of Hertfordshire Press.

Kenrick, D. and Clark, C. (1999) *Moving on: The Gypsies and Travellers of Britain*, Hatfield: University of Hertfordshire Press.

Kenrick, D. and Puxon, G. (2009) *Gypsies under the swastika*, Hatfield: University of Hertfordshire Press.

Khattab, N. (2009) 'Ethno-religious background as a determinant of educational and occupational attainment in Britain', *Sociology*, vol 43, no 2, pp 304-322.

Kisby, B. (2010) 'The Big Society: power to the people?', *The Political Quarterly*, vol 81, no 4, pp 484–91.

Kloostermann, R. and Rath, J. (eds) (2003) *Immigrant entrepreneurs: Venturing abroad in the age of globalisation*, Oxford: Berg.

Knight, P. (2010) *Gypsy Roma Traveller History Month Report,* London: GRTHM www.grthm.co.uk/report_2009/GRTHM%202009%20 report_v2.pdf.

Kovats, M. (2003) 'The politics of Roma identity: between nationalism and destitution', *Open Democracy*, 29 July, pp 1-8.

Kundnani, A (2004) 'Anger grows over *Daily Express* reporting of Roma', Institute of Race Relations, online at: www.irr.org.uk/news/ anger-grows-over-daily-express-reporting-of-roma.

Kwiek, G.D. (1998) 'I am the common Rom', in I. Hancock, S. Dowd and R. Djurić, *The roads of the Roma,* Hatfield, University of Hertfordshire Press, p 106.

Kwiek, G.D. (2010) 'Afterword: Rom, Roma, Romani, Kale, Gypsies, Travellers & Sinti … Pick a name and stick with it, already!', in D. Le Bas and T. Acton (eds) *All change: Romani studies through Romani eyes,* , Hatfield: University of Hertfordshire Press.

Laclau, E. and Mouffe, C. (2001) *Hegemony and socialist strategy: Towards a radical democratic politics*, 2nd edn, London: Verso.

Le Bas, D. (2010) 'The possible implications of diasporic consciousness for Romani Identity', in D. Le Bas and T. Acton (eds) *All All change: Romani studies through Romani eyes*, Hatfield: University of Hertfordshire Press.

Le Bas, D. and Acton, T. (eds) *All change: Romani studies through Romani eyes*, Hatfield: University of Hertfordshire Press.

Lefebvre, H. (1991) *The production of space*, Oxford: Blackwell.

Lehti, A., and Mattson, B. (2001) 'Health, attitude to care and pattern of attendance among Gypsy women: a general practice perspective', *Family Practice*, vol 18, no 4, pp 445-8.

Lemon, A. (2001) *Between two fires: Gypsy performance and Romani memory from Pushkin to Postsocialism*, Michigan: Duke University Press.

Lengyel, G. (ed) (2009) *Deliberative methods in local society research (the Kaposvar experiences)*, Budapest: Corvinus University.

Lewis, M. (2005) *Asylum: Understanding public attitudes'* London: IPPR.

Lewis, G. and Drife, J. (2001) *Why mothers die 1997–1999: The confidential enquiries into maternal deaths in the United Kingdom*, London: RCOG.

Liégeois, J.P. (2007) 'Roma in Europe', Council of Europe, Strasbourg.

Light, I. and Gold, S. (2000) *Ethnic economies*, San Diego, CA: Academic Press.

Local Government Association (2008) *Narrowing the gap: Final guidance Year 1*, London: LGA.

Local Government Improvement and Development (2011) *Culturally responsive JSNAs: A review of race equality and joint strategic needs assessment (JSNA) practice*, London: LGID.

Lukes, S. (1974) *Power: A radical view*, Basingstoke: Macmillan Press.

Lukes, S. (ed) (1986) *Power*, Oxford: Basil Blackwell.

Lundy P. and McGovern, M. (2006) 'Participation, truth and partiality: participatory action research, community-based truth-telling and post-conflict transition in Northern Ireland', *Sociology*, vol 40, pp 71-88.

Macionis J. and Plummer, K. (2002) 'Racism, ethnicities and migration', in *Sociology: A global introduction,* 2nd edn, Harlow: Personal Education Limited, pp 259-64.

Macpherson, W. (1999) *The Stephen Lawrence Inquiry*, London: HMSO.

Marks, K. (2004) *Traveller education: Changing times, changing technologies*, Staffordshire: Trentham Books.

Marmot, M. (2005) 'Social determinants of health inequalities', *The Lancet*, vol 365, pp 1099-104.

Marsh, A. (2010) 'The Gypsies in Turkey: History, ethnicity and identity – an action research strategy in practice', in D. Le Bas and T. Acton (eds) *All change: Romani studies through Romani eyes*, Hatfield: University of Hertfordshire Press.

Marsh, A. and Strand, E. (eds) (2006) *Gypsies and the problem of identities*, London: IB Tauris/Istanbul: Swedish Institute in Istanbul.

Matras, Y. (2002) *Romani: A linguistic introduction*, Cambridge: Cambridge University Press.

McCarthy, P. (1994) 'The sub-culture of poverty reconsidered', in M. McCann, S. Ó Síocháin and J. Ruane (eds) *Irish Travellers: Culture and ethnicity,* Belfast: The Institute of Irish Studies, The Queen's University of Belfast/The Anthropological Association of Ireland..

McCready, T. [misspelled on website as Mcreay] (2010) *Porrajmos*, Transcript of speech at the launch of Gypsy Roma Traveller History Month, 1 June 2010, online at: www.grthm.co.uk/bigger-picture-porrajmos.php.

McGarry, A. (2010) *Who speaks for Roma? Political representation of a transnational minority community*, London: Continuum.

McNiff, J. and Whitehead, D. (2009) *Doing and writing action research*, London: Sage Publications.

McVeigh, R. (1997) 'Theorising sedentarism: the roots of anti-nomadism', in T. Acton (ed), *Gypsy politics and identity*, Hatfield: University of Hertfordshire Press.

McVeigh, R. (2007) 'Ethnicity denial and racism: the case of the Government of Ireland Against Irish Travellers', The Irish Migration, Race and Social Transformation Review, vol 2, no 1, online at: www.dcu.ie/imrstr/volume1issue2/volume1issue2-6.htm.

Mee, K. and Dowling, R. (2000) 'Tales of the city: Western Sydney at the end of the millennium', in J. Connell (ed) *Sydney, South Melbourne*, Oxford: Oxford University Press.

Memedova, A. (2004) 'Romani Men and Romani Women Roma Human Rights Movement: a missing element', European Roma Rights Centre, 27 May, online at: www.errc.org/cikk.php?cikk=1850.

Meyer, H., Barber, S. and Luenen, C. (2010) 'The Open Method of Coordination (OMC) – A governance mechanism for the G20?', *Social Europe Journal*, online at: http://eprints.lse.ac.uk/39365/1/The_open_method_of_coordination_a_governance_mechanism_for_the_G20_(LSE_RO).pdf.

Meyer, J. (2004) 'What is action research', in C. Seal (ed) *Social research methods: A reader*, Oxford: Routledge.

Millar, S. (1999) 'Straw's Travellers gaffe "misconstrued"', The *Guardian*, 20 August, online at: www.guardian.co.uk/world/1999/aug/20/race.politicalnews.

Morris, E. (1997) 'Equality and the sum of its parts', *Times Educational Supplement*, 26 September, online at www.tes.co.uk/article.aspx?storycode=71411.

Morris, R. and Clements, L. (2002) *At what cost? The economics of Gypsy and Traveller encampments*, Bristol: The Policy Press.

NatCen (National Centre for Social Research) (2009) *Pupils with declining attainment at Key Stages 3 and 4: Profiles, experiences and impacts of underachievement and disengagement*, DCSF RR-086, London: DCSF.

Neff-Smith M., Erickson G. and Campbell J. (1996) 'Gypsies: health problems and nursing needs', *The Journal of Multicultural Nursing and Health*, vol 2, no 4, pp 36-42.

Nettleton, S. (2001) 'Social inequalities and health status', in S. Nettleton (ed) *The sociology of health and illness*, Cambridge: Polity Press.

NHS PCC (National Health Service Primary Care Contracting) (2009) *Primary Care Service Framework: Gypsy & Traveller Communities*, London: NHS, online at: www.pcc.nhs.uk/uploads/primary_care_service_frameworks/2009/ehrg_gypsies_and_travellers_pcsf_190509.pdf.

Ní Shuinéar, S. (1997) 'Why do Gaujos hate Gypsies so much, anyway?', in T. Acton (ed) *Gypsy politics and identity*, Hatfield: University of Hertfordshire Press.

Ní Shuinéar, S. (1994) 'Irish Travellers, ethnicity and the origins question', in M. McCann, S. Síocháin and J. Ruane (eds) *Irish Travellers and cultural identity*, Belfast: Institute of Irish Studies.

Niner, P. (2002) *The provision and condition of local authority Gypsy/Traveller sites in England*, London: Office of the Deputy Prime Minister' (ODPM).

Nirenberg, J. (2009) 'Romani political mobilization from the First International Romani Union Congress to the European Roma, Sinti and Travellers Forum', in N. Sigona and N. Trehan (eds), *Romani politics in contemporary Europe: Poverty, ethnic mobilisation, and the neoliberal order*, London: Palgrave Macmillan.

Nowotny, H. (1981) 'Women in public life in Austria', in C.F. Epstein and R.L. Coser (eds) *Access to power: Cross-national studies of women and elites*, Boston: George Allen and Unwin, pp 147-56.

Nozick, R. (1974) *Anarchy, state and Utopia*, New York: Basic Books.

NUT (National Union of Teachers) (2010) On-line NUT survey, November 2010 (unpublished).

O'Higgins, K. (1993) 'Travelling children in substitute care', in K. O'Higgins (ed) *Surviving childhood adversity*, Belfast: The Institute of Irish Studies.

ODPM (Office of the Deputy Prime Minister) (2004) *Gypsy and Traveller sites*, Housing, Planning, Local Government and the Regions Committee, Thirteenth Report of Session 2003/04, online at: www.publications.parliament.uk/pa/cm200304/cmselect/cmodpm/633/633pdf.

ODPM (2006) *Circular 01/06 (ODPM): Planning for Gypsy and Traveller caravan sites*, London: ODPM.

Ofsted (1996) 'The education of Travelling children', London: Ofsted, online at: www.ofsted.gov.uk/sites/default/files/documents/surveys-and-good-practice/e/Education%20of%20Travelling%20children%20%28The%29%20%28PDF%20format%29.pdf.

Ofsted (1999) 'Raising the attainment of minority ethnic pupils: school and lea responses', Ofsted HMI report No 170, online at: www.ofsted.gov.uk/resources/raising-attainment-of-minority-ethnic-pupils-school-and-lea-responses.

Ofsted (2003) 'Provision and support for Traveller pupils', London: Ofsted, online at: www.ippr.org/images/media/files/publication/2011/05/public%20services%20commission%20summary%20new_1672.pdf.

Ofsted (2006) *Joint area review of Hackney Children's Services*, online at: www.ofsted.gov.uk/local-authorities/hackney.

Okely, J. (1983) *The Traveller Gypsies*, Cambridge: Cambridge University Press.

Okun, A. (1981) *Prices and quantities: A macroeconomic analysis*, Washington DC: Brookings Institution.

Open Society Institute (2011) 'EU policies for Roma inclusion', Policy Assessment, Brussels: Open Society Institute.

The Ormiston Trust (2007) *Consultation with Gypsy and Traveller communities on policy options for the draft revision to the Regional Spatial Strategy for the East of England to address the provision of Gypsy and Traveller caravan sites*, Ipswich: Ormiston Children and Families Trust.

Orr, K. and Bennett, M. (2010) 'Editorial', *Public Money and Management*, vol 30, no 4, pp 199-203.

OSRI (Open Society Roma Initiatives) (2011) 'Beyond rhetoric: Roma integration roadmap for 2020', Hungary: Open Society Foundation.

Ostrom, E. (1990) *Governing the commons: The evolution of institutions for collective action*, New York: Cambridge University Press.

Pahl J. and Vaile, M. (1986) 'Health and health care among Travellers', *Journal of Social Policy*, vol 17, pp 195-213.

Parkin, F. (1979) *Marxism and class theory: A bourgeois critique*, Cambridge: Tavistock.

Parry, G., Van Cleemput, P., Peters, J., Moore, J., Walters, S., Thomas, K. and Cooper, C. (2004) *The health status of Gypsies and Travellers in England: Report of Department of Health Inequalities in Health Research Initiative Project 121/7500*, Sheffield: University of Sheffield Press.

Parvin, P. (2009) 'Against localism: does decentralising power to communities fail minorities?', *The Political Quarterly*, vol 80, no 3, pp 351-60.

Parvin, P. (2011) 'Localism and the Left', *Renewal*, vol 19, no 2, pp 37-49.

Patel, P. (2010) House of Commons debate, 7 December, *Hansard*, col 7WH.

Patrin (2000) *The Patrin web journal, timeline of Romani (Gypsy) history*, online at: www.geocities.com/Paris/5121/timeline.htm.

Peattie, K. and Morley, A. (2008) 'Social enterprises: diversity and dynamics, contexts and contributions, a research monograph', ESRC Monograph, Cardiff: BRASS.

Penny, L. (2010) 'Michael Gove and the imperialists', *New Statesman*, 1 June, online at: www.newstatesman.com/blogs/the-staggers/2010/06/history-british-ferguson.

Phillips, T. (2003) 'Speech to launch CRE Gypsy and Traveller Strategy', Commission for Racial Equality, October.

Phillips, T. (2005) 'It's bad – but real solutions can be found', The *Observer*, 27 March, online at: www.guardian.co.uk/uk/2005/mar/27/race.comment.

Polányi, K. (1957 [1944]) *The great transformation: The political and economic origins of our time*, Boston: Beacon Press.

Pollner, M. and Rosenfeld, D. (2000) 'The cross–culturing work of gay and lesbian elderly', *Advances in Life Course Research*, vol 5, pp 99-117.

Poole, L. and Adamson, K. (2008) *Report on the situation of the Roma Community in Govanhill,* University of the West of Scotland.

Porter, L. (2010) *Unlearning the colonial cultures of planning,* Farnham: Ashgate.

Powell, D. and Sze, F. (2004) *Interculturalism: Exploring critical issues,* Oxford: Inter-disciplinary Press.

Putnam, R. (2000) *Bowling alone: The collapse and revival of American community,* London: Simon and Schuster.

Rawls, J.B. (1971) *A theory of justice,* Massachussets: Belknap Press.

Reason, P. and Bradbury, H. (2008) *Handbook of action research: participative inquiry and practice,* 2nd edition, London: Sage Publications.

Reid, A. (1963) *Password: Places, poems, preoccupations,* Boston: Little Brown.

Richards, P. (2011) 'Gypsies: tramps and thieves?', *ProgressOnline,* 12 February, online at: www.progressives.org.uk.

Richardson, J. (2006a) *The Gypsy debate: Can discourse control?,* Exeter: Imprint Academic.

Richardson, J. (2006b) 'Talking about Gypsies: the notion of discourse as control', *Housing Studies,* vol 22, no 1, pp 77-96.

Richardson, J. (2007a) *Contentious spaces: The Gypsy/Traveller site issue,* York/Coventry: JRF/CIH.

Richardson, J. (2007b) 'Policing Gypsies and Travellers', in M. Hayes and T. Acton (eds) *Travellers, Gypsies, Roma: The demonisation of difference,* Cambridge, Cambridge Scholars Press.

Richardson, J. (ed) (2010a) *From recession to renewal: The impact of the financial crisis on public services and local government,* Bristol: The Policy Press.

Richardson, J. (2010b) 'Discourse dissonance: an examination of media, political and public discourse and its impact on policy implementation for Roma, Gypsies and Travellers at a local level', Romani Mobilities conference, Harris Manchester College, University of Oxford, January.

Richardson, J. (2011a) *The impact of Planning Circular 1/06 on Gypsies and Travellers in England,* Leicester: De Montfort University.

Richardson, J. (2011b) 'Articulation of Gypsies and Travellers within antagonistic practices', Unpublished notes..

Richardson, J. and Ryder, A. (2009a) 'New Labour's policies and their effectiveness for the provision of sites for Gypsies and Travellers in England', in N. Sigona and N. Trehan (eds) *Gypsies and Travellers in Europe,* Basingstoke: Palgrave Macmillan.

Richardson, J. and Ryder, A. (2009b) 'Stamp on the camps – a case study of a moral panic, othering and political furore in the UK', Extremism and the Roma and Sinti in Europe: Challenges, Risks and Responses conference (supported by OSCE/ODIHR), September 2009, London, .

Riches, R. (2007) *Early years outreach practice: Supporting early years practitioners working with Gypsy, Roma & Traveller Families with transferable ideas for other outreach workers*, London: Save the Children..

Roberts, K. (1991) 'Informal economy and family strategies', *International Journal of Urban and Regional Research,* vol 18, no 1, pp 90–96.

Robinson, J. and Tansey, J. (2006) 'Co-production, emergent properties and strong interactive social research: the Georgia Basin Futures Project', *Science and Public Policy*, vol 33, no 2, pp 151–60.

Robson, C. (1993) *Real world research,* Oxford: Blackwell.

Roma Education Fund (2009) 'School as ghetto: Systemic overrepresentation of Roma in special education in Slovakia', on-line at www.romaeducationfund.hu.

Roma Participation Program (2002) *Reporter,* Special Desegregation Issue, online at: www.soros.org/sites/default/files/rppl.pdf.

Roma Press Agency (2005) '"The European approach to tackling the problem of human rights for the Roma is concealed racism" (says chairman of Dzeno Association Ivan Veselý in an interview for the Roma Press Agency)', 21 February.

Roma Support Group (2010) *Improving engagement with the Roma community,* Research Report: London: Roma Support Group.

Rostas, I. (2009) 'The Romani Movement in Romania: institutionalization and (de)mobilization in England', in C. Trehan and N. Sigona (eds) *Contemporary Romani politics: Recognition, mobilisation and participation,* London: Palgrave Macmillan.

Ryder, A. (2009) NATT Conference Record, online at: www.natt.org.uk/speeches-day-2.

Ryder, A. (2011) *Gypsies and Travellers and the third sector,* Third Sector Research Centre Discussion Paper.

Ryder, A. and Greenfields, M. (2010) *Roads to success: routes to economic and social inclusion for Gypsies and Travellers,* Report by the Irish Traveller Movement in Britain.

Ryder, A., Acton, T., Alexander, S., Cemlyn, S., Van Cleemput, P., Greenfields, M., Richardson, J. and Smith, D. (2011) *A big or divided society? Report of the Panel Review into the Impact of the Localism Bill and Coalition Government Policy on Gypsies and Travellers*, Kidwelly: Travellers Aid Trust..

Ryder, A., Cemlyn, S., Greenfields, M., Richardson, J., and Van Cleemput, P. (2012) 'A critique of UK Coalition Government policy on Gypsy, Roma and Traveller communities', hosted on Equality and Diversity Forum website, www.edf.org.uk/blog/wp-content/uploads/2012/06/Coalition.

Salway, S., Nazroo ,J., Ghazala, M., Craig, G., Johnson, M. and Gerrish, K. (2010) 'Fair society, healthy lives: a missed opportunity to address ethnic inequalities in health', *British Medical Journal*, vol 340, p 684.

Sapstead, D. (2005) 'Protests as police spend £10,000 on anti-racism CD guide for Gipsies', The *Telegraph*, online at: www.telegraph.co.uk,.

Sartori, G. (1987) *The theory of democracy revisited*, Chatham: Chatham House Publishers.

Scott, J.C. (1990) *Domination and the arts of resistance: Hidden transcripts*, New Haven: Yale University Press.

Sepulveda, L., Syrett, S. and Calvo, S. (2010) *Social enterprise and ethnic minorities*, Third Sector Research Centre Working Paper 48, Birmingham: TSRC.

Shaull, R. (1970) 'Foreword', in P. Freire, *Pedagogy of the oppressed*, New York, Continuum Publishing Company.

Shelter (2007) *Good practice guide: Working with housed Gypsies and Travellers,* London: Shelter.

Sigona, N. and Trehan, N. (eds) (2009) *Romani politics in contemporary Europe: Poverty, ethnic mobilisation and the neoliberal order*, London: Palgrave Macmillan.

Smart, H., Titterton, M. and Clark, C. (2003) 'A literature review of the health of Gypsy/Traveller families in Scotland: the challenges for health promotion', *Health Education*, vol 103, no 3, pp 156-65.

Smith, A. (1776 [2008]) *An inquiry into the nature and causes of the wealth of nations*, ed. K. Sutherland, Oxford: Oxford Paperbacks.

Smith, M. (1975) *Gypsies*, London: Fabian Society.

Smith, R. (2010) *Social Work, Risk, Power, Sociological Research Online*, 4 February, at: www.socresonline.org.uk/15/1/4.html.

Smith, D. and Greenfields, M. (2012) 'Housed Gypsies and Travellers in the UK: work, exclusion and adaptation', *Race and Class*, vol 53, no 3, pp 48-65.

Smith, J.A., Flowers, B. and Larkin, M. (2009) *Doing interpretive phenomenological analysis*, London: Sage.

Smith-Bendell, M. (2009) *Our forgotten years: A Gypsy woman's life on the road*, Hatfield: University of Hertfordshire Press.

Spear, S. (2005) 'Living on the front line', Chartered Institute of Environmental Health, 15 April, online at: www.cieh.org/ehp/living_on_the_front_line.html.

Stevenson, B. (2007) *A8 nationals in Glasgow*, Glasgow City Council.

Stewart, M. (1997) *Time of the Gypsies*, Boulder: Westview Press.

Strand, S. (2008) 'Minority ethnic pupils in the longitudinal study of young people', in *England Extension Report on Performance in Public Examinations at Age 16*, Research Report DCSF RR-002, Warwick: Warwick University.

Sturcke, J. (2005) 'Tories announce crackdown on Travellers', The *Guardian*, 21 March, online at: www.guardian.co.uk/uk/2005/mar/21/race.conservatives.

Sturzaker, J. and Shucksmith, M. (2011) 'Planning for housing in rural england: discursive power and spatial exclusion', *Town Planning Review*, vol 82, no 2, pp 169-93.

Sutherland, A. (1992) 'Cross-cultural medicine: a decade later', *Western Journal of Medicine*, vol 157, pp 276-80.

Sweney, M. (2012) 'ASA to formally investigate "Bigger. Fatter. Gypsier" ad campaign', *The Guardian*, 28 May, online at: www.guardian.co.uk/media/2012/may/28/asa-bigger-fatter-gypsier-ad-campaign.

Taba, M. and Ryder, A. (2012) 'An overview of Roma education segregation and desegregation' in I. Rostas (ed) *Ten years after: A history of Roma School desegregation in Central and Eastern Europe*, Budapest: Central European Press.

Taske, N., Taylor, L., Mulvihill, C. and Doyle, N. (2005) 'Housing and public health: a review of reviews of interventions for improving health – evidence briefing', NICE, online at: www.nice.org.uk/page.aspx?o=526671.

Taylor, S., Repetti, R. and Seeman, T. (1997) 'Health psychology: what is an unhealthy environment and how does it get under the skin?', *Annual Reviews Psychology*, vol 48, pp 411-47.

The Economist (2010) 'Dale Farm's Gypsies, Travellers travails, conflicts are growing between Gypsies and residents', 12 August, online at: www.economist.com.

The *Sun*, (2005) 'Editorial', 9 March.

Thomas, J. (1985) 'Gypsies and American medical care', *Annals of Internal Medicine*, vol 102, no 6, pp 842-5.

Titmuss, R. (1974) *Social policy*, London: Allen and Unwin.

Trehan, N. (2001) 'In the name of the Roma', in *Between past and future: The Roma of Central and Eastern Europe*, Hatfield: Hertfordshire University Press.

UNICEF (2007) 'Breaking the cycle of exclusion: Roma children in South East Europe', online at www.unicef.org.

Ureche, H. and Franks, M. (2007) *This is who we are: A study of the views and identities of Roma, Gypsy and Traveller young people in England*, London: Children's Society.

Valentine, G. and McDonald, I. (2004) *Understanding Prejudice: Attitudes Towards Minorities*, London: Stonewall.

Van Cleemput, P. (2004) *The health status of Gypsies and Travellers in England: Report of qualitative findings*, Sheffield: University of Sheffield.

Van Cleemput, P (2008) *Gypsies and Travellers accessing primary health care: Interactions with health staff and requirements for 'culturally safe' services*, PhD thesis, Sheffield: University of Sheffield.

Van Cleemput, P. (2008) 'Health empact of Gypsy sites policy in the UK', *Social Policy and Society*, vol 7, no 1, pp 103-117.

Van Cleemput, P., Bissell, P. and Harris, J. (2010) 'Pacesetters Programme: Gypsy, Roma and Traveller core strand evaluation report for the Department of Health', www.shef.ac.uk/scharr/sections/ph/research/h_i/hiresearch.

Van Cleemput, P., Parry, G., Thomas, K., et al (2007) 'The health related beliefs and experience of Gypsies and Travellers: a qualitative study, *Journal of Epidemiology and Community Health*, vol 61, no 3, pp 205-10.

Vertovec, S. and Wessendorf, S. (2010) *The multiculturalism backlash: European Discourses, Policies and Practices*, London: Routledge.

Webb, R. and Vuillamy, G. (2006) 'Coming full circle? The impact of New Labour's education policies on primary school teachers' work', University of York/Association of Teachers and Lecturers.

Webster, L. and Millar, J. (2001) *Making a living: Social security, social exclusion and new Travellers*, Bristol: The Policy Press.

Which? Magazine (2007) 'Measures to stop doorstep conmen under threat – OFT Questions legality of no cold-calling zones', 30 August.

WHO CSDH (World Health Organization Commission on Social Determinants in Health) (2007) 'Achieving Health Equity: From Root Causes to Fair Outcomes', Interim Statement of the Commission on Social Determinants of Health, online at: www.who.int/social_determinants/en/.

Wilkin, A., Derrington, C. and Foster, B. (2009a) *Literature review: Improving outcomes for Gypsy, Roma and Traveller pupils*, National Foundation for Educational Research.

Wilkin, A., Derrington, C., Foster, B., White, R. and Martin, K. (2009b) *Improving the outcomes for Gypsy, Roma and Traveller pupils: What works*, online at https://www.education.gov.uk/publications/RSG/SchoolsSO/Page10/DCSF-RR170.

Wilkin, A., Derrington, C., White, R., Martin, K., Foster, B., Kinder, K and Rutt, S. (2010) *Improving the outcomes for Gypsy, Roma and Traveller Pupils: Final Report*, Research Report DFE-RR043, London: Department for Education.

Wilkinson, R.G. (1999) 'Putting the picture together: prosperity, redistribution, health and welfare', in M. Marmot and R. Wilkinson (eds) *Social determinants of health*, Oxford: Oxford University Press.

Wilkinson, R.G. (2005) *The impact of inequality: How to make sick societies healthier,* New York: The New Press.

Wilkinson, R.G. (1996) *Unhealthy societies: The afflictions of inequality*, London: Routledge.

Wilkinson, R. and Marmot, M. (2003) *The solid facts*, Copenhagen: World Health Organization.

Willems, W. (1997) *In search of the true Gypsy: From Enlightenment to final solution*, trans by D. Bloch, London: Frank Cass.

Williamson, G. (2010) House of Commons Debate, 7 December, *Hansard*, col 1WH.

Wilson, R. and Bloomfield, J. (2010) *Building the good society: A new form of progressive politics*, Compass.

Wolf, A. (2010) *Review of vocational education: The Wolf Report*, online at: https://www.education.gov.uk/publications/standard/publicationDetail/Page1/DFE-00031-2011.

Worthington, A. (ed) (2005) *The Battle of the Beanfield*, Teignmouth: Enabler Publications.

Zeman, C.L., Depken, D.E. and Senchina, D.S. (2003) 'Roma health issues: a review of the literature and discussion', *Ethnicity & Health*, vol 8, pp 223-49.

Index

Page references for notes are followed by n

AN OLD ROM AND HIS SON
A poem by Romani Poet
Valdemar Kalinin

There is no warmth beneath the oak,
Where an old Rom sits by his son,
A walking-stick in his hand
        To give strength,
He reflects upon his past...

When like a lord,
He led horses away from a tricky deal
        With a smile,
His eyes still shine young and courageous,
From a face that has become wrinkled.

His well-educated son
        Holds a newspaper,
"How will Roma survive?"
        Father asks son,
"Nearly everybody has rushed to trade...
"So who will care for the horses?"

"My father, don't presume
That everyone will change horses for cloth!
I will throw away my diploma,
Rather than see Romani heritage forgotten."